EFFECTIVE HELPING

Interviewing
and
Counseling
Techniques

EFFECTIVE HELPING

Interviewing and Counseling Techniques

BARBARA F. OKUN

Northeastern University

DUXBURY PRESS

North Scituate, Massachusetts

Duxbury Press

A DIVISION OF WADSWORTH PUBLISHING COMPANY, INC.

Effective Helping: Interviewing and Counseling Techniques was edited and pre-pared for composition by Sylvia Stein. Interior design was provided by Jane Pitts and Dorothy Thompson. The cover was designed by Nancy Gardner and Joseph Landry.

L.C. Cat. Card No.: 76-9916
ISBN 0-87872-119-3

PRINTED IN THE UNITED STATES OF AMERICA

5 6 7 8 9 -- 80 79 78

IN MEMORIAM

Catherine A. Brenner

who personified the effective
helper in both her personal and
professional life.

CONTENTS

PREFACE

My goal in writing *Effective Helping* was to provide students in human services and counseling programs with an integrated approach to basic helping skills, utilizing theory, practice, and case application. As a result, this book developed as an introduction to interviewing and counseling skills for use in both professional and paraprofessional settings. The content is appropriate primarily for beginning courses in human relations and counseling theory and process. It can also be valuable for training programs in human services institutions and agencies. Both uses will depend upon effective utilization of the integrated approach upon which the book is built.

The human relations counseling model presented in this book is concerned with skills, helping stages, and issues. The communication skills include hearing verbal messages, perceiving non-verbal messages, and responsive listening to both verbal and non-verbal messages. These listening skills enable helpers to progress through the helping stages: the relationship stage, during which rapport, trust, and problem clarification occur; and the strategies stage, which involves selecting and applying an appropriate helping strategy. The issues include values, ethics, and societal and professional topics which can positively or negatively affect a helping relationship. All three dimensions are crucial to effective helping.

This book is unique in that it integrates theory, practice, and application by providing for didactic and experiential learning. Key features include realistic exercises, dialogue excerpts, examples, and two full-length cases. The book provides an overview to helping relations and does not purport to produce professional helpers. It does, however, attempt to demystify by description and example the counseling practice, and to expose students to the major aspects of effective helping.

The first four chapters present the three-dimensional human relations counseling model and explore the nature of a helping relationship. Extensive practice and theory in communications skills and relationship building are interwoven into these chapters. Chapters 5 through 7 describe major theories, approaches, and strategies of helping. Chapter 8 discusses helpers' values, ethical and professional issues which effect helping relationships.

I wish to thank all of the people who have encouraged and helped me. Jackie and Frank Gagliardi, former students, introduced me to Bob Gormley of Duxbury Press. Ensuing discussions with Bob directly led to the writing of this book. My colleagues and students have been continuously sensitive and supportive, and my classes have willingly participated in field-testing this material. Particular thanks go to Peg and Bob Read for allowing me the use of their mountain cabin to concentrate on rewriting the original manuscript.

Without my husband Sherman and my children Marcia, Jeffrey, and Douglas, this book could never have been completed. Their devotion and tolerance sustained me throughout. There were many weekends and nights when they allowed me to work uninterrupted and took over some of my chores and responsibilities. Sherman patiently and thoroughly read, re-read, suggested content and concepts, organized, edited, and encouraged from beginning to end.

My thanks also to the reviewers who provided invaluable comments: Susan Uzan, Elizabeth Carollo, Paul Whisenand, Gerald O'Connor, Arline Lyle, Leonard Romney, Willa Reichbach, Ronna Krozy, and Steven Danish.

Barbara F. Okun

CHAPTER 1

INTRODUCTION

A major impact of recent counter-culture movements on American society has been the heightened awareness of the need for more positive "relating" between people—within families, neighborhoods, communities, at work, and in schools. We see reactions in the growth of the "encounter movement," the popularity of communal living, and the increase in the number of people choosing human services careers. The mass media have highlighted different forms of alienation and loneliness as sources of many of today's social ills. More people now want to care about and help one another, but much misunderstanding results from their inability to communicate these desires.

Ineffective or faulty communications appears to be at the root of most interpersonal difficulties. Conversely, effective communications are necessary to develop and maintain any type of positive interpersonal relationship. Unfortunately, written communications skills rather than face-to-face or interpersonal communications have been traditionally considered legitimate curriculum concerns in our schools. Although schools teach us to respond to information, they do not really encourage or teach us to hear, to perceive, and to respond to less apparent, underlying verbal and nonverbal messages. Thus, communications skills training becomes essential for any human relations endeavor.

PURPOSE OF THIS BOOK

The basic purpose of this book is to provide the foundation for individuals to develop human relations skills they need to incorporate in

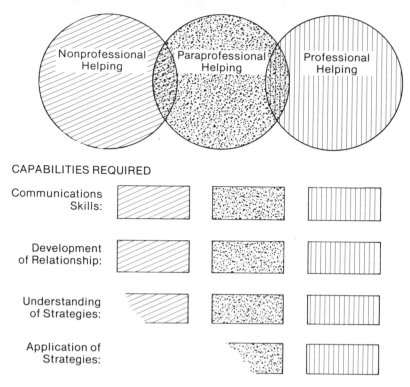

Figure 1-1   *Helping Relationships*

effective helping relationships. As part of this foundation, an introductory overview of the counseling process is presented to familiarize helpers with the knowledge and skills used for immediate, short-term, and long-term helping.

The book is intended for use both by groups and by individuals, in formal and informal human relations training. The content focuses upon the knowledge and skills needed by individuals in human services positions (such as mental health assistants, counselors, probation officers, employment service workers) or those involved in other helping roles (such as marriage partner, friend, supervisor, teacher, colleague).

The material is oriented for use in training either beginning students entering a helping profession or those who need or want to improve their human relations effectiveness. Because it provides foundation skills, this material will be useful to people continuing on for professional training in counseling, for people in non-professional settings, as well as for people who find themselves in informal helping relationships in their day-to-day encounters. Although some of the examples and case studies are slanted toward the professional end of the spectrum (see figure 1-1), they are useful to all helpers for illustrating the material in the text and acquainting them with what goes on in professional helping relationships. Technical terms, with which you may be unfamiliar, will sometimes be used in the book. The first time they appear they will be in bold-face type to indicate their inclusion in the glossary at the end of the book.

Overall, the book is intended to be more of a practical, applied manual than a theoretical treatise. However, it does include a basic overview of the major theoretical approaches to helping as background for understanding the strategies covered in the book. It is an introduction to applied human relations, where the users are encouraged to employ their knowledge, to learn from their own experiences, and to integrate the new knowledge with their own capabilities. Remember, though, that human relations, the interactions between people, is a vast subject. Only a limited understanding of this field can be gained from a book such as this. You cannot expect to become expert in these matters from the introductory exposure to theory, skills, and practice that can be covered in one book.

Even though you will not be able to utilize the strategies presented in this book without further training, you will be able to begin to use the communications skills and you should know about the strategies and their applications to be able to relate your work to the work performed by professional counselors in the human services field. For example, if you are working as a probation officer and find that one or more of your charges has difficulty meeting the terms of probation, it could be very helpful and important for you to know about the existence of behavior modification strategies and how they can help your clients gain some control over their environments and their own behaviors. You may need some assistance in formulating and applying these strategies, but you would at least know what you need further knowledge and training in.

WHO IS THE HELPER?

The helper is anyone who assists persons to overcome or to deal with problems. These problems may be caused by (1) external or environmental conditions, such as job, societal, or economic factors over which we have no control; (2) interpersonal conditions, such as clashes with family members, friends, or fellow workers; and (3) internal conditions, such as illness or inability to cope with day-to-day stresses.

We often think of human relations helpers as trained specialists such as psychiatrists, psychologists, social workers, and counselors. These are the professional helpers (representing one end of the spectrum of helpers shown in figure 1-1) who undergo extensive graduate level training in the study of human behavior and applied

helping strategies and supervised clinical training helping individuals and groups in order to develop their expertise.

Overlapping this category of helpers are paraprofessional
human services workers such as psychiatric aides or technicians,
youth street workers, day care staff, probation officers, and church
workers. They normally receive specialized human relations training
at the undergraduate college level and usually work on a team with
professionals or have professionals available for consultation and
supervision.

We certainly must also include the nonprofessionals in our discussion. Although they probably do not receive formal training as
helpers, they provide important helping assistance as individuals.
This group includes people who help on a formal basis (inter-
viewers, supervisors, teachers) and on an informal basis (friends,
relatives, colleagues).

The common denominator of these three groups of helpers is
that they all must effectively use communications skills (see chapter
3) to initiate and to develop their helping relationships (see chapter
4) with the people whom they are assisting. In order to provide this
support for more extensive kinds of problems, helpers apply certain
strategies (see chapters 6 and 7). The application of these strategies
requires formal training and experience and their utilization by
professional and some paraprofessional helpers is illustrated
throughout the book.

POINT OF VIEW

The overall philosophy of this book is that (1) effective communications are the underlying core of any helping relationship; (2)
more than one strategy can be used with any client; (3) continuous
self-evaluation of the helper and evaluation of "where the helping
relationship is" are necessary for effective helping; and (4)
awareness of the helper's own values, feelings, and thoughts is
necessary to be able to accept helpees for their needs, not for the
helper's needs. All helpers need to become familiar with the material
in this book to understand the part that counseling plays in the
delivery of human services.

The approach to helping presented in this book is flexible and
adaptable; whatever strategies or techniques are considered most
useful in a given situation will be used rather than applying one or
only a few theoretical modalities to all helping situations. The
strategies (see chapters 6 and 7) that work for a particular client may
be modified or rejected for another client in another situation.

The successful helper is familiar with many approaches and
strategies. Having a broad range of alternatives enables helpers to

select those strategies most likely to meet the needs of a particular client or client system. Underlying the use of any given strategy, however, is the trust relationship between the helper and the helpee developed during the first phase of helping. The strategy is applied using communications skills, which are essential throughout the whole helping process.

In order to be comfortable applying a variety of helping strategies, the helper must be able to deal with others in the **affective** domain (one's awareness of feelings), the **cognitive** domain (one's understanding of thinking), and the **behavioral** domain (one's acting or doing). In turn, the helper must help the client learn to function more effectively in these three domains. Therefore helpers must continually develop an understanding of themselves; they need to clarify their own social, economic, and cultural values and needs to be able to recognize and separate their needs and problems from their clients' needs and problems.

The selected strategy for formally helping a particular client may depend upon the helper's assessment of deficits in a particular domain (affective, cognitive, or behavioral). The following examples demonstrate this point.

A client was once referred to me by a colleague specifically for **systematic desensitization,** a precise behavioral technique developed by Joseph Wolpe aimed at reducing anxiety by associating the undesirable response with relaxation, an antagonistic response to anxiety, in order to extinguish the undesirable response. This client was a thirty-year-old male who experienced rage at what he considered undue noise: his wife's chewing, his coworkers' tapping pencils, his baby's crying all enraged him. After several sessions, it was determined that the client was functioning for the most part in the cognitive and behavioral domains and was completely detached from any of his own or anyone else's feelings. Thus he was unable to experience any effective human relationships and his marriage was in danger. During the following few sessions we unsuccessfully attempted systematic desensitization to satisfy the client's expectations. At the same time, I endeavored to establish a trusting relationship. When he began to trust me and to feel more comfortable, I suggested that we use some **client-centered** and **Gestalt** strategies to tap his affective domain, to help him become aware of and explore his feelings. The client's wife was eventually brought into the counseling sessions and she verified his reports that as he began to learn to experience and explore his emotions, he was better able to relate to her and others and his tolerance of outside noises began to increase.

A young lady was babysitting for a family of three children while the parents were away on a trip. A recently widowed grandmother had moved in with this family and was also there. The babysitter had been told by the parents that the grandmother was in the depressed stage of a manic-depressive illness. During the first two days, the babysitter observed that Grandma really controlled the family by refusing to eat, by talking about her poor self, and by continuous moping. Grandma was so miserable and the whole family always felt guilty and could never cheer her up, no matter what they did! Familiar with behavioral principles and reality therapy techniques and unable to endure the oppressive climate in this house, the babysitter pointed out to the three children how they were feeding into this situation and she modeled the kind of reinforcing behavior she wished them to adopt: ignoring Grandma's complaints and refusal to eat, but sitting down and talking to her and giving her lots of **strokes** (loving attention) when she expressed interest in anything other than herself. At the same time, the babysitter told Grandma that she was on to her, how she pulled the strings on members of the family. She told her that she would not accept Grandma being depressed or refusing to eat. This was done in a loving, but firm, manner. By the end of the week, Grandma was discussing the Watergate hearings with whoever would listen, was taking walks with neighbors, and was reading newspapers and books as well as eating adequate meals. She had desperately wanted attention, to feel worthwhile. Now she learned to get this attention by positive behavior because she was given the attention she desired every time she showed positive behavior.

A salesman for a large manufacturing company complained to the personnel counselor that he was under too much pressure, that he didn't think he could really do his job. He talked at length about the symptoms of his anxiety—how he couldn't sleep, how his appetite had waned. He had always been successful and now the thought of not making his quota and not receiving approval from his manager was more than he could bear. The counselor felt he was focusing excessively on his feelings, bordering on hysteria. Thus, he decided to try some **cognitive restructuring,** based on Rational-Emotive-Therapy. After several sessions and some homework reading, the salesman was able to correct some of his faulty thinking. He no longer had to tell himself that he had to achieve the highest quota in his department in order to be a worthwhile person and he owned responsibility for putting this pressure on himself and ceased blaming his manager. As he changed his thinking, his symptoms decreased. Actually, his sales increased as his self-expectations seemed to become more realistic.

We can see from these examples that (1) different people need help in different areas of functioning, (2) more successful outcomes are likely if we fit the strategy to the helpee's individual needs, and (3) sometimes the effective strategy is relatively simple and can be utilized by someone lacking lengthy, professional training.

COUNSELING

Counseling as referred to in this book encompasses the professional form of helping. The terms "counselor" and "helper" will be used interchangeably, as will the terms "helpee" and "client."

The counseling skills and knowledge covered in this book can apply to different degrees to professional, paraprofessional, or non-professional helpers. As the basic communications skills involved in formal or informal helping and in professional, paraprofessional, or nonprofessional helping relationships are the same, much of what constitutes professional training has proven to be effective for paraprofessional and lay helpers. With more training and ex-perience, the helper can deal with a greater variety of people and concerns on a more intensive or theoretical basis.

Many people consider counseling both an art and a science. It is an "art" in the sense that the personality, values, and demeanor of the counselor are important variables (along with the skills and knowledge) that are subjective and difficult to define or to measure. It is a "science" in that much of what we know about human behavior and some of the helping strategies has been developed as structured, measurable, objective systems. Similarly, counseling itself involves a two-part, although overlapping, process. The first part is more an "art" and the second part is more a "science." The process of delivery is perhaps again more an art that runs through the entire helping relationship.

Empathy, defined as understanding another person from that person's frame of reference, is a concept that underlies the entire helping relationship and is necessarily focused upon during the rapport-building initiation of a helping relationship.

The first stage of the counseling process is that of building a trust relationship. The purpose of this relationship building is to create support, trust, and open disclosure in order to uncover and explore as much information and as many feelings as possible. This exploration enables the helper and the helpee to determine mutually the goals and objectives for helping and, thus, the direction of the helping relationship. Figure 1-1 shows that this first relationship stage applies to nonprofessional, paraprofessional, and professional helpers alike.

The skills involved in relationship building on a one-to-one (i.e., one helper with one helpee) basis are fundamental skills that can be used when interacting with others at home, at school, at work, or in your community. These relationship skills are based upon the work of Carkhuff (1967, 1969, 1971, 1972, 1973), Gordon (1970), and others who have developed systematic helper training systems that derive from basic Rogerian client-centered theory (see chapter 5).

The second stage of the helping process consists of strategy planning, implementation, and evaluation, leading to termination and follow-up. This stage of the helping process is of some concern to paraprofessional helpers and normally within the province of professional helpers. The nonprofessional helper needs a rudimen-tary knowledge about the process and application of helping strategies in professional and paraprofessional helping relationships in order to understand and effect appropriate use of human services. The success of this strategies stage depends greatly upon the effectiveness of the communications skills in establishing a positive helping relationship during the first rapport-building stage (chapter 7).

HUMAN RELATIONS COUNSELING MODEL

The counseling model upon which this book is based draws upon facets of the major formal theoretical views discussed in chapter 5. It emphasizes a client-centered, problem-solving helping relationship in which behavior changes and action can result from one or both of the following: (1) the client's exploration and understanding of his or her feelings, thoughts, and actions or (2) the client's understanding of and decision to modify pertinent environmental and systemic variables. Cognitive, affective, or behavioral strategies are used alone or in concert when both the helper and the helpee determine the appropriate need and timing.

The theoretical assumptions of the human relations counseling model reflect **existential** as well as behavioristic influences. A list of those influences follows:

1. People are responsible and capable of making their own choices and decisions.

2. People are controlled to a certain extent by their environment, but they are able to direct their lives more than they realize. They always have choices and freedom, along with responsibility, even if they have restricted options due to environmental variables or inherent biological or personality predispositions.

3. Behaviors are purposive and goal directed. People are continuously striving toward meeting their own needs, ranging from basic physiological needs to abstract self-actualization (fulfilling physiological, psychological, sociological, and aesthetic needs).

4. People want to feel good about themselves and continuously need positive confirmation of their own self-worth from **significant others.** They want to feel and behave **congruently,** to reduce **dissonance** between internal and external realities.

5. People are capable of learning new behaviors and unlearning existing behaviors and they are subject to environmental and internal consequences of their behaviors, which in turn serve as **reinforcements.** They strive for reinforcements that are meaningful and congruent with their personal values and belief system.

6. People's personal problems may arise from unfinished business (unresolved conflicts) stemming from the past (concerning

events and relationships) and, although some exploration of causation may be beneficial in some cases, most problems can be worked through by focusing on the here and now, on what choices the person has now. Problems are also caused by **incongruencies** between internal (how you see things inside) and external (how you see things outside) perceptions in the present.

7.   Many problems experienced by people today are societal or systemic rather than personal or interpersonal. People are capable of learning to effect choices and changes from within the system as well as from without.

The human relations counseling model emphasizes a client-centered helping relationship and the mutual identification of goals, objectives, and intervention strategies that can ultimately be evaluated by observable behavioral change in the helpee's life. It is an eclectic approach in that it utilizes a variety of techniques and strategies, but the major vehicle for change is the development and maintenance of a warm, personally involving, empathic relationship.

The helper is encouraged to learn when and how to use different techniques and strategies and to use different approaches with the same helpee in order to deal with as many areas of concern as possible within the cognitive, affective, and behavioral domains. The goals of helping are to integrate these three domains, to help the helpee become emotionally and cognitively aware of his or her responsibility and choices, and to see this awareness translated into action. When helpees are able to assume responsibility for their feelings, thoughts, and actions and to reduce the contradictions between them, they are able to feel good about themselves and about the world and make choices that reflect the integration of internal and external variables.

The helping relationship is considered the essential foundation of the helping process. It is the *process* of verbal and nonverbal communication, not the content of verbal conversation, upon which this relationship is based. As long as there is an effective helping relationship that communicates the helper's understanding, humanness, strength, and ability to give permission and protection to the helpee, flexibility to select and utilize different strategies remains.

Strategies are secondary to the helping relationship. If a particular strategy does not work but the helping relationship is solid, the helping process is not likely to be negatively affected. For example, if you have developed a trusting relationship with a helpee and you ask her to dialogue (Gestalt technique, see chapter 5) with her mother, taking both roles to become more aware of her positive and negative feelings toward her mother, and she is unable to get into it, she will not think you are crazy or incompetent for having tried this strategy. If she trusts and respects you, she will continue to explore with you, seeking strategies that will be more helpful. This helping relationship is reciprocal, in that the helper is considered an equal of the helpee rather than an expert or magician. They work together toward achieving agreed-upon objectives. By equal, I mean that there is reduced social distance and that the responsibility for what occurs is mutual. At the same time, the helper must be able to communicate to clients an understanding of human behavior and the skills to help clients change their behaviors. This relationship aims to increase the helpee's self-understanding and exploration, but it does not provide false reassurance and support. Rather, it is honest and accepts the possibility that discomfort and pain may be involved in the helping process. This honesty enables helpers to tolerate their own and helpees' discomfort without needing to cover it up with false reassurance and distancing.

The major implications for helpers of the human relations counseling model are listed below. This model:

1. defines communications skills as the core of effective human relationships

2. allows that these communications skills can be taught to all helpers in all types of helping relationships

3. provides room for diversity and flexibility for helpers to learn a variety of intervention strategies that can be effective if the basic helping relationship is developed and maintained

4. modifies and integrates a variety of established approaches and strategies

5. provides the versatility and flexibility necessary to meet the needs of a heterogeneous population

6. provides for dealing with feelings, thoughts, and behaviors in a short-term, practical manner relating to the helpee's real life

7. focuses on the positive rather than the negative aspects of the helpee's life (i.e., what one can do to change one's life or environment rather than adjust to given outside pressures)

8. places responsibility for living and decision making upon the helpee while affording as much facilitating as humanly possible.

Dimensions of the Human Relations Counseling Model

There are three integrated dimensions of counseling: stages, skills, and issues.

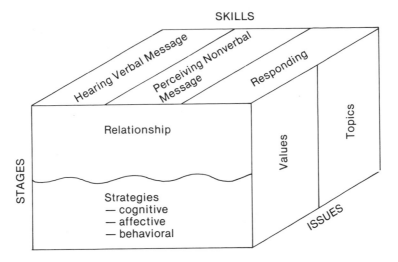

Figure 1-2   *The Counseling Model in Dimensional Terms*

Figure 1-2 shows that helping is encompassed in two overlapping stages of the first dimension. Within this dimension, the two stages of helping are accomplished in the following steps:

1. relationship (development of trust, genuineness, empathy)
    (1) initiation/entry
    (2) clarification of problem being presented
    (3) structure/contract for helping relationship
    (4) intensive exploration of problem(s)
    (5) possible goals and objectives of helping relationship

2. strategies
    (1) mutual acceptance of defined goals and objectives of helping relationship
    (2) planning of strategies
    (3) use of strategies
    (4) evaluation of strategies
    (5) termination
    (6) follow-up

The top dimension represents communications skills: hearing verbal messages, perceiving nonverbal messages, and responding to verbal and nonverbal messages. These communications skills are required to accomplish the two stages of helping (relationship and strategies) that constitute the first dimension.

The side or third dimension represents the issues, which are the values and cognitive topics that cut across the other two dimensions. These issues involve not only how an individual relates to others and his or her environment, but also such subjects as sexism, racism, ageism, and poverty. Furthermore, this dimension includes professional matters of ethics, training, and practice, as well as the personal values and attitudes of the helper.

Outlining a counseling model in diagrammatic form necessitates some formalizing and systematizing that appear rigid and arbitrary. However, this multidimensional view is useful in presenting a simple overview of what happens in and what constitutes effective helping relationships. It thereby provides a useful framework for learning about counseling and developing necessary skills. Naturally, the helper will modify or redesign this conceptual model into whatever form works for him or her.

Stages in Applying the Counseling Model

Relationship   The thesis of this book is that the development of a warm, trusting relationship between the helper and the helpee underlies any strategy or approach to the helping process and, therefore, is a core condition for any effective helping process. Developing a relationship is a time-consuming process; however, a skilled helper can guide this development so that the relationship can aid the helpee within a short period of time.

This development starts with the initial contact between the helper and the helpee. A climate is provided for the helpee to explore concerns and to begin to identify underlying as well as apparent concerns. Later, the client begins to understand these concerns and their implications for living and starts to clarify his or her needs and expectations from the helping relationship in order to facilitate self-exploration, self-understanding, and choices of action. This relationship is crucial to the mutual determination of appropriate goals and objectives and of the limits and nature of the relationship.

Strategies   Once the goals and objectives are mutually decided, the helper reviews all available effective strategies (or courses of action for effective helping) and discusses with the helpee the rationale for a suggested strategy. The possible consequences and ramifications of any strategy are explored.

When agreement on a course of action is reached, the helper applies the strategy, keeping his or her mind open to modifying or refining, depending upon the needs of the helpee. There must be continuous evaluation of the effectiveness of a particular strategy. As stated previously, the effectiveness of any strategy depends more upon the relationship between the helper and the helpee than upon the efficacy of the particular strategy.

When the desired outcomes as agreed upon by both helper and helpee are achieved, the helping relationship is either terminated or attention is focused on another set of objectives and goals. If termination is decided upon, the helper informally or formally checks up on the continued progress of the helpee at a later time.

Skills Needed to Apply the Counseling Model

The communications skills presented in this model are based upon the responsive listening format, which focuses upon hearing verbal messages, perceiving nonverbal messages, and responding to these messages both verbally and nonverbally. The model assumes consistency between the helper's verbal and nonverbal messages. It further relies upon the helper's ability to respond to the helpee by clarifying the latter's underlying feelings and thoughts in such a way as to add to the helpee's self-understanding.

By developing these communications skills, helpers also develop their own self-awareness. As they learn to use their own intuitive feelings as guidelines for hearing other people's messages, they sharpen their helping skills. Helpers are always asking themselves, "What is this person really trying to say to me?", "Why is s/he really feeling?" and they are trying to communicate their understanding of this real feeling and message back to the helpee.

Hearing Verbal Messages Verbal messages are the apparent and underlying cognitive and affective content of the helpee's statements. Understanding the content, implicit and explicit, is usually secondary to understanding the underlying messages and feelings communicated by this content.

Perceiving Nonverbal Messages Nonverbal messages refer to body language, vocal tone, facial expressions, and other cues that accompany verbal messages. The helper learns to recognize inconsistencies between verbal and nonverbal messages and to develop the helpee's awareness of these incongruencies or inconsistencies.

Responding Responding requires immediate, genuine, concrete, and empathic reaction to the verbal and nonverbal messages. Both apparent and underlying significances of messages as well as their relationships and inconsistencies affect responses.

Issues Affecting the Counseling Model

Pervasive issues affect both stages of helping. By exposing and clarifying these issues, the helper is able to achieve the type of helping relationship in which these issues do not interfere with helping.

Responsive listening skills are effective techniques for discovering and exploring these issues.

Values   Values clarification is a part of helping relationships in that the helper and the helpee both take responsibility for their own attitudes, beliefs, and values. For example, a male counselor in a high school who tells a female student that she cannot enroll or should not consider a carpentry course may be allowing his sexist values to distort or interfere with his counseling. If helpers are not aware of their own biases, the effects will be harmful. However, recognizing your own values will help you avoid imposing them on clients. Research has shown that helpers do communicate their values to helpees, whether or not they do so consciously. Bringing them out into the open and being constantly aware of your values can help you avoid imposing them.

Topics   Some of the pervasive concerns affecting the helping process are issues such as involuntary (or reluctant) clients; helper's dislike of helpees; and ethics, including confidentiality and the helper's responsibility to the sponsoring institution.

CONTENT OF THE BOOK

The human relations counseling model will be further discussed in the following chapters. Chapter 2 defines and illustrates effective and ineffective helping relationships. Chapter 3 presents materials for use in developing techniques for effective communications. Chapter 4 explores the relationship stage in depth and chapter 5 presents an overview of theoretical approaches that relate to the strategies discussed in chapter 6. In chapter 7 the application of strategies and crisis intervention are explored and chapter 8 gives a brief overview of issues affecting the helping relationship. A final postscript summarizes the entire model.

Interspersed within these chapters are case materials and exercises designed to provide an opportunity to try out your conceptual and practical understanding of the material covered in the text. The exercises are designed to be used primarily in supervised group settings.

SUMMARY

In this chapter we defined the intent and orientation of the book as providing a fundamental introduction to the skills and knowledge necessary for effective helping relationships. These skills and knowledge are needed, to varying degrees, by nonprofessional, paraprofessional, and professional human services workers. Counseling, one important part of human services, is used to represent the helping relationship.

The human relations counseling model consists of three equally important dimensions: stages (relationship and strategies), skills, and issues. These three dimensions are interdependent and cannot be considered mutually exclusive. The helping process depends upon the development of a trusting relationship between the helper(s) and the helpee(s). Effective communications skills enhance this relationship and also provide a way for dealing with controversial issues. Strategies are the various approaches that helpers use to promote self-exploration, understanding, and behavior change with helpees.

REFERENCES AND FURTHER READINGS

Carkhuff, R. *The Counselor's Contribution to Facilitative Processes.* Urbana, Il.: Parkinson, 1967.

———. *Helping and Human Relations,* vols. 1 and 2. New York: Holt, Rinehart, and Winston, 1969.

———. *The Development of Human Resources.* New York: Holt, Rinehart, and Winston, 1971.

———. *The Art of Helping.* Amherst, Ma.: Human Resource Development Press, 1972.

———. *The Art of Problem Solving.* Amherst, Ma.: Human Resource Development Press, 1973.

Carkhuff, R., and Berenson, B. *Beyond Counseling and Therapy.* New York: Holt, Rinehart, and Winston, 1967.

Gazda, G. *Human Relations Development.* Boston: Allyn and Bacon, 1973.

Gordon, T. *Parent Effectiveness Training.* New York: Wyden, 1970.

Ivey, A. *Microcounseling: Innovations in Interviewing Training.* Springfield, Il.: Thomas, 1971.

Rogers, C., ed. *The Therapeutic Relationship and Its Impact.* Madison: University of Wisconsin Press, 1967.

CHAPTER 2

THE
HELPING
RELATIONSHIP

In this chapter, I will first describe helping relationships, with particular emphasis on the communications involved. An overall view of what occurs in a helping relationship will increase your understanding of the following chapters, where we begin to talk about and practice how the helping skills and theoretical knowledge interrelate.

The purpose of a helping relationship is to meet the needs of the helpee, not those of the helper. It is meant largely to enable the helpee to assume responsibility for himself and to make his or her own decisions. Therefore, helpers neither solve helpees' problems nor reassure them merely to make them feel better.

Helpers assist and support helpees so they may come to terms with their problems by exploration, understanding, and action. For instance, if an employee comes to you and says he or she cannot continue working for the same supervisor, you may, after exploration, focus on helping the employee learn to get along better in that work setting. On the other hand, helping may well involve some direct form of environmental rearranging or systems change that has the effect of aiding someone in the system. If, in this instance, exploration determines that the supervisor is the source of the trouble and is hampering the employee's contributions to production or service, you may focus on transferring the employee to a more suitable setting, work directly with the supervisor to improve relations, or do both. A helping situation does not involve doing something to someone else to make him or her better; it does involve working together to seek the best solution and, if possible, to help in implementation of that solution.

Therefore, a helping relationship that benefits the helpee is a two-way mutual learning process between two (or more) people. The relationship is dependent for its effectiveness upon the helper possessing the skill to communicate his or her understanding of the helpee's feelings and behaviors and the ability to apply appropriate helping strategies in order to facilitate the recipient's self-exploration, self-understanding, problem solving, and decision making, all of which lead to constructive action on the part of the helpee. These capabilities can be learned by people desiring to improve their human relations skills.

There are different kinds of helping relationships, although all are similar in concept and strategies used, and they correspond to the three groups of helpers described in chapter 1. There are professional relationships (doctor - patient, pastor - congregant, counselor - client, social worker - client), where the professional helper has received intensive formal training in human behavior, problem solving, and communications related to helping. There are paraprofessional relationships (employment interviewer - applicant, case aide - client, street worker - youth, recreation leader - youth, probation officer - probationer), where shorter term formal training such as courses or workshops in human relations may be involved. There are also nonprofessional helping relationships (receptionist - customer, salesperson - customer, stewardess - passenger), where the helping process may be incidental to the relationship.

Within the category of professional relationships there are formal relationships, which usually occur in an institutional setting such as an office, a school, or a hospital, and there are informal relationships, which can occur any place—between friends, relatives, neighbors, peers or in the office, school, or hospital. Formal situations are ones in which the helper - helpee roles are stated or implied by position or contract, where the specific reason for con-

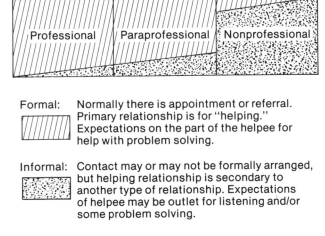

Formal: Normally there is appointment or referral. Primary relationship is for "helping." Expectations on the part of the helpee for help with problem solving.

Informal: Contact may or may not be formally arranged, but helping relationship is secondary to another type of relationship. Expectations of helpee may be outlet for listening and/or some problem solving.

Figure 2-1 *Helping Relationships*

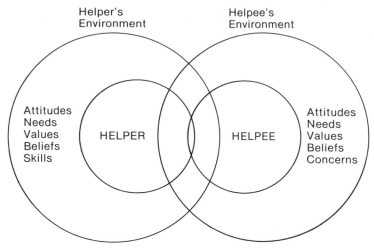

Figure 2-2 *The Helping Relationship in Its Primary Form*

tact is known to be for some kind of help. Informal helping is where the helping relationship is secondary to another relationship, whether it be a formal or informal relationship, such as principal - teacher or friend - friend. Figure 2-1 shows that as you go from professional to nonprofessional helping relationships there is less structure, shorter time involvement, and more limited expectations for problem solving and relationships tend to become less formal.

ESSENTIAL COMMUNICATIONS

Regardless of the setting or nature of the helping relationship, regardless of the personal values and beliefs of the people involved, and regardless of the theoretical orientation of the professional helper, the underlying prerequisite skill in any helping relationship is effective communication. The author's experience and a wide spectrum of research verifies this conclusion.

Figure 2-2 shows the helping relationship in its primary form. The helper and the helpee are always engaged in mutual communication. The principal difference between them is that the helper possesses some skills (expertise) and the helpee possesses some concerns (problems). Put any names in the circles and put the circles in any context and the relationships are still essentially the same.

How can we help someone if we cannot learn their concerns and impart to them our feelings or thoughts? Both processes are dependent upon the ability to communicate. Communication in this sense means the capacity to listen, to pay attention, to perceive, and to respond verbally and nonverbally to the helpee. This ability can be learned by most people, regardless of their educational background or personality. It is a skill that requires continuous practice, as does any type of skill learning. Not surprisingly, it is found that those people considered by others to be most helpful in formal or informal settings possess heightened communication skills.

Research indicates that communication problems are the major source of interpersonal difficulties. For example, most marital and family problems stem from misunderstanding or other ineffective communications, resulting in frustration and anger when implicit expectations and desires are not fulfilled. Yet a major problem of the people who seek professional help is their inability to communicate these problems or concerns. Therefore, it is necessary to look closely at the process (a sequence of events that takes place over a period of time) of communication within helping relationships.

POSITIVE AND NEGATIVE COMMUNICATIONS BEHAVIORS

Most of us have been helpees on numerous occasions; so, based on our own experience, we should be able to recognize helpers' communications behaviors that have aided or hindered our receiving help. If you were asked to list those verbal and nonverbal behaviors that you, as the helpee, found supportive in any kind of helping relationship, what would your list look like? Table 2-1 lists behaviors typically cited by beginning counseling students. Most students can more easily state verbal behaviors than nonverbal. See if you agree with these lists or can add to them.

The gist of both these lists is that in the helping relationships

Table 2-1 *Helping Behaviors*

Verbal	Nonverbal
uses understandable words	tone of voice similar to helpee's
reflects back and clarifies helpee statements	maintains good eye contact
appropriately interprets	occasional head nodding
summarizes for helpee	facial animation
responds to primary message	occasional smiling
uses verbal reinforcers e.g., "mm-mm," "I see," "Yes"	occasional hand gesturing
calls helpee by first name or "you"	close physical proximity
appropriately gives information	moderate rate of speech
answers questions about self	body leans toward helpee
uses humor occasionally to reduce tension	occasional touching
is nonjudgmental	
adds greater understanding to helpee's statement	
phrases interpretations tentatively so as to elicit genuine feedback from helpee	

students judge most effective, helpers show listening and attending behaviors that communicate empathy, encouragement, support, honesty, caring, concern, respect, sharing, affection, protection, potency, and nonjudgmental acceptance. Clients are helped because they feel worthwhile as human beings, feel accepted by another human being, and are therefore permitted to be their true selves and to explore their true concerns.

Similarly, you can undoubtedly recognize indications of non-helping communications behavior. Would you add to or change the lists presented in table 2-2? We can see that these verbal and nonverbal behaviors involve inattentiveness, imposition of the helper's values and beliefs on the helpee, judgment, and "I know what's best for you" or "I'm better than you" attitudes. They hinder because they put the helpees on the defensive immediately and make them feel so worthless that they will naturally choose avoidance rather than approach behaviors.

Table 2-2 *Nonhelping Behaviors*

Verbal	Nonverbal
advice giving	looking away from helpee
preaching	sitting far apart or turned from
placating	helpee
blaming	physical sneers
cajoling	frowning
exhorting	scowling
extensive probing and questioning—	tight mouth
especially "why" questions	shaking pointed finger
directing, demanding	distracting gestures
patronizing attitude	yawning
overinterpretation	closing eyes
using words helpee doesn't understand	unpleasant tone of voice
straying from topic	too slow or too fast rate of speech
intellectualizing	
overanalyzing	
talking about self too much	

The purpose of presenting the case interactions in exercises 2-1 through 2-5 is to determine whether or not you can recognize what is effective and what is not effective in a helping relationship in the following exchanges. Read each of the excerpts, transcribed from actual helping encounters, and then rank the helper's responses on a 0 - 5 scale (0=least helpful, 5=most helpful) before reading my comments and discussing your fellow students' reactions. Obviously, you can only respond to the verbal content. A variation of this might involve acting out the roles in the excerpt. Comments on the exercises are found at the end of the chapter. For these and all the exercises in this book please remember that there is usually no right or wrong answer. They should be used as a focus for discussion of peoples' differences in perceptions and responses.

Exercise 2-1. Ms. James is a twenty-six-year-old clerk-typist in the marketing department of a large publishing firm. She has worked there for sixteen months and her overall annual job evaluation rating was "Fair." Specific comments that contributed to this rating were "late for work," "does not accept criticism well," "scowls when asked to retype assignments." Ms. James has come into the personnel office to request a job change.

(1) *Personnel clerk:* I see Ms. James, that you haven't been doing too ~judgemental~ well in the marketing department. What's going on down there?

    Ms. James: Mr. Barber is very difficult to work for. He picks on everything I do and I just know he doesn't like me.

(2) *Personnel clerk:* Well, Mr. Barber feels that *your* attitude is poor and that you are not doing your work as fast or as accurately as he needs it.

    Ms. James: I'm doing it as well as I can. I'm much faster than the other girls in the office and he never picks on them. Why doesn't he leave me alone? He always hovers over my desk (shudders).

(3) *Personnel clerk:* Look, Ms. James, we both know that jobs are tight now and that you need to work. With such a poor reference from Mr. Barber, I couldn't possibly place you anywhere else in this company. Try real hard in the next couple of months to do better and then after your eighteen-month evaluation, we'll see what we can do.

    Ms. James: (sighing) O.K. I guess I'm stuck. I still don't think I can ever make him like me, though.

How would you rate each of the personnel clerk's (helper) statements?

(1)

0	1	2	3	4	5
NOT HELPFUL		MODERATELY HELPFUL			HELPFUL

(2)

0	1	2	3	4	5
NOT HELPFUL		MODERATELY HELPFUL			HELPFUL

(3)

0	1	2	3	4	5
NOT HELPFUL		MODERATELY HELPFUL			HELPFUL

What were your reasons for these ratings? What verbal behaviors from tables 2-1 and 2-2 can you identify? Think about these and then write in what you might have said if you were the personnel clerk. You can then look at my comments at the end of the chapter. How do you think Ms. James was feeling during this session? What was the personnel clerk doing? What do you think the problem really was and whose problem was it? These are the kinds of questions we continually ponder when participating in or observing helping relationships.

Exercise 2-2. Ms. Smith is a luncheon aide at the neighborhood elementary school. One day, while she is supervising a fourth grade class during the lunch hour, Tommy runs up to her and angrily denounces Steven for stealing his yogurt from his lunchbag. In reviewing the situation, Ms. Smith discovers that Steven has indeed taken and consumed Tommy's yogurt.

(1) *Ms. Smith:*   Steven, why did you take Tommy's yogurt? *why*

Steven: I dunno.

(2) *Ms. Smith:*   Don't you know that it's wrong to steal? *preach*

Steven: Uh-huh.

(3) *Ms. Smith:*   I'm going to have to tell Mr. Singer about this. *punish*
You go sit in the corner until he comes back.

Steven: O.K.

How would you rate each of Ms. Smith's statements?

(1)

0	1	2	3	4	5
NOT HELPFUL		MODERATELY HELPFUL			HELPFUL

(2)

0	1	2	3	4	5
NOT HELPFUL		MODERATELY HELPFUL			HELPFUL

(3)

0	1	2	3	4	5
NOT HELPFUL		MODERATELY HELPFUL			HELPFUL

Again, try to determine what your reasons were for these ratings. What verbal behaviors from tables 2-1 and 2-2 can you identify? How might you have handled this situation? How do you think Steven feels? How does Ms. Smith feel? What is she doing?

Exercise 2-3. Julie, age twenty-two, came in to see her college counselor. She has been married for two years and is seriously contemplating divorce. (This information was given over the telephone to the counselor when the appointment was made.) The following is an excerpt from the middle part of the first session:

(1) *Counselor:* Can you tell me about how things are in your marriage now?

Julie: Pretty bad. He's always working—we never do anything together. We really have nothing to say to each other. I'm so bored I could scream!

(2) *Counselor:* Things are pretty tough for you.

Julie: (beginning to cry) He never wants to go anywhere or do anything. He doesn't like to be with people. We don't have any friends together at all.

(3) *Counselor:* You feel angry, as if you can't go out and do what you want on your own.

Julie: Yes. But sometimes I do go out. Like last Sunday I asked Steve if he wanted to go to the ballet with me. I asked him three times. He said no, I should go by myself. I did, too!

(4) *Counselor:* Yet you felt bad about leaving him.

Julie: I don't want to hurt him.

(5) *Counselor:* You feel as if you are responsible for him.

Julie: Well, yes, of course . . . everything I do . . . I worry about what's going to happen to him.

(6) *Counselor:* Wow! That's quite a burden of responsibility you're carrying around on your shoulders.

Julie: What do you mean?

(7) *Counselor:* I was just thinking that it's hard enough to be responsible for one's self. You can be responsible *to* someone else, but if you take on the responsibility *for* all of their feelings, thoughts, and actions, that's quite a load! It would scare me.

Julie: Yeah, I see what you mean. But aren't I responsible for my husband's feelings?

(8) *Counselor:* You tell me.

Julie: Maybe that's why I always feel so hemmed in. I never seem to have any fun.

(9) *Counselor:* Tell me about the last time you had fun.

Julie: Last summer I worked as a waitress in a restaurant. It was great. I loved it. I felt so alive and I was with people all the time. I really loved it.

(10) *Counselor:*   You seem to miss that a lot.

       Julie: I had to stop to go back to school. I didn't want to stop though.

(11) *Counselor:*   You think a lot about going back to that kind of job.

       Julie: Yes, I wish I could. I really liked all the attention I got.

(12) *Counselor:*   It was exciting to have people notice you and respond to you.

       Julie: Um-mm. I don't want to miss it all.

(13) *Counselor:*   Miss?

       Julie: You know, the fun and the excitement . . .

(14) *Counselor:*   You feel as if you don't have any fun and excitement with Steve.

       Julie: That's right. Not for a long time, probably never.

(15) *Counselor:*   You're really very angry at Steve. You feel cheated, as if he is keeping you from having any fun and excitement.

       Julie: Yes, that's it. Please, can you help me?

Although this was a rather lengthy excerpt, let's see if you can go through the same process as before and rate each response.

(1) _____

0	1	2	3	4	5
NOT HELPFUL		MODERATELY HELPFUL			HELPFUL

(2) _____

0	1	2	3	4	5
NOT HELPFUL		MODERATELY HELPFUL			HELPFUL

(3) _____

0	1	2	3	4	5
NOT HELPFUL		MODERATELY HELPFUL			HELPFUL

(4) _____

0	1	2	3	4	5
NOT HELPFUL		MODERATELY HELPFUL			HELPFUL

(5) _____

| 0 | 1 | 2 | 3 | 4 | 5 |

NOT
HELPFUL

MODERATELY
HELPFUL

HELPFUL

(6) _____

| 0 | 1 | 2 | 3 | 4 | 5 |

NOT
HELPFUL

MODERATELY
HELPFUL

HELPFUL

(7) _____

| 0 | 1 | 2 | 3 | 4 | 5 |

NOT
HELPFUL

MODERATELY
HELPFUL

HELPFUL

(8) _____

| 0 | 1 | 2 | 3 | 4 | 5 |

NOT
HELPFUL

MODERATELY
HELPFUL

HELPFUL

(9) _____

| 0 | 1 | 2 | 3 | 4 | 5 |

NOT
HELPFUL

MODERATELY
HELPFUL

HELPFUL

(10) _____

| 0 | 1 | 2 | 3 | 4 | 5 |

NOT
HELPFUL

MODERATELY
HELPFUL

HELPFUL

(11) _____

| 0 | 1 | 2 | 3 | 4 | 5 |

NOT
HELPFUL

MODERATELY
HELPFUL

HELPFUL

(12) _____

| 0 | 1 | 2 | 3 | 4 | 5 |

NOT
HELPFUL

MODERATELY
HELPFUL

HELPFUL

(13) _____

| 0 | 1 | 2 | 3 | 4 | 5 |

NOT
HELPFUL

MODERATELY
HELPFUL

HELPFUL

(14) _____

| 0 | 1 | 2 | 3 | 4 | 5 |

NOT
HELPFUL

MODERATELY
HELPFUL

HELPFUL

0	1	2	3	4	5
NOT HELPFUL		MODERATELY HELPFUL			HELPFUL

You will be able to identify several different verbal behaviors and feelings of both the counselor and the client in this lengthier transcript. What do you think the counselor is doing and why? See if you can trace Julie's feelings through the excerpt.

Exercise 2-4. Danny, age seventeen, comes into his counselor's office during his senior year in high school. Danny is a B+ student with above average SAT scores and a very good extracurricular record. His counselor has known him for two and one-half years and knows that he is the oldest of three children, that his parents are of moderate means and eager for him to go to college but concerned about the financial aspect. Danny has recently been awarded a full tuition state scholarship at the university or college of his choice within his home state.

(1) *Counselor:* Danny, congratulations! I was so pleased to hear about your scholarship.

Danny: Thanks, Mr. Dawson. But, you know, I really want to go to Miami University in Ohio.

(2) *Counselor:* Why, Danny! How could you think of such a thing! Think how much money you'll save your folks if you stay in the state. There are some fine schools here.

Danny: Yeah . . . my folks say I should do whatever I really want to do. They suggested I come talk to you about it.

(3) *Counselor:* Yes, Danny. I'm sure they want you to do what you want. Your folks really are wonderful. But they're probably not telling you what they really think. You know they've been worried about college costs and this just works out beautifully for all of you.

Danny: Well, I don't know. I guess I'll go back and talk to them.

How would you rate each of the counselor's statements in this excerpt?

(1)

0	1	②	3	4	5
NOT HELPFUL		MODERATELY HELPFUL			HELPFUL

positive toward client

(2) _ignores his message - imposes values_

0	1	2	3	4	5
NOT HELPFUL		MODERATELY HELPFUL			HELPFUL

(3) _Assuming_

0	1	2	3	4	5
NOT HELPFUL		MODERATELY HELPFUL			HELPFUL

Exercise 2-5. Mr. Williams, age thirty-two, is seeing his employment counselor about some forthcoming job interviews. He has been laid off for three months now and has a wife and two young children to support. He has had several unsuccessful job interviews over the past two months.

Mr. Williams: I'm really uptight. And so's my wife. She gets mad when I come home from these job interviews with no job. Who's gonna pay the bills she asks?

(1) *Counselor:* It really is rough to be in your position. Sounds to me like you're pretty worried about the job interviews we've set up.

Mr. Williams: (nodding) Well, I must be doing something wrong. None of them have even given me a chance. I must be a real dud. Why should these be any different?

(2) *Counselor:* You really want to be able to do better and you're worried that maybe you can't.

Mr. Williams: I don't know. I never used to flub interviews. I get so nervous now.

(3) *Counselor:* The tension of being out of work is really affecting everything.

Mr. Williams: Yes. I think I come on too strong . . . too wound up. You know, it's like I'm trying to please too much. I just can't seem to help it.

(4) *Counselor:* Since your next interview is tomorrow, let's take the rest of our time to practice interviewing. It might help you to feel more comfortable.

How would you rate each of the counselor's comments?

(1) _____

0	1	2	3	4	5
NOT HELPFUL		MODERATELY HELPFUL			HELPFUL

(2)

0	1	2	3	4	5
NOT HELPFUL		MODERATELY HELPFUL			HELPFUL

(3)

0	1	2	3	4	5
NOT HELPFUL		MODERATELY HELPFUL			HELPFUL

(4)

0	1	2	3	4	5
NOT HELPFUL		MODERATELY HELPFUL			HELPFUL

RESEARCH FINDINGS

Now that we have spent some time differentiating between helpful and nonhelpful verbal communications in terms of specific examples, we can look at what researchers have found about the characteristics of the helper in a helping relationship. Review the list of desirable versus undesirable behaviors, which we may have modified since our first reading, and we can start to generalize about helpful and nonhelpful traits for the effective helper. However, let's not be too quick in drawing conclusions.

Human relations trainers are aware that some students who come into their programs with certain personal attitudes and traits seem to absorb and to integrate their academic training with their living style more easily than some other students. Yet when we try to identify the traits that support students' progress as helpers, we—both teachers and students—become rather vague. We make references to "emotional maturity," "flexibility," "open-mindedness," "intelligence," "warmth," and "sensitivity." Yet these subjective terms tell us little that we can use directly for professional growth.

Professional training traditionally involves the study of the academic disciplines of psychology, sociology, anthropology, and the specialized knowledge and skill areas of counseling. Yet an increasing body of evidence supports the idea that helpers are only as effective helpers as they are self-aware and able to use their own selves as vehicles of change. Therefore, training in content may not be as important as training in process, skills, and self-knowledge. Knowledge in academic disciplines and underlying theory are important, but human relations training programs need to focus more on trainees' self-awareness and communications skills. Integration of personal experience with supervised field experience and academic training becomes essential for developing ability as a helper.

An initial review of the research about helper characteristics can be overwhelming in that we may wonder if "self-actualized" human beings (those who have achieved self-understanding and fulfillment) really exist! However, if we focus on the commonalities in key research studies, we should be able to identify the "characteristics" of effective helpers. We can find some initial answers in a few milestone studies.

Combs, et al. (1969) in their University of Florida research found that effective helping practitioners in school and college teaching, counseling, nursing, and ministering share certain beliefs about the following:

1. *Knowledge.* For effective professional helping, practitioners must be personally committed to specialized knowledge in their field and must find this knowledge personally meaningful.

2. *People.* People are viewed as able rather than unable, worthy rather than unworthy, internally rather than externally motivated, dependable rather than undependable, helpful rather than hindering.

3. *Self-concept.* Helper's self-concept involves feeling personally adequate rather than inadequate, identifying with rather than apart from others, feeling trustworthy rather than untrustworthy, feeling wanted rather than unwanted, feeling worthy rather than unworthy.

4. *Helping purposes.* Helpers are freeing rather than controlling people, deal with larger rather than smaller issues, are more self-revealing than self-concealing, are more involved with than alienated from clients, are more process oriented than goal oriented in helping relationships.

5. *Approaches to helping.* Helpers are more directed toward people than things, are more likely to approach helpees subjectively or **phenomenologically** than objectively or factually.

Rogers (1958) believes that helpers must be open and that the following conditions are necessary for helpee development in a helping relationship:

1. *Unconditional positive regard.* Helpers should communicate acceptance of helpees as worthwhile persons, regardless of who they are or what they say or do.

2. *Congruence.* Helpers should evidence congruence between their sayings and behavior. In other words, they should practice what they preach.

3. *Genuineness.* Helpers should be real and sincere, honest and clear.

4. *Empathic.* Helpers should be able to communicate empathic understanding of helpees' frames of reference and should let them know they feel and understand helpees' concerns from the helpees' points of view.

Developing Rogers' theoretical formulations into applied research, Carkhuff and Truax (1967, pp. 26 - 30) have identified four core dimensions that facilitate effective helping relationships if communicated at high levels. They have demonstrated that paraprofessionals as well as professionals can receive training to increase their levels of communication of these four dimensions and that this increased communications ability has a positive effect on the helpee's development and change. The dimensions are

1. *Empathy.* Helpers are able to communicate to the helpee their own self-awareness and understanding in relation to the helpee, providing the helpee with an experiential base for change.

2. *Respect and positive regard.* Helpers can communicate their own warmth and caring.

3. *Genuineness.* Helpers can be honest with themselves and their helpees.

4. *Concreteness.* Helpers can be accurate, clear, specific, and immediate in their responses to client statements.

Brammer (1973, pp. 21 - 26) believes that the following conditions are necessary:

1. *Self-awareness.* Helpers should be aware of their own values and feelings, of the use (and power) of their ability to function as models for helpees.

2. *Interest.* Helpers should show interest in people and in social change.

3. *Ethical behavior.* Helpers should demonstrate commitment to behaviors that are reflections of their own moral standards, of society's codes, and of the norms of the helping profession.

Thus, we see that helpers' self-awareness and communications skills are common threads from the above lists. It is hard to separate the helper's personality characteristics from his or her levels and styles of functioning, as both are interrelated. Likewise, it is difficult to assess which variable (the knowledge base of understanding behavior or the ability to communicate this understanding) has greater influence on a helping relationship.

HELPING CHARACTERISTICS

You may draw your own conclusions from the cited studies and other findings on what characterizes effective helping and on the role of communications. Nevertheless, let us look at what they mean in an applied context. I believe that the following qualities, behaviors, and knowledge of helpers are most influential in affecting the behaviors, attitudes, and feelings of helpees. And these qualities, behaviors, and knowledge are the same for professional, paraprofessional, and nonprofessional helpers in any context.

Qualities

Self-awareness   Individuals who continually develop their own self-understanding and awareness are more likely to be effective as helpers than those who do not, because they are then able to separate their needs, perceptions, and feelings from those of their clients and are better able to use their self-awareness as a basis for helping others develop their own self-awareness. Development of self-awareness also allows us personally to experience the process, both happy and painful, of human development and the impact of societal, cultural, and familial influences on behavior. This ability can result in more effective use of the self as a vehicle for the helper to transmit change. Helpers who are self-aware continually ask themselves questions such as, "What's really going on here?", "How come I'm feeling this way?", "Am I really listening to what is being said or am I projecting my own perceptions and feelings?", and "Whose problem is this—mine or the helpee's?"

To illustrate, consider the following example:

Sara Jane was a counseling intern in an elementary school and was working with a sixth-grade student named Elizabeth. Elizabeth was telling Sara Jane how upset she was with her mother because her mother would not let her drop out of Girl Scouts and participate instead in after-school sports.

> *Elizabeth:* I really want to stay for after-school sports, but my mom just won't let me. She says I've been in Girl Scouts for so long that it would be a shame to drop it now.

> *Counselor:* You are angry with your mother for not letting you do what you want to do.

Elizabeth:	She's always on my back, always telling me what I can and can't do. I just wish she'd leave me alone.
Counselor:	I don't blame you for being so angry, Elizabeth. Why don't you just tell her that you're old enough to make your own decisions and that you want her to leave you alone.
Elizabeth:	Do you really think I can do that? Boy, she might really cream me.
Counselor:	She has to learn to let you lead your own life.

Remember that this client is an eleven-year-old girl! Although she may be experiencing a normal developmental desire for more independence, should she lead her own life? Instead of helping Elizabeth to explore and understand her independence - dependence conflict, the counselor is giving her permission to rebel. A discussion of this excerpt with the counselor made it apparent that the counselor was overidentifying with Elizabeth and putting words into her mouth that she, the counselor, would like to be able to say to her mother. A more self-aware counselor might say to herself, "This sounds familiar to me. I can certainly understand Elizabeth's feelings, but I must be careful not to let my own needs and feelings interfere with hers."

Honesty One of the major variables in developing trust, honesty is a crucial ingredient for any effective interpersonal relationship. We may not always agree with what someone says, but if we believe the other person is being honest, we can respect that person. Helpers can communicate honesty by being open with clients, by answering questions to the best of their ability, and by admitting mistakes or lack of knowledge.

Honesty is more than just being truthful; it is also being open to exploration and being fair in evaluation. One way to assess your own honesty as a helper is to invite honest feedback from clients and peers to see how they view you. Consider the following example of honesty in a helping relationship:

Ms. Barnes is a registered nurse who has had specialized training in rape counseling. She is on call at a city hospital emergency ward that provides follow-up counseling to rape victims. Ms. Barnes is talking with a 23-year-old woman who was assaulted three days earlier.

Ms. Barnes:	You're feeling a lot of pressure from your family and the police to press charges against this guy, aren't you?
Woman:	It's been just awful and I don't know what to do. Everyone's been telling me what I should do,

	what the right thing is. Please tell me—you've been involved with this kind of business before. What do you think I should do?
Ms. Barnes:	It's quite a dilemma and one that only you can resolve. There really is no one right answer for everyone, you know.
Woman:	What would you do if you were me?
Ms. Barnes:	I honestly don't know, and I've thought about that a lot. I'd like to think I'd have the guts to testify, but after what I've seen, I'm not so sure. It's very rough going, takes a lot of time and there's continuous harassment and you really have to be tough to take it. Not many people can take it and it doesn't mean that you're not brave or good if you don't.

Ms. Barnes was then able to provide factual information about the judicial process in these types of cases and help the woman explore and understand her feelings and thoughts about this. Because the counselor was open about her own views on the matter, she created a climate of trust and openness. This attitude is more than honesty. But at one point later in the session, the woman verbally expressed appreciation of Ms. Barnes' "no nonsense, honest approach."

You may be wondering how you can be honest in a situation where you find yourself unable to like or agree with the helpee. These situations do occur and, short of referral to another helper, we need to admit to ourselves these negative reactions and to separate them from our dealings. This will be further explored in chapter 8.

Congruence A commonly voiced criticism of the adult generation by today's youth is that of "hypocrisy"—incongruence or inconsistency between the words and actions of their elders. Perhaps this incongruence occurs when we have not engaged ourselves in a conscious process of examining, clarifying, and acknowledging our own values and beliefs.

An individual who experiences congruence between his or her own values and beliefs and his or her life style communicates more credibility and exerts more modeling potency than someone whose energy is used to deny incongruence. Further, if one has clarified and "owned" one's value system, one is better able to express one's values and beliefs without imposing them on others, thus allowing a more honest, nonjudgmental relationship.

If you believe that the purpose of a helping relationship is to facilitate the helpee's self-understanding and decision making and not to impose the helper's standards and values on the helpee, then you will agree that this congruence, which in turn depends upon the helper's own self-awareness, is an important factor for effective helping relationships. This point of view does not imply that there is a "right" or "wrong" value system for helpers. Rather it simply advocates congruence between what we believe, what we say, and what we live. Furthermore, it has been the author's experience that people who are aware of and secure in their own values and beliefs are not threatened when faced with divergent or contrasting values and beliefs. Therefore, they are better able to help effectively a broader spectrum of people. An example of congruence is seen in the following exchange:

Ms. Jones is a welfare worker who is making a home visit to the Becker family. The Beckers have six children, live in a two-room apartment, and have been on welfare since Mr. Becker lost his job a year ago. They are having a very difficult time budgeting for sufficient food.

Ms. Jones:	I don't know how anyone can survive a visit to the market these days, food stamps or not!
Ms. Becker:	I just can't manage, that's all. We're lucky if we have meat once a week, the way things are. There just isn't enough.
Ms. Jones:	It is frustrating and also challenging. I do believe we can all find creative ways and change our eating habits for the better.
Ms. Becker:	It's impossible, believe me. Easy for people like you to say. You try and feed a family of eight on this kind of money. . . .
Ms. Jones:	I'm not saying it's easy, but it is being done. Let me tell you what I've been doing—collecting new casserole and leftover recipes and now we're having more fish, cheese, and poultry and much less beef. Several of us in the office have started to collect a pool of new recipes from ourselves and our clients. I'd be glad to send you some and maybe you could give us some of yours to spread around.
Ms. Becker:	No fooling! You people are really doing that?

This incident actually did occur and is an example of a helper implementing with action what she says (practicing what she preaches). The point is that phoniness comes through and contaminates the helper's credibility and potency.

Behaviors

As discussed earlier in this chapter, the ability to communicate what we perceive, feel, and believe is an extremely crucial aspect of any interpersonal relationship. Research substantiates that developing and utilizing these skills has a positive effect on helping relationships. Let's carry this a step further by suggesting that we can effect positive human relations by continuously teaching (instructionally and by modeling) these same communication skills that we attempt to master to our clients and anyone else in our orbit, formally or informally. Examples of these skills are illustrated in chapter 3.

Knowledge

As you will see in chapter 5, a knowledge of the theories upon which effective helping is based is essential to the professional practitioner. To a lesser degree, this is also true for the paraprofessional. Likewise, the knowledge of research and applied findings make it possible for the nonprofessional helper to do a meaningful job.

An example of how disastrous a lack of theoretical knowledge can be is illustrated in this actual situation:

> Mr. Howard, a sixth-grade teacher, referred two of his female students to a consulting psychiatrist because he was concerned about their "homosexual tendencies." When asked to share his observations, Mr. Howard said that these two girls held hands, wrote notes to each other during class, always went to the girls' room together, and were really inseparable. Although Mr. Howard was a counselor-in-training, he claimed that his role as a teacher prohibited him from talking to the girls directly about his concerns.

The consulting psychiatrist was quick to point out that there was no basis whatsoever for Mr. Howard's conclusions about these two girls. A basic knowledge in developmental psychology (as well as awareness of his personal values) would have assured Mr. Howard that same-sex peer affiliation is indeed "normal" at preadolescent ages, that the need for close relationships is prevalent at this age.

SUMMARY

A helping relationship involves communications between two or more people to explore the helpee's beliefs, values, attitudes, feelings, and behaviors in order to increase his or her self-understanding (and understanding of others) and to facilitate his or her deciding upon a course of action, taking this action, and assuming responsibility for the consequences of this action. There are many different kinds and levels of helping relationships and many different approaches to helping people, but communications is the basic dimension of any and all helping relationships. In informal helping relationships, there is a mutuality that does not exist in more formal helping relationships. Helpers and helpees can switch roles in informal relationships.

Both our experience and research indicate that certain traits and characteristics of helpers appear to affect positively helping relationships. Whatever these traits and characteristics, the more in touch a person is with his or her own beliefs, behaviors, and feelings and the better he or she is able to communicate genuinely, clearly, and empathically self-understanding and understanding of the helpee and others, the more likely the helper is to be effective. Certain communications behaviors seem to translate the needed traits and characteristics. The exercises in this chapter were intended to enable you to recognize what verbal communications are and are not facilitative.

COMMENTS ON EXERCISES

Exercise 2-1.

From this excerpt, we really don't know whose problem this is —Mrs. James's or Mr. Barber's. The personnel clerk assumed that the problem was Ms. James's and made no attempt to verify this assumption by gathering new data from her. By learning more about Ms. James's thoughts, feelings, and behaviors the personnel clerk might have begun to help her clarify the nature of the problem, what part of it she can own, and what are her options and other alternatives for coping with the problem. In order to be helpful, the personnel clerk should have helped Ms. James feel worthwhile as a human being, regardless of what she is or is not doing (so that she may retain her dignity), and at the same time encouraged Ms. James to explore more fully and understand what is happening to her, to take responsibility for herself. The personnel clerk's three statements were not helpful; no clarification or change occurred. Behaviors that the personnel clerk utilized were judging, blaming, and telling the client what to do. Ms. James was feeling defensive, as one is likely to feel when attacked. She had come to the personnel office to see about a job change and she never really got the chance to do so; she was immediately pushed into a corner.

Exercise 2-2.

This short excerpt is all too typical of the interactions between adults, who see themselves as being helpful, and youngsters, who have been "caught in the act" of doing something wrong. Ms. Smith is not being helpful in that she is not helping Steven to retain his feeling of self-worth and dignity or to understand his own behavior.

Nor is he being helped even to begin to verbalize what it really was all about, much less what he can do in the future about this type of behavior. Ms. Smith is apparently not concerned with Steven's feelings nor is she concerned with trying to understand him. Behaviors that she utilized were judging, punishing, threatening, and blaming. Asking "why" questions insures defensiveness. If people knew why they did something, they would not have to get into such compromising situations. Asking questions such as Ms. Smith did cuts off communications and encourages denial and withdrawal. Exploration and understanding cannot occur if communications are cut off. Like Ms. James, Ms. Smith most likely feels angry and frustrated at not being able to control a situation. A more appropriate response for Ms. Smith would have been, "Steven, it's very difficult when somebody else has something that you really want to have." This response would have allowed Steven the opportunity to tell his side of the story to an empathic listener.

Exercise 2-3.

Julie's counselor demonstrated effective responsive listening skills and succeeded in eliciting much affect (feeling) and **content** (information) from her. Some of the responses are more helpful than others, but overall this was a helpful first session in what subsequently became a short-term helping relationship. (At the end of this helping relationship, Julie was able to decide for herself and take responsibility for her decision and action regarding her marriage.) Behaviors that the counselor utilized were reflection, empathy, clarification, and interpretation. This is a lengthy excerpt, so let's take each counselor statement.

(1) This is a good "opener," eliciting more information on an open-ended level.

(2) This is a reflective, empathic statement in that it conveys the counselor's understanding of Julie's intense feeling.

(3) Again, this adds clarity by focusing on Julie's feelings.

(4) Some interpretation is here in that the counselor was interpreting the nonverbal behavior that accompanied this statement.

(5) Again, there is some interpretation. The client's response indicates that the counselor was on target.

(6) and (7) Counselor focuses on the responsibility issue, adding some possible materials for client to consider.

(8) Counselor backs away from imposing own values here but succeeds in putting the issue back in the client's hands.

(9) Another exploratory statement—open ended.

(10) There is some interpretation of the underlying message here.

(11) This is a probing statement. The counselor is not quite sure if this is the right track.

(12) Again, probing.

(13) Strictly reflection.

(14) This is reflecting the client's statement but bringing it back to her relationship with her husband.

(15) The counselor is responding to the intense underlying feeling and focusing this feeling on the husband.

The counselor had to make some decisions during this excerpt about what she would focus on with the client; there were many alternative directions she could have followed and one is not necessarily "more right" than another. Julie was helped to begin to explore what was bothering her and to begin to understand some of her feelings. This is only the beginning—from here, continuing to develop the relationship, the counselor can help Julie assume responsibility for herself and make her own decisions.

Exercise 2-4.

Danny's counselor did not even recognize Danny's feelings, much less show concern for them. He was not helpful to Danny at all because he was imposing his own values and beliefs on Danny and telling him what the "right" thing was to do. If allowed to explore all the options and ramifications, Danny might very well have decided to remain within the state, but he, not the counselor, would have made the decision. He might also have found some ways of being able to attend the university of his choice, through a work program or some other means. Behaviors used here were projection, telling what to do, and judging. The first statement was moderately helpful in that it allowed Danny the opportunity to pursue what was on his mind and conveyed genuine pleasure and caring. However, the second and third counselor statements were not helpful in that they took over and did not allow Danny to work this through on his own.

Exercise 2-5.

Mr. Williams's counselor demonstrated helpful communications skills. He took his time in drawing out his client so that it was the client, not the counselor, who clarified the problem by elaborating on his "coming on too strong" in job interviews. A less patient counselor might have aided the client in bemoaning his misfortune rather than seeing what might be done about it. Each of the three counselor responses demonstrates empathy, reflection, and congruence. The last counselor statement is action oriented, taking into consideration the nature of the problem and the available time for intervention.

REFERENCES AND FURTHER READINGS

Brammer, L. *The Helping Relationship.* Englewood Cliffs, N.J.: Prentice-Hall, 1973.

Brammer, L., and Shostrum, E. *Therapeutic Psychology: Fundamentals of Actualization Counseling and Psychotherapy.* 2d ed. Englewood Cliffs, N.J.: Prentice-Hall, 1968.

Carkhuff, R. *The Art of Helping.* Amherst, Ma.: Human Resource Development Press, 1972.

Carkhuff, R., and Truax, C. *Beyond Counseling and Therapy.* New York: Holt, Rinehart, & Winston, 1967.

Combs, A., et al. *Florida Studies in the Helping Professions.* Gainsville: University of Florida Press, 1969.

Combs, A.; Avila, D.; and Purkey, W. *Helping Relationships, Basic Concepts for the Helping Profession.* Boston: Allyn and Bacon, 1971.

Pietrofesa, J.; Leonard, G.; and Van Hoose, W. *The Authentic Helper.* Chicago: Rand McNally, 1971.

Rogers, C. "The Characteristics of a Helping Relationship." *Personnel and Guidance Journal* 37 (1958): 6 - 16.

———. *Client-centered Therapy.* Boston: Houghton Mifflin, 1951.

CHAPTER 3

COMMUNICATIONS
SKILLS

To be effective, helpers must utilize communications skills involving hearing verbal messages (cognitive and affective content), perceiving nonverbal messages (affective and behavioral content), and responding verbally and nonverbally to heard and perceived messages. The verbal and nonverbal communications behaviors were reviewed briefly in the previous chapter. To ensure that these communications skills become an integral part of your techniques as a helper, you must practice them frequently. When you start learning these skills, you may find yourself concentrating harder than ever before on your communicating behaviors. You may feel uncomfortable at first with this concentration and the resulting fatigue. Because we take so many of our communicating behaviors for granted, you may not previously have had the opportunity to focus on them and to develop your awareness. It is relatively easy to talk about communications skills and to understand theoretically their importance for effective helping relationships. It is quite another matter to put into practice your conceptualizations. Actual verbal practice is more difficult than written exercises!

The exercises suggested in this chapter are most effective and valuable when incorporated with group discussion. Sharing what you have experienced during the exercises, your feelings and your recognition of what you are willing to do and what you tend to shy away from (**approach** and **avoidance reactions**), are the most beneficial aspects of the exercises. More understanding comes from this kind of discussion after completion of an exercise than from the actual exercise. In this kind of discussion, called processing, one talks about one's feelings and reactions rather than about the actual content.

HEARING VERBAL MESSAGES

We are all aware of the need to listen to verbal messages and we can sometimes restate simple verbal messages back to their senders in a one-to-one situation. But if we think back to the game "telephone" that groups play at parties, we can remember how simple verbal messages become distorted as they pass through different people.

As difficult as it sometimes is to hear even apparent verbal messages, it is much more difficult to hear underlying messages, particularly the affective content. One of the reasons for this problem is that we tend to respond more to the cognitive content than to the affective content. We fail to recognize inconsistencies and underlying dynamics of the "hidden agenda."

Cognitive content concerns the actual facts and words of the message. Affective messages may be verbal or nonverbal and concern feelings, attitudes, and behaviors. Receiving verbal messages really involves both hearing cognitive and affective content and being able to discriminate between them. The cognitive content is usually easier to hear; it is stated. The affective content sometimes differs from the cognitive content and is often less apparent. The difference between hearing only the apparent verbal message and hearing it as well as the underlying message is the difference between ineffective listeners and effective listeners.

Your response to a client's statement will depend upon your ability to hear what is being said and to uncover the underlying message. Your response will, in turn, influence the direction of the client's next statement. Thus, before you can learn to respond appropriately to a client's statement, you must learn to hear and discriminate between his or her apparent and underlying cognitive and affective messages.

Verbal Cognitive Messages

Verbal cognitive messages are easier for us to recognize than affective messages, for our schooling stresses cognitive content. Cognitive messages usually concern things, people, or events and may involve one or several simple or complex themes. The client is often more comfortable talking about thoughts or behaviors than actually feeling them.

If we find ourselves responding only to the client's cognitive concerns, we never really get down to the underlying feelings and concerns. For example, a client may come in and talk about trouble with a supervisor. If the helper asks only "What happened?," "What did your supervisor say?", and "What did you say then?" the entire session can pass without uncovering the client's underlying concerns and feelings. The only possible outcome of this type of helper response would be the helper's suggestion that the client make different verbal responses or offer different behaviors to the supervisor. The helper's suggestions may work out, but they really don't contribute to the client's understanding and choosing his or her own course of action. Problem solving in itself might not target the underlying concern.

The theme (problem or concern) that is focused on affects the direction of the ensuing discussion. A helper hopes to choose the theme that will be the most productive in developing the helping relationship. It is difficult to determine which cognitive theme is most important and there could actually be several of equal importance, but it is necessary to respond to and focus upon one major theme at a time in order to clarify and explore all aspects of the situation. The objective of the following exercises is to help you identify cognitive themes in communications.

Exercise 3-1. Read the following client statements and pick out as many different cognitive topics as you can.

(1) "I'm really up a tree at this point as I have so many bills to pay and Tom isn't working and I don't know what to do. This job doesn't pay enough and I guess I should see if I can get an extra evening job, like waitressing or telephone soliciting. I wanted to go back to school at night this term, but that doesn't seem possible now."

(2) "Why should I stay in school when there are so many people with degrees who can't get jobs anyway? I don't feel as if I'm learning anything here anyway, nobody seems to care what happens to anybody and the classes are so large and impersonal. It's a waste of money."

(3) "I couldn't find a parking place today so I missed this morning's briefing session. Somebody ought to do something about this situation. I can't find that memorandum and I'm not sure what to say to Mr. Jones when he calls this afternoon."

(4) "Look, I've got a sick kid, we just moved here and don't know anyone, the landlord won't turn on the heat, and I need to find a job to pay the bills. I don't know where to turn to first, but I also need to get the rest of my furniture delivered."

(5) "Wow, what a time we had! We went swimming every day, bicycling at night, fishing several times, and just had a great time. Oh yes, we sailed the Meyers's boat—did you know they were down there?"

Now go over your answers and see if you can rank them in order of importance or immediacy of concern. In other words, if you had to respond to only one of the themes, which would it be? Then check your answers with mine. Remember, just cognitive content, not feelings!

(1)   a.   I don't have enough money.
      b.   I have bills to pay.
      c.   Should I take another job?
      d.   Should I go back to school?

(2)   a.   Is school worth the money it costs?
      b.   I'm not learning anything here.
      c.   People who go to school don't get jobs later.
      d.   People get lost in such a big, impersonal place.

(3)   a.   I don't know what to say to Mr. Jones when he calls later.
      b.   Somebody ought to fix the parking situation.
      c.   I need to be able to park in order to get here on time.
      d.   I lost a memorandum.
      e.   There aren't enough parking places here.

(4)   a.   My apartment is not satisfactory because there is no heat.
      b.   My kid is sick.
      c.   I don't know what to do or where to start.
      d.   I need money to pay the bills.
      e.   I need a job.
      f.   I am alone here.
      g.   I just moved here.
      h.   I have not received all my furniture.
      i.   I have a disagreeable landlord.

(5)   a.   We had a great time.
      b.   The Meyers were down there.
      c.   through f could be interchangeable: swimming, bicycling, fishing, sailing.

Without other cues it is obviously difficult to rank objectively the cognitive content in terms of importance to the client. However, once you have learned to hear the verbal cognitive content, you will be able to use affective content as clues for establishing priorities. It is amazing how, in verbal communications, we more often respond to the most recent verbal theme rather than to the most important one. We need to train ourselves to hear the whole message and discriminate among themes. A variation of this exercise would be to read aloud the excerpts and have your partner verbally recall the cognitive themes.

Exercise 3-2. This exercise has many different forms and has been called different names by different people. The purpose is to develop attending skills by repeating verbal cognitive messages. It is effective in groups that divide either into pairs (helper, helpee roles) or into triads (helper, helpee, observer roles). One person, the helpee, communicates a dialogue no longer than three minutes about some personal or imagined concern to the helper, who must then restate the verbal message back to the helpee to the latter's satisfaction. The helpee and the observer (if there is a triad) then process this interaction by evaluating the effectiveness of the helper's restatement of the helpee's verbal cognitive content. Everyone in the dyad or triad has the chance to be the helpee and helper. The observer can jot down what he or she has heard and compare it to what the helper restates. After the pairs or triads have completed this exercise, they process their experiences as a larger group by sharing difficulties and concerns emerging from the exercise and their suggestions for dealing with these difficulties and concerns. Observers share their observations about the helper's verbal and nonverbal behaviors, such as posture, eye contact, and gestures.

Exercise 3-2 helps us to realize how we spend more energy preparing what we are going to respond than listening to what is actually being said to us. It is also a good exercise to show us how we often hear another person's verbal message through our own filters ("selective perception"). We often hear and see what we need or want to hear and see rather than what is actually being communicated.

Exercise 3-3. This exercise highlights the incongruities that can exist between verbal and nonverbal communications in cognitive messages. Remaining in your pairs or triads, repeat exercise 3-2 with one difference: the helpee deliberately attempts to use facial expressions, vocal tones, posture, and gestures that are opposite to the cognitive messages being sent. For example, if I am talking about my concern about finding a legitimate parking place in time to get to a downtown meeting, I would smile, be relaxed and nonverbally express casualness. The point of this exercise is for the helper to experience how these incongruities between verbal and nonverbal behaviors can affect perception of cognitive messages. Helpees also discover discomfort in communicating incongruous messages on a conscious level.

Verbal Affective Messages

Affective messages are communicated to us both verbally and non-verbally, but for the present we will restrict ourselves to verbal communications. Affective messages are feelings, emotions that may be directly or indirectly expressed. They are much more difficult to communicate than cognitive messages and much more difficult to perceive and hear. Clients are often so much more aware of thoughts than feelings that the helper's responses clarifying and identifying feelings come as a surprise to them and uncover a whole new area for exploration and experiencing. By hearing affective messages and, in turn, responding to them, the helper is communicating not only acceptance of these emotions but also permission for the client to experience and own these feelings.

Feelings usually occur in four major areas: anger, sadness, fear, or happiness. Very often one area covers up another feelings area (e.g., sadness sometimes masks anger or vice versa or anger masks fear). There are many different words that we can use to identify feelings and it is helpful to select vocabulary that is comfortable for the client. For example, if a teenager is using the current vernacular of his peer group, instead of using the word "angry" when identifying his feelings, you may say "pissed off" as long as you feel comfortable doing this (and do not come across as a phoney). Identifying underlying feelings from verbal messages is difficult at first and is related to how comfortable and proficient you are in recognizing and expressing your own feelings. It is crucial that you listen to the client's messages and identify his or her feelings rather than project your own on the client. Again, this requires continuous, repeated practice.

Exercise 3-4. The purpose of this exercise is to clarify your own ways of expressing feelings and emotions. Individually, write down all the words that you can think of that express each of the following four major emotions: happiness, anger, fear, and sadness. What words do you use to express these feelings? For example, under "happiness" you may write "glad," "groovy," "tip-top," and so forth. When you have completed your list, share it with one or two others and see if there are many differences.

Exercise 3-5. Now take each of the four major emotions (happiness, anger, fear, and sadness) and list as many verbal behaviors as possible that you are aware of enacting when you feel each of them. For example, when you're mad, you may swear, use short clipped sentences or monosyllables, yell. Share these in small groups and learn how different people express the same emotion.

Exercise 3-6. This exercise is called listening for feelings. For each of the following statements, write what you think the person is really feeling. Ask yourself "What is the underlying feeling here?"

(1) Two big boys were picking on me when I was coming home from Boy Scouts today.

(2) The doctor told me to come over here and have all these tests. I'll sit over here and wait until you're ready for me.

(3) Poor Lenny! He works so hard and he never gets home for dinner anymore.

(4) I can't wait until final exams are over.

(5) I'm really too busy to take a coffee break now, although I'd love to talk to you.

(6) I can't type that report today. Professor Greene gave me four rush letters to get out by three o'clock and I still have the exams to type.

(7) Please put down that newspaper. You never talk to me anymore.

(8) I think people are out to get what they can for themselves.

(9) If Jim hadn't been transferred, this project would have gotten off the ground in plenty of time.

(10) Have you heard anything about the new social worker? I'm supposed to see her at three o'clock.

(11) I hear the new office manager is a real clock watcher.

(12) Only two more weeks until vacation!

(13) Look, Ms. Jones, if *you* can't get this typing done, I'll have to see if the typing pool can do it.

(14) My husband is out of work and I don't know how we're going to pay the rent next month.

(15) All children steal at that age, don't you think?

(16) Young people today really have a lot more sexual freedom than we did in my day!

(17) John, I want to tell you that after much careful consideration, I'm stepping down as chairperson so as to have more time for my family and to do my research.

(18) Ms. Green is a lousy teacher. She doesn't know how to explain things.

(19) Please bring the car home by eight o'clock. I don't want you driving in the dark.

(20) Why should I stay in school? I don't know what I want to do. What do you think?

(21) I hate staff meetings. No one ever gives me a chance to talk.

(22) Coming to see you just doesn't seem to be helping me. We talk about the same stuff over and over and I still don't know what to do.

(23) No one ever picks me to be on their team at school.

(24) Are you going to see me again this week, doctor?

(25) I'd like to talk to you when you have a minute. Be sure and see me before you leave the office tonight.

After you have completed this exercise, discuss your answers either in small groups or as a large group. Then you may look at the answers at the end of the chapter. You will note that different people identify different underlying feelings for the same stimulus statement and that, in discussing these statements, various projections begin to emerge. For example, one group of students told me that some members felt so threatened by statement (25) that they identified the underlying feeling as "anger," whereas other members perceived it as "eager," hypothesizing a situation where someone in an office wants to invite someone over but doesn't want others in the office to know about it and feel excluded. Try reading aloud with different affect and intonation the statements on which the group disagrees and see what differences occur.

Exercise 3-7. This exercise is similar to exercise 3-2 (cognitive verbal messages) but now you'll identify the feelings rather than the cognitive content. In dyads, with backs to each other to block out nonverbal cues, have the helpee talk for up to three minutes and have the helper identify the feelings that were being communicated. The helpees should not verbally identify their own feelings for the helpers, but should make the same types of comments as they did in exercise 3-2 and allow the helper to identify the underlying feeling. This should be processed in the same manner as exercise 3-2.

Exercise 3-8. Have two dyads or triads work with each other, with two people identified as helpers, two as helpees, and two as observers. The purpose of this exercise is to show each helper how two different people may express the same feeling with different verbal messages and different nonverbal cues. The two helpees are to separate themselves from the rest of the group, select one feeling (e.g., elation, frustration, or boredom) and tell the two observers secretly which feeling they have selected. Then each helpee is to make verbal statements expressing, but not identifying verbally, this feeling to each of the two helpers separately. The helper is to identify the feeling. The observer will let the helper know when he or she is correct and the helpee is encouraged to continue making statements until this identification occurs.

Hearing and discriminating among affective and cognitive verbal messages without body language cues is extremely difficult and is, naturally, hampered by the artificiality of out-of-context role playing. Nevertheless, as you become used to role playing, you will become less artificial and more comfortable. After you have practiced identifying cognitive and affective contents separately, try exercise 3-9.

Exercise 3-9. In pairs or triads assign helpee, helper, and observer roles. The helpee is to talk for five to ten minutes about a real or imagined concern. The helper is not to ask any questions, but can make exploratory statements, such as "Tell me more about that" and "I'm wondering if" to probe for more data. At the end of the agreed-upon time, the helpee is to stop and the helper is to identify both the cognitive and affective messages to the helpee's satisfaction. A suggested format is "You are feeling _____ when _____ because _____." Allow everyone the opportunity to be helpee and process in small and large groups. The purpose of this exercise is to sharpen helpers' discrimination skills and to focus their attention on the helpee's message and the development of messages. It helps client-centered listening in that it does not allow the asking of questions.

Questions are usually more detracting than additive. We have learned to hide behind questions and, as they are second nature to us, it is strongly recommended that we rephrase questions into statements until we have mastered communications skills and become aware of when and how to ask questions. For example, instead of asking, "What did you do next?" say, "Tell me what happened then."

PERCEIVING NONVERBAL MESSAGES

Because perceiving nonverbal messages has not been emphasized in our culture, exercise 3-7 usually produces frustration and tension as we become aware of our dependence on nonverbal cues for understanding verbal messages. In chapter 2 we listed various nonverbal behaviors that were deemed facilitative and nonfacilitative for effective helping relationships. The kinds of nonverbal cues that we attend to in a communicative relationship are listed in table 3-1. We look to see if this nonverbal behavior is consistent with the verbal behavior and if we can pick up clues from it that will help us to identify the affective messages (underlying feelings) we are hearing. The nonverbal perceptions provide us with clues, not conclusive proofs, of these underlying feelings. However, experience has proven that nonverbal clues tend to be more reliable than verbal clues!

Exercise 3-10. Cut out some pictures of people from a magazine. Remove the captions and ask your partner what he or she believes is being communicated. Then, in groups of four to six, ask other people to respond to the same picture. Talk about the various responses and see if it is possible to reach some concensus. After you have identified the feelings that are being communicated in several pictures, see if you can establish some patterns for your group's identifications. The purpose of this exercise is to examine different responses to the same nonverbal stimulus. What were the reasons given for a particular identification? In cases of disagreement, what were the major variables of difference? What kinds of projections could you perceive from the verbal discussions of those identifications? How can you explain the variety of perceptions?

Exercise 3-11. The purpose of this exercise is to afford you the opportunity to identify feelings from another person's nonverbal behavior. In triads or small groups, have one person identify a specific feeling or emotion and tell it to an observer. The person who has selected this emotion nonverbally tries to communicate it to his partner or to the other members of a small group. When the emotion has been properly identified, someone else chooses a feeling and attempts to communicate it to the group. Process your experiences as you did in exercise 3-10.

Exercise 3-12. Another way to achieve this same goal of identifying nonverbal messages is to play a nonverbal form of "telephone." A group sits in a circle and one person selects a feeling to start the game. Everyone closes his or her eyes and the starter taps the person on the right who opens his or her eyes, tries to understand the nonverbal communication, and then repeats the communications process, tapping the person on the right, who opens his or her eyes and receives and sends the nonverbal message. This entire exercise is nonverbal until the last person in the circle receives the message and verbally identifies the feeling. The group then processes what happened, where and how the message became distorted, if it did, and what people were feeling about nonverbal communication.

Exercise 3-13. This exercise helps us to identify more complex nonverbal messages, coming from a scene, rather than an isolated feeling. A pair go out of the room, plan a ten-minute role play scene of, perhaps, a couple talking over the dinner table, a teacher and principal conferring, or whatever seems appropriate (and fun!). They come back into the room and, using nonsense syllables, carry on a dialogue between themselves that has no verbal meaning for the observers. The observers are to attempt to reconstruct and identify what is occurring strictly by observing nonverbal behavior. During the processing of this exercise, the role players can contribute by sharing their intentions and feelings. The observers usually find that they can perceive a lot of the true message by just observing nonverbal behaviors.

Exercise 3-14. The purpose of this exercise is to become more aware of your own nonverbal behaviors associated with feelings. List all of the nonverbal behaviors you can for each of the four major emotions: anger, fear, happiness, and sadness. For example, "When I'm mad, I frown, clench my fists, pull my body tight, sit away from people, and feel knots in my stomach." Share these in small groups and note similarities and differences.

Exercise 3-15. Now return to exercise 3-1 and see if you can list the major feelings in each of the situations. This is more complex than identifying the underlying feeling in exercise 3-6 because there is more than one cognitive theme. Are these your feelings or what you believe the subject is feeling? How can you tell? How did you decide? Discuss in small groups.

Table 3-1   *Nonverbal Cues in a Communicative Relationship*

Feature	Examples
body position	tense, relaxed, leaning toward or away
eyes	teary, open, closed, excessive blinking, twitching
eye contact	steady, avoiding, shifty
body movement	knee jerks, taps, hand and leg gestures, fidgeting, head nodding, pointing fingers, dependence on arms and hands for expressing message, touching
body posture	stooped shoulders, slouching, legs crossed, rigid, relaxed
mouth	smiling, lip biting, licking lips, tight, loose
facial expression	animated, bland, distracting, frowning, puckers, grimaces
skin	blushing, rashes, perspiration, paleness
general appearance	clean, neat, sloppy, well-groomed
voice	fast, slow, jerky, high pitched, whispers

Exercise 3-16. This is a variation of exercise 3-3. In pairs or triads, take turns being helper, helpee, and observer. The helpee tells about a real or imagined concern and uses facial expressions, vocal tones, postures, and gestures that are opposite to the feelings he or she is expressing in the verbal message. For example, I may tell you how excited I am about a trip I'm going to make this weekend and slump, frown, and slur my words. What feelings do you perceive? The helper states what he or she perceives the major expressed feeling to be. Then members discuss their experiences with verbal and nonverbal incongruence. Which cues did you find yourself giving most attention to? What did you make of this?

RESPONDING VERBALLY AND NONVERBALLY

Responsive listening is defined as responding verbally and nonverbally to both the apparent and underlying thoughts and feelings of the client. This is easier said than done and involves developing awareness of one's self as a communicator as well as hearing and perceiving skills. It is essential that the helper be congruent in his or her own verbal and nonverbal communications or else the helpee will be just as confused by double messages from the helper as the helper is when he or she receives double messages from the helpee.

Responsive listening implies that the helper is able to communicate his or her genuine understanding (empathy), acceptance, and concern for the helpee and, at the same time, add some understanding of the issue by clarifying the helpee's statement. Thus, helpers must be able to communicate to the client their identification and understanding of the primary cognitive concern and the underlying feeling, as well as their own caring.

The following is an example of responsive listening:

> *Helpee:* I know I'm too fat. That's why nobody ever asks me out.
>
> *Helper:* You really feel sad when you see everyone around you having a good time and you're scared, wondering what will happen to you if you don't improve your appearance.

Saying "don't worry" or "you should go on a diet" is not helpful. Those kinds of responses do not help clients increase their self-understanding.

We will work with more examples of responsive listening as we proceed through this chapter. What makes the above an example of responsive listening is that it identifies an underlying feeling, relates it to the major cognitive concern, and adds clarity and understanding to the helpee's statement. Let's focus first on developing our awareness of our own nonverbal communications behaviors.

Exercise 3-17. An important Gestalt exercise that helps us get in touch with our own comfort or discomfort with nonverbal behavior is to have pairs sit facing each other. They are to communicate for three to five minutes by eye contact only. No other body language or verbal language is permitted. After this time is up, they can continue their eye contact, but also communicate with their hands for three to five minutes. Then they are allowed to communicate nonverbally any way they choose. At the end of this exercise, the pairs are to process verbally, by sharing their feelings and thoughts, their intentions and reactions. Then, in small or large groups, people can share their experiences. Many people find themselves very uncomfortable maintaining eye contact at first, but this form of communications becomes more comfortable and meaningful with practice and experience.

Exercise 3-18. Another significant Gestalt exercise is called "mirroring" by many Gestalt facilitators. In pairs, sit and face each other. One person is the communicator, the other is the nonverbal mirror. The communicators talk about anything they desire for five minutes. The mirrors nonverbally mirror each gesture, movement, and expression of the communicators. (They do not verbally mirror what they think the other is saying, because they are concentrating on the nonverbal.) At the end of five minutes, the mirrors express their feelings, the communicators share their feelings, and they both share what they have learned from participating in this exercise. If you do not have a partner, you can do this alone by talking to yourself in front of a mirror. We rarely see ourselves communicating and are unaware of our nonverbal behaviors. We can then discuss whether our nonverbal behaviors are facilitative or nonfacilitative. For example, one student discovered that by sitting back and rocking on his chair, he was distancing himself from others and not being facilitative.

Exercise 3-19. In triads, the helpee communicates a real or imagined stress situation or crisis. The helper attempts to respond to these messages and the helpee and the observer give direct feedback to the helper about his or her nonverbal behavior. The checklist in appendix A can be utilized by the observers in this exercise which serves to confirm and develop the awareness of our nonverbal behaviors arising from the previous exercises.

Desirable nonverbal behaviors for effective helping relationships include occasional nodding, smiling, touching, and hand gesturing; good eye contact; facial animation; leaning toward the helpee (sitting near without a desk barrier); a moderate rate of speech; and a firm tone of voice.

Verbal Responding

With verbal responses, we attempt to communicate to helpees that we are truly hearing and understanding them and their perspective; to communicate our ability to help, our warmth, acceptance, and caring; and to help the client's efforts toward self-understanding and self-exploration as well as understanding others by focusing on major themes, clarifying inconsistencies, reflecting back the underlying feelings, and synthesizing the major apparent and underlying concerns and feelings.

We have already begun to focus on verbal responding by identifying major affective and cognitive contents of helpee statements. Now we must begin to develop patterns of verbal responding to ensure that we clearly get our messages across to the helpee and meet the above aims.

The ten major verbal responses are making the minimal verbal response, paraphrasing, probing, reflecting, **clarifying**, checking out, **interpreting**, **confronting**, informing, and summarizing.

Minimal Verbal Response.   Minimal responses are the verbal counterpart of occasional head nodding. These are verbal clues such as "mm-mm," "yes," "I see," "uh-huh" to indicate that the helper is listening and following what the client is saying.

Paraphrasing.   Paraphrasing is a verbal statement that is interchangeable with the client's statement, although the words may be synonyms of words the client has used. For example:

> *Helpee:*   I had a lousy day today.
>
> *Helper:*   Things didn't go well for you today.

Probing.   Probing is an open-ended attempt to obtain more information about something and is most effective when used in the form of a statement such as "Tell me more," "Let's talk about that," "I'm wondering about . . ." rather than "how," "what," "when," "where," or "who" questions.

Reflecting.   Reflecting refers to communicating our understanding of the helpee and his or her concerns and perspectives to the client. We can reflect stated or implied feelings, what we have observed nonverbally, inclusions and exclusions of the statements that we have observed, and specific content. Examples of reflecting are "You're feeling uncomfortable about seeing him," "You really resent being treated like a child," and "Sounds as if you're really angry at your mother."

Clarifying.   Clarifying is an attempt to focus upon or understand the basic nature of a helpee statement. Examples are "I'm having trouble understanding what you are saying. Is it that . . . ," "I'm confused about. . . . Could you go over that again, please.", and "Sounds to me like you're saying. . . ."

Checking Out.   Checking out occurs when the helper is genuinely confused about his or her perceptions of verbal or nonverbal behavior or when the helper has a hunch that bears trying out. Examples are "I feel that you're upset with me. Can we talk about that?", "Does it seem as if . . .", and "I have a hunch that this feeling is familiar to you." The helper asks the helpee to confirm or correct the helper's perception or understanding.

Interpreting.   Interpreting occurs when the helper adds something to the client's statement, when the helper tries to help the client gain an understanding of his or her underlying feelings, their relation to the verbal message, and the relation of what he or she is communicating to the present situation. For example:

> *Helpee:* I just can't bring myself to write that report. I always put it off and it's hanging me up right now.
>
> *Helper:* You seem to resent having to do something you don't want to do.

If this interpretation is useful, it will add to the helpee's understanding and you will receive a reaction reflecting "Yes, that's it." If it is not useful, the helpee may say, "No, not that but. . . ."

Confronting.   Confronting involves honest feedback about what the helper really thinks is going on with the helpee. The confrontation may focus on genuineness, such as "I feel you really don't want to talk about this.", "It seems to me you're playing games in here.", and "I'm wondering why you feel you always have to take the blame. What do you get out of that?" The confrontation may focus on discrepancy, such as "You say you're angry, yet you're smiling." or "On the one hand, you seem to be hurt by not getting that job, but on the other hand you seem sort of relieved, too." An effective way of using confrontation is to send "I messages," to own your responsibility for the confrontation by sharing openly your own genuine feelings with the helpee or by focusing on the helpee's avoidance or resistant behaviors.

Informing.   Informing occurs when you share objective and factual information such as telling a person what you know about a particular college in terms of student enrollment, types of programs, etc. It is important for the helper to separate informing from advising, the latter having a subjective aura of suggestibility to it. Advising is all right as long as it is tentatively suggested with no strings attached and as long as it is labeled as advice, not as a demand.

Summarizing.   Summarizing is a clarifying type of statement by which the helper synthesizes what has been communicated and highlights the major affective and cognitive themes. This is important at the end of a session or during the first part of a subsequent session. Summarizing is beneficial when both the helper and the helpee participate and agree with the summarizing message. It is also an opportunity to encourage the helpee to share his or her feelings about the helper and the session.

The following are some general guideline themes running through these major verbal responses:

1. phrasing them in the same type of vocabulary as the helpee uses

2. speaking slowly enough so that the helpee understands each word

3. using concise rather than rambling statements

4. pursuing the topic introduced by clients

5. talking directly to clients, not about them

6. sending "I statements" to own your feelings and allowing clients to reject, accept, or modify your messages

7. encouraging clients to talk about their feelings

8. timing your responses to facilitate, not block, communications

Exercise 3-20. The purpose of this exercise is to see if you can recognize and identify the types of major verbal responses just discussed. This exercise will help you become aware of your own verbal responses and, perhaps, encourage you to expand your repertoire. Read the following client and counselor statements and then identify the counselor's response, as one of the above ten major verbal responses: minimal verbal response, paraphrasing, probing, reflecting, clarifying, checking out, interpreting, confronting, informing, or summarizing.

(1) _Checkout_   *Helpee:* That's why I'm here. Jim said you were a good one to talk to.

                Helper: Let's see now. You want me to help you decide whether or not you should accept the transfer. Is that right?

(2) _inform_   *Helpee:* Do you think they have a good benefits package there?

                Helper: The National Conference Board reports that that particular company ranks in the top third for employee benefits.

(3) _probe_   *Helpee:* Eddie made me get kicked out of class today.

                Helper: Tell me more about it.

(4) _MVR_   *Helpee:* I have to get the house cleaned before we can have company over.

                Helper: I see.

(5) _paraphr._ *Helpee:* In my family, my dad and brother don't do any of the work around the house.

Helper: The men in your family don't do any housework.

(6) _interpret_ *Helpee:* I can't decide what to do. Nothing seems right.

Helper: You're feeling pretty frustrated and you want me to tell you what to do.

(7) _Confront_ *Helpee:* I don't want to talk about it.

Helper: You always seem to back away when things get personal. It seems to me that it's much easier for you to talk about the situation than feel it.

(8) _Clarify_ *Helpee:* Anyway, I'm unable to do it because it's too expensive and besides they won't help me anyway.

Helper: Let me get this straight. You feel the tests will cost too much and the results won't be worth the cost. Is that it?

(9) _reflect_ *Helpee:* Nobody in this world cares about anyone else.

Helper: It's scary to feel that nobody at all cares about you.

(10) _Summarize_ *Helpee:* I guess that about covers it.

Helper: Let's see if we can review what we've talked about today. . . . Does this seem right to you?

Check your answers with mine:

- (1) checking out
- (2) informing
- (3) probing
- (4) minimal verbal response
- (5) paraphrasing
- (6) reflecting
- (7) confronting
- (8) clarifying
- (9) interpreting
- (10) summarizing

We have already referred to general guidelines for effective verbal responding. Remember that our primary goals are to communicate understanding, warmth, acceptance, genuineness; communicate our ability and willingness to listen and facilitate; and help the clients further understand and explore themselves and others and decide for themselves their courses of action while keeping the door open to develop further communications.

The following are some specific guidelines for effecting the type of communication that will actualize these goals:

1. Listen to the helpee's basic message.

2. Respond to the most important part of the helpee's statement that coincides with the basic apparent or underlying verbal and nonverbal message.

3. Reflect the helpee's feelings at a greater level of intensity than originally expressed by the helpee.

4. Reflect both implicit and explicit feelings of the helpee.

5. Respond to the helpee's behaviors.

6. When the helpee changes topics, respond to the primary cognitive or affective common theme of the topics.

7. Always allow the helpee to modify or reject your perceptions.

8. Use your own feelings as bases for checking out, confronting, **leading,** etc.

9. If you are unable to rephrase your questions into statements, ask only open-ended questions that clarify for the helpee or that elicit feelings.

10. If the helpee doesn't pause to give you a chance to respond and you feel lost or confused, break in with an "I feel confused . . ." to focus on the major themes. By the same token, don't feel that you have to respond to every single helpee statement.

The next exercise will give you an opportunity to identify responses that are interchangeable, subtractive, or additive in terms of communicating your goals to the helpee. At the same time that you are learning to differentiate between facilitative and non-facilitative responses, you are learning, through **modeling,** what are facilitative responses.

Exercise 3-21. Rate these responses to helpee statements as either - (subtractive—one that detracts from where helpee is at), = (interchangeable— one that neither adds to nor subtracts from where helpee is at), or + (additive—one that adds to helpee's understanding). There is not necessarily one of each response in each set.

(1) *Helpee:* I need to find a job quick. I've got a family to support.

Helper: _____ a. Why did you leave your last job?
_____ b. You really are scared about how you're going to make ends meet.
_____ c. You want to find a job right away so you can take care of your family.

In this situation, the first response would be rated - because it asks a "why" question and puts the helpee on the defensive, not adding to his understanding. Response b is +, identifying the underlying feeling and communicating empathy. Response c is = because it neither adds nor detracts, but merely paraphrases the message. Now continue along and check the answers at the end of the exercise.

(2) *Helpee:*   Put the flowers over there and the newspaper there, and bring me my slippers and robe, please.

Helper: _____ a.   You really want me to be able to give you more attention.

_____ b.   You want your flowers and newspaper put down so I can bring you your slippers and robe.

_____ c.   Here you go again. I have other patients to care for too!

(3) *Helpee:*   I'm not going to be able to come back to school next year.

Helper: _____ a.   Why?

_____ b.   People who graduate have a better chance of getting jobs.

_____ c.   You're not coming back for your junior year.

(4) *Helpee:*   Yeah, well you gotta be tough if you're gonna make it on the outside. Nobody gives an ex-con a chance anyway, so you gotta take what you can get and see that you get it.

Helper: _____ a.   You really feel that no one's gonna give you a break.

_____ b.   You're wondering if you're tough and smart enough to make it. It's scary.

_____ c.   Ex-cons don't have a very good track record, you know.

(5) *Helpee:*   When I'm at home, my mom lets me eat whatever I want.

Helper: _____ a.   Wow! Your mom sure spoils you!

_____ b.   You don't want to have to eat what you don't like.

_____ c.   You're unhappy that you can't always do what you want to here.

(6) *Helpee:*   I'm so angry at my mother that I'd like to kill her! She never says a nice thing to or about me. I wish I never had to see her again.

Helper: _____ a.   It makes you really angry that you seem to need her approval, doesn't it?

_____ b. It's wrong to even think about your mother like that.

_____ c. You're really angry with your mother. Tell me more.

(7) *Helpee:* This is an awful place to work. No one is ever where they should be.

Helper: _____ a. You don't like working here.

_____ b. All offices are like this in this kind of business.

_____ c. It seems to you that nobody cares about you here and that nobody wants to help you.

(8) *Helpee:* It's unfair that you can't find more money for me. How am I supposed to manage? I've got a wife and four kids.

Helper: _____ a. You're concerned about making ends meet.

_____ b. You're getting as much as you're entitled to under the law.

_____ c. Why do you think you should get more than anyone else?

(9) *Helpee:* People today care more about money than they do about each other.

Helper: _____ a. You feel lonely and scared that people don't seem to care about you.

_____ b. It makes you angry that people are so materialistic.

_____ c. Yes, that's the world we live in today.

(10) *Helpee:* That's a lousy course. I've had all that stuff before and it's a waste of my time and money. Most of the courses around here are pretty bad.

Helper: _____ a. You're not sure you should be in that course.

_____ b. It's a required course for this program.

_____ c. You seem to have ambivalent feelings about being in this program. Can we talk about this?

(11) *Helpee:* I'd love to go back to work, but my husband feels I should be home when the kids get back from school.

Helper: _____ a. I can see why he feels that way. It's much better for the children when their mom is home.

_____ b. You're not sure whether to work or stay home.

_____+_____ c. Sounds like you feel some anger toward your husband imposing his expectations on you.

(12) *Helpee:* I've really had a rough year.
  Helper: _____=_____ a. You've had a tough time this year.
  _____ b. Everyone has a bad year at some time or another.
  _____+_____ c. You seem to be pretty uptight about how you've handled things this year.

(13) *Helpee:* Well, he's got a hell of a nerve telling me what to do in that tone of voice. Who does he think he is?
  Helper: _____−_____ a. Bosses are known to do that. Don't take it to heart. I'm sure his bark is worse than his bite.
  _____=_____ b. You sure get angry when someone pushes you around!
  _____+_____ c. You're really angry that he doesn't treat you with respect and accept you as a person who has feelings.

(14) *Helpee:* Look, I'm only here because Mr. Smith sent me. I've got nothing to talk about.
  Helper: _____=_____ a. Mr. Smith wanted you to come see me.
  _____+_____ b. You don't want to be here and you're angry you got yourself into this.
  _____−_____ c. He must have had some reason for sending you here.

(15) *Helpee:* Every night my wife complains about everything that's happened during the day. It's getting so I don't want to go home anymore. I'd much rather stay in town and drink with the boys.
  Helper: _____−_____ a. All wives are like that. After all, what else have they to do?
  _____+_____ b. You find it so intolerable at home that it's easier for you to stay away. Sounds as if you're pretty angry at your wife.
  _____=_____ c. Your wife really rides roughshod on you when you get home every night.

Note that the subtractive responses in exercise 3-21 neither add understanding to what the helpee has said nor focus upon the helpee's underlying feelings. Rather, they tend to moralize or preach and avoid effective parts of helpee statements. The interchangeable responses do not close the door for further development, but they do not add to what has already been stated. Helpers who continually make interchangeable responses need to examine carefully their own avoidance behavior. Are they afraid to risk testing out their understanding? The additive responses communicate the helper's listening, understanding, and caring; help focus on the implicit and explicit affective and cognitive content; and encourage further exploration. Even a helper's response that incorrectly identifies the underlying feeling would be considered additive. As long as the helpee has the opportunity and encouragement to say something like "No, not that, but . . ." further exploration is facilitated. So it is not as much a question of a "right" or "wrong" response as it is a question of how facilitative in terms of empathy, honesty, and open-endedness a response is.

At this point, you may be thinking to yourself, "But isn't this kind of verbal responding putting ideas and thoughts into the helpee's head?" The answer to this question is that genuine, client-centered, empathic responses are your best insurance against putting words, ideas, or your values or needs into your client's head because you are hearing client messages and responding to them and, at the same time, continually allowing for feedback and reactions to your responses. By your manner and responses, you can communicate to helpees your respect and confidence in their ability to think, feel, and act for themselves. You neither want to nor must do that for them. If the client does not like or agree with what you say, that is fine; it does not mean that you are a "no good" helper or that the helpee is "resisting" you. It does mean, however, that you can both continue to explore what is going on until you can agree on what it is all about.

Here are the answers to exercise 3-21:

(2)	a. +	(7)	a. =	(12)	a. =
	b. =		b. −		b. −
	c. −		c. +		c. +
(3)	a. −	(8)	a. +	(13)	a. −
	b. −		b. −		b. =
	c. =		c. −		c. +
(4)	a. =	(9)	a. +	(14)	a. =
	b. +		b. =		b. +
	c. −		c. −		c. −
(5)	a. −	(10)	a. =	(15)	a. −
	b. =		b. −		b. +
	c. +		c. +		c. =
(6)	a. +	(11)	a. −		
	b. −		b. =		
	c. =		c. +		

Exercise 3-22 asks you to write what you consider an additive response to each client statement. Check your responses against mine at the end of the chapter to see if you're in the right ball park. There is no one right response to any statement. Discuss your responses with others in your group.

Exercise 3-22. Write the best verbal response you can think of to meet the communications goals discussed in this chapter. Remember that this is out of context and, therefore, you can only respond to verbal cues.

(1) *Helpee:* I had a great time last night. I didn't think about Dave one minute!

Helper: (Possible answer: You're relieved that you were able to have fun and not think about Dave.)

(2) *Helpee:* John was smoking pot at the party and he wanted Tom and me to do it, too. But I was scared we'd get into trouble.

Helper: You feel Apprehensive About smoking pot

(3) *Helpee:* We'd like to get married, but we know we have many problems. What do you think we should do?

Helper: Tell me About the problems you think you

(4) *Helpee:* You know, I wrote that financial report; but because I'm only an assistant I can't even get credit for it.

Helper: you would like to recieve recognition for your work.

(5) *Helpee:* We don't need his folks' help. We can do it ourselves and I wish Jack would realize that his mother's always butting into our affairs.

Helper: You feel you + Jack cAn be independent + resent his mothers interfervence.

(6) *Helpee:* I refuse to let my kid be sent to that school with all those kinds of kids. She's gonna stay right here where she belongs.

Helper: You feel that being w other types of kids is not good for your dAughter.

(7) *Helpee:* I'm not so sure that I can handle this job. It may be too much for me.

Helper: It sounds like you're AfrAid of fAiling At the job.

(8) *Helpee:* Listen, mister, you better believe that once I get outta here, there's no way you're gonna get me back. I'll die first and I'll take some of your kind with me, you wait and see.

Helper: You Are sure of your Ability to MAke it on the outside.

(9)   *Helpee:*   The boys won't let me play ball with them. They're always teasing me and calling me names. I hate them!

       Helper:

(10) *Helpee:*   I think people are two-faced.

       Helper:

(11) *Helpee:*   You're always late. I've got more important things to do than sit around your office waiting for you, you know.

       Helper:

(12) *Helpee:*   I can't take that test. I have a splitting headache. Will you talk to Ms. Smith for me?

       Helper:

(13) *Helpee:*   I didn't do nothin'. You're always picking on me.

       Helper:

(14) *Helpee:*   I made it through school on my own. Why should I pay his tuition? Let him work like I did.

       Helper:

(15) *Helpee:*   I'm always telling Jim not to argue with his father. His father has a terrible temper.

       Helper:

(16) *Helpee:*   I'm so mad at my boss! I'd like to wring his neck. I do all the work around here and he doesn't even recognize that.

       Helper:

(17) *Helpee:*   How can he expect me to work, take care of the house, and raise the children? He better find work pretty soon so we can afford some help.

       Helper:

(18) *Helpee:*   I managed just fine until the accident. I'm blind now and I just have to face the fact that I can't do what I used to do.

       Helper:

(19) *Helpee:*   Other people have no idea how expensive it is to care for a handicapped child. We have to keep borrowing from my family.

       Helper:

(20) *Helpee:* I now have a job, Johnny is in day care, and I just can't believe how wonderful everything is. For the first time in forty-four years, I feel like a whole person!

Helper:

You might label your answers from the list of ten major verbal responses before looking at my responses at the end of the chapter.

Now that you have had an opportunity to respond in writing to client statements, it is time to try out verbal responses. The next few exercises allow you to practice this type of responsive listening in small groups. A useful adjunct to these exercises is to tape record sessions with actual helpees or with a friend or member of your family and then analyze your tape. Remember that this is a learning process, that practicing what you can conceptualize is very difficult, and that it will take continuous practice and time to achieve effective responsive listening skills.

Exercise 3-23. The purpose of this exercise is to begin to verbalize responses that demonstrate responsive listening. Students are divided into triads (it is recommended that these triads remain stable for the duration of the course so that, as trust develops within the group process, students will feel freer to use real concerns rather than role play). Each triad meets for at least one hour per week, in or out of class settings. In each triad, each member has the opportunity to be helper, helpee, and observer for at least fifteen minutes at each triad meeting. The helpee may present a real personal issue or concern (it does not have to be a crisis or even a negative issue) or role play a concern. The helper demonstrates effective responsive listening skills. Problem solving and solution giving are to be avoided. The purpose of these interactions is for the helpees to express their concerns and for the helpers to make the helpees feel understood and to facilitate further exploration. The observers are free to break in if they feel the helper is getting off the track or getting into problem solving. At the end of ten or fifteen minutes, the triad processes this microcounseling session. It is as important for observers to give honest feedback to helpers as it is for helpees to share their reactions and feelings. You may find that you best learn the impact of effective and noneffective listening skills when you take the helpee role. The helper and helpee can see if they felt "connectedness" the same times. You are free to use the observer's guide in appendix A.

In regard to observer ratings, Kagan and Schauble (1969, p. 310) have found the interpersonal process recall helpful in processing counselor interactions. The observer may use this to ask questions of the helper in processing the triad sessions:

1. What do you think the helpee was trying to say?

2. What do you think the helpee was feeling at this point?

3. Can you pick up any clues from the nonverbal behavior?

4. What was running through your mind when the helpee said that?

5. Can you recall some of the feelings you were having then?

6. Was there anything that prevented you from sharing some of your feelings and concerns about the person?

7. If you had another chance, would you like to have said something different?

8. What kind of risk would there have been if you said what you really wanted to say?

9. What kind of person do you want the client to see you as?

10. What do you think the client's perceptions of you are?

The observer may also use a rating scale (see appendix A) to aid in providing feedback to the helper or make audio or video tapes of the session and then analyze the playback. The rating scale focuses upon the verbal and nonverbal behaviors desired in microhelping situations for skill development in responsive listening. It also provides feedback about the type of communications the helper uses. In general, there is "over-participation," where helpers feel they must say something at all pauses and put much of their own energy into filling up gaps; there is "O.K. participation," where the energy levels of the helper and helpee are about equal and the helper feels comfortable with occasional silences and pauses; and there is "under-participation," where helpers are so insecure about their verbal respondings that they allow helpees to go on and on and never intervene. In the last case, the helpee has a higher level of energy invested in the communications than the helper. Once you become aware of your own patterns and styles of communications, you will be able to modify your responses in the best interests of the helpee.

Exercise 3-24. This is a variation of exercise 3-23, whereby small groups of six to ten people are arranged in a circle. One person volunteers to be the helpee and begins to communicate a personal concern. For each helpee statement, a different person in the circle makes a facilitative response, going around the circle. For example, the helpee makes an opening statement and person A responds, then the helpee replies to person A and person B responds to that and so forth around the circle. This exercise is processed in a similar manner to exercise 3-23. It has the advantage of involving more people in the processing and producing various levels of responses to the same person. Thus, the helpee is able to provide valuable feedback: whose responses were more helpful, why, and whose were not helpful. Actually, the most important benefit of this exercise is for the helpee, in that he or she is able to feel the effects of "connected" and "unconnected" responses.

SELF-AWARENESS

In order to avoid a dependent relationship with a helpee, it is important for you to be aware of your own needs, feelings, and problems. As discussed previously, self-awareness enables you to communicate better your equality to, respect for, and confidence in the helpee and your ability to understand empathically the helpee's problems without adding to them by projecting your own feelings and needs. Unfortunately, helpees are not always quick to recognize relationships where the helper becomes dependent on the helpee, perhaps because helpees are often looking for someone to take over for them and to tell them what to do. Part of your responsibility is to refuse to do this and to encourage helpees to take responsibility for themselves.

It is useful for helpers to assess continually their own needs and feelings, to think about where they are at any particular time by asking themselves the following kinds of questions and by discussing them with peers and supervisors:

1.   Am I aware when I find myself feeling uncomfortable with a client or with a particular subject area?

Very often, helpers find themselves uneasy with a certain type of client who represents something threatening or with a controversial subject such as sex or drugs. It is important for helpers to recognize this discomfort, to own it for themselves, and to decide upon an honest approach (deal with discomfort and proceed) or avoidance (refer client to another helper). "I messages" can be helpful here, for example, "Look, I find I don't know enough about drugs to really discuss this with you."

2.   Am I aware of my own avoidance strategies?

Do I recognize when I avoid certain topics, allow the client to wander off, or ask many questions to cover up my own insecurities? Helpers who are aware of their avoidance can say to themselves, "This seems to be really bothering me and I better figure out what is going on so I can be truly facilitative with this helpee." One can, therefore, risk failure.

3.   Can I really be honest with the helpee?

Is my fear that the client won't like me making me afraid to confront or help him or her focus upon something unpleasant? Do I have to be perfect and right all the time, or can I be me? If helpers have a strong need to be liked all the time, they will use reassuring, supportive responses to an excess and diminish the possibility for client development of responsibility and independence.

4.   Do I always feel as if I need to be in control of situations?

You may have some need for structure and direction in order to be accountable and achieve goals and objectives, but you should be aware of how you feel when a helpee disagrees or wants to pursue something different. For example, there may be times when you want to try a different approach with the helpee, such as a Gestalt exercise, and the helpee refuses to participate. If you have a need to control, you may feel angry and rebuffed in this situation. If you do not have this need to control, you can accept the helpee's feelings without feeling personally attacked and can propose alternatives or delay introducing another approach. Responsive listening is a safeguard against controlling the communications.

5.   Do I often feel as if I must be omnipotent in that I must do something to make the helpee "get better" so I can be successful?

If you find yourself often experiencing this feeling, you may question whether you are in the right field! It is your relationship with helpees that will facilitate their resolving their problems to their satisfaction, not that you have waved your magic wand and done something to them. You can feel good about yourself when you see helpees acting for themselves and taking responsibility for themselves.

6.   Am I so problem-oriented that I'm always looking for the negative. for a problem, and I never respond to the positive, to the good?

This is a common concern of helpers in that they are exposed more to negative feelings than to positive ones. However, it is important to identify and respond to positive affective and cognitive content to balance perspective and, more importantly, to reinforce positive conditions.

7.   Am I able to be as open with clients as I want them to be with me?

A common problem of people in helping professions is that they want to avoid their own feelings and problems by focusing on their clients' feelings and problems. A good rule of thumb is never to ask anyone to do anything or talk about something that you would not be willing to talk about or do in that or other situations.

Some of the above deal directly with communications and some are more related to the issues discussed in chapter 8. Your ability to utilize effective communications is integrated with your continuing development of sensitivity and self-awareness.

SUMMARY

In this chapter we have identified and elaborated upon the elements of responsive listening. A progressive series of individual and group exercises was presented first to develop awareness of your own styles of verbal and nonverbal communications behaviors, then to test out your understanding of the conceptualization of responsive listening, and then to allow you to practice and develop more effective communications skills. Guidelines for developing these skills and continued self-awareness were also presented.

The effectiveness of these exercises will depend largely on the supervisory and modeling capabilities of your supervising trainer, but an instructor cannot spend a great deal of supervisory time with any one individual. Members of a group, however, can learn to be effective observers and provide individual trainees with beneficial instruction in the form of genuine feedback. Communications skills are the fundamental basis of the helping relationship. We will next proceed to examine the stages of the helping process.

EXERCISE ANSWERS

Exercise 3-6.

(1) scared of bullies

(2) fear of illness or pleased at attention from doctor

(3) sympathy for Lenny or anger at Lenny for never getting home

(4) anxiety about coming exams or anticipation of vacation after exams

(5) feeling pressured and rushed or bitter and angry about not being able to take coffee break

(6) anger at being overworked by Professor Greene or distressed that she's too busy to type report

(7) frustration and anger or loneliness

(8) fear of being hurt or anger at others' selfishness

(9) exasperation and frustration about delay or anger at dependence on Jim

(10) anxiety about new social worker or excitement about meeting her

(11) fear

(12) anticipation

(13) anger at Ms. Jones or concern for Ms. Jones

(14) desperation

(15) fear that something is wrong with child

(16) anger at young people for having more sexual freedom or jealousy

(17) relief at stepping down or bitterness about pressures

(18) frustration at inability to learn

(19) concern

(20) confusion, fear

(21) anger at being ignored

(22) futility about not getting anywhere or anger at helper for not being better helper

(23) anger at rejection or loneliness

(24) fear of rejection or loneliness

(25) anger or concern

Exercise 3-22. Possible helper responses might be

(2) Sounds to me like you were annoyed at them for tempting you.

(3) You're confused as to whether or not your marriage will work if you haven't worked through your problems.

(4) It makes you feel angry and inadequate when you're not given credit for your work.

(5) You're pretty angry at Jack for not being able to wean himself away from his folks.

(6) You're afraid something will happen to her and you care so much.

(7) You're afraid that you may be inadequate and may fail on this job.

(8) I hear how determined you are to make a go of it. That's terrific.

(9) It makes you feel sad and lonely when they won't let you play with them.

(10) You've been hurt often and you're afraid to trust people.

(11) You feel like I don't care enough about you if I keep you waiting.

(12) You're so afraid you won't do well on that test.

(13) It seems to you that I don't like you, that I'm unfair to you.

(14) You're angry that he wants your help when you were strong enough to do it on your own.

(15) You're afraid of anger.

(16) You don't feel appreciated.

(17) You're really scared and overwhelmed with responsibilities.

(18) You're very independent and you seem determined and proud.

(19) You're very angry that you have to be dependent on your family.

(20) Things are finally going well for you and you don't want anything to happen.

REFERENCES AND FURTHER READINGS

Benjamin, A. *The Helping Interview*. Boston: Houghton Mifflin, 1974.

Brammer, L. *The Helping Relationship*. Englewood Cliffs, N.J.: Prentice-Hall, 1973.

Gazda, G. *Human Relations Development*. Boston: Allyn and Bacon, 1973.

Gordon, T. *Parent Effectiveness Training*. New York: Wyden, 1970.

Hackney, H., and Nye, S. *Counseling Strategies and Objectives*. Englewood Cliffs, N.J.: Prentice-Hall, 1973.

Ivey, A. *Microcounseling: [Interviewing Skills Manual]*. Springfield, Il.: Thomas, 1972.

Kagan, N., and Schauble, P. "Affect Simulation in Interpersonal Process Recall." *Journal of Counseling Psychology* 16 (1969): 309-313.

CHAPTER 4

STAGE 1: THE RELATIONSHIP STAGE

The development of a helping relationship underlies the effectiveness of any helping strategy. In this chapter we will review the necessary conditions and steps for creating the type of empathic climate in which the helpee can begin to explore his or her world and gain self-awareness. The communications skills discussed in chapter 3 are crucial to the effectiveness of this stage.

CONDITIONS

Before discussing the five steps of the relationship stage itself, let's look at the inherent conditions affecting this stage. These conditions may appear obvious to you, but unless they are taken into account, they may hinder the helping relationship.

Initial Contact

The term "interview" is often used to describe the first one or two helping periods because these sessions are usually for information gathering. For some people, this word is formal and carries a threatening connotation—we can all think of job and school interviews we've endured that have been more like inquisitions. Whether the interview is initiated by the helper, the helpee, or a third party, the helpee often feels anxiety about being accepted and fears saying the "wrong" things.

Let us use the term interview then for the initial meeting, where contact is first made and information gained. Subsequent meetings can be called "sessions." The first interview is really a testing period for both parties—helpers ask themselves if they will be able to work effectively with the helpees and helpees ask themselves if they will be able to trust and respect their helpers and share their real concerns.

The tone of an interview is actually set at the first moment of initial contact, whether that be appointment setting or the actual interview. The first step in a helping relationship is to establish a mutually convenient meeting time for both parties. Right away, the helper can show frankness. If unable to devote adequate time to the helpee at that particular moment, rather than hurriedly trying to rush through a few frantic exchanges in a corridor, the helper is better off saying, "I see you really need to talk to me about that. I'm tied up now. Could you come back at three o'clock?"

The helper must quickly determine the realities and priorities of any given situation: Is this a crisis? Can I rearrange my schedule? Can this person wait until later to see me? Sometimes the only way to determine this is to ask helpees whether or not they can wait. The point is that at this critical contact moment the helper can communicate genuine concern and willingness to be available to the helpee. The following are some points to remember:

1. Schedule a specific time for an appointment, avoiding "later," "next week," or "soon" and suggest specific alternatives.

2. Tell the helpee that you want to be available to him or her when you both can give your full time and attention to the helpee's concerns.

3. Communicate support (reinforcement) to the helpee for initiating contact (e.g., "I'm so glad you've come to see me about this."). People often feel a bit foolish and unsure about asking for help and they need reassurance.

If you work in a setting where appointments are made for you, it is important for you to assume responsibility for seeing that whoever makes appointments (a receptionist, clerk, or secretary) communicates the same kind of concern and helpfulness to the client. There is nothing more deflating to a person seeking help than to be rudely put off by an appointment maker who delays appointments, refers to how busy you are, or is too inquistive and asks too many personal questions.

If at all possible, it is helpful to have a corner where people waiting to see you may be unobserved by others in your setting. Many people feel uncomfortable if a peer knows they are talking to a supervisor, a counselor, or some other helping person.

If you are initiating the first interview, tell the person why you are arranging this meeting, preferably at the appointment-making time or at the outset of the first contact. It is necessary that the helpee understand why you've arranged this contact so that he or she can learn to trust you and to offset his or her resistances and defenses.

Duration

A helping relationship may last one, few, or many sessions. The number depends upon:

1. the nature of the relationship (whether it is formal or informal, voluntary or involuntary, etc.),

2. the nature of the problem (whether it is short-term or long-term; how easily it is defined, clarified, and accepted; whether it is crisis or preventive or developmental), and

3. the setting in which this relationship occurs (whether it is a counseling center, a human services institution, a business, etc.).

In many cases, it is unlikely that the nature and timing of the helping relationship can be predetermined until the nature of the problem is clarified. Thus, most initial sessions begin in a similar fashion, with the dual purposes of having the involved parties establish rapport and identify the problems.

Applications and Forms

If applications or forms are necessary to the process, it is usually better to ask the helpee to complete them before you begin the interview so that the meeting time can best be used in establishing a positive relationship. However, if your time allows, it can sometimes be mutually beneficial to establishing a helping relationship if you aid the helpee in filling out the forms. Just remember not to become so involved in the content of the forms that you miss what is really being communicated.

Facilities

In order to establish trust and support, it is necessary to provide a meeting place where confidentiality can be ensured. Conferences in open offices with thin partitions or the corner of an occupied room can be difficult situations in which to uncover a client's real concerns. If a private room is not available, you can try to find an out-of-the-way section in a stairwell or corridor or go out of the building.

If you do have a private office, try to arrange the furniture so that you can sit facing the helpee without any barriers. For example, you can sit on one side of your desk next to the helpee, rather than across from him or her. Some people prefer to work away from their desks and arrange chairs facing each other in another part of the room.

Timing

Except in unusual circumstances, try to keep appointments as scheduled. It is terribly frustrating when someone comes to see you or is planning to come to see you and you are not available.

You can let the helpee know just how much time you have at the outset, if this is not already understood. During all interviews and sessions, it is important that you demonstrate your involvement with the helpee by refusing to accept telephone calls and by not allowing interruptions of any kind. A common complaint voiced by people seeking help is that they just began to get down to their real concerns when the mood was broken by an interruption.

Record Keeping

If you intend to take written notes or use a video or audio tape recorder during the interview, you can begin by explaining your rationale for this and by clarifying who will or will not have access to the recorded data. Do not assume that a helpee who doesn't bring it up doesn't have questions and feelings about this. You bring it up and frankly discuss what it is all about. Both the helper and the helpee usually become oblivious to recording devices after the first few moments. Very often, helpees ask to review video and audio tapes which can prove to be an excellent strategy for furthering the helpee's and the helper's self-awareness.

Third Party

Sometimes a helpee will bring someone, such as a friend, a relative, or an interpreter, along to the interview. Depending upon the nature of the situation and setting, you will have to decide whether the presence of a third party will help or hinder and act accordingly.

Some of the above conditions fall under the heading of common courtesy. We can all think of situations when we, as helpees, have been stymied by neglect of one or more of them.

STEPS

Think back to interviews that you have participated in. What conditions did you find threatening and what conditions did you find helpful? Try to relate them to what we're now discussing. We are going to cover the five steps in the relationship stage; they are initiation/ entry, clarification of presenting problem, structure/ contract for the helping relationship, intensive exploration of problem(s), and establishing possible goals and objectives of the helping relationship.

Initiation/Entry

A warm, smiling welcome is the best way I know to begin any interview or session. The obvious purpose is to put the helpee at ease and then to get down to the business of identifying issues and concerns as quickly as possible. And, of course, you want to let helpees know that you are genuinely glad to see them. Often some informal conversation about the weather, parking, and so forth, is necessary in order to help the client relax. Ice-breaking remarks, such as "Tell me what I can do for you" or "I'm interested in what's going on with you now" can help focus on the reason for the meeting.

Refer back to chapter 3 for discussion and practice in listening to verbal messages and observing nonverbal messages. You can get more information by responsive listening statements than by asking questions. Some examples of drawing out the helpee follow:

> *Helpee:* My husband has never been out of work so long before. It's having a terrible effect on the kids. That's why I'm here, I guess.

> *Helper:* That's a scary situation for all of you, I know. Let's talk more about what it's doing to your family.

The helper is communicating support and understanding, while, at the same time, steering the conversation onto specific effects of the husband's unemployment on his family.

> *Helpee:* My friend Joan Astin said you helped her decide if she should go back to work. I thought I'd come in and see what you can do for me.

> *Helper:* She's quite a woman. You seem to be in a quandry about what you want to do. Can you tell me about the options you've been considering?

The helper is acknowledging the helpee's relationship with Ms. Astin and, at the same time, seeking clarification on the nature of the situation.

> *Helpee:* (fidgeting and avoiding eye contact) I dunno why you sent for me. I ain't done nothin' wrong.
>
> *Helper:* You feel uncomfortable because you think you wouldn't be here unless you were going to be landed on. I've asked you to come in so that I can get to know you better and find out more how you're doing in shop. Mr. Jones seems to feel you're having some difficulties there.

The helper responds honestly to the request for explanation of the interview in a nonthreatening manner.

> *Helpee:* I don't know whether I should come to you with this. I hate to complain. My daughter is awfully unhappy with Betty (her camp counselor).
>
> *Helper:* I'm glad you've come to see me, Ms. Brown. Tell me what you think is troubling Sue about Betty.

The helper is assuring the helpee that it's O.K. to deal with this issue, while asking for some further information.

> *Friend:* Hi! Got time for a cup of coffee?
>
> *Friend:* Just a sec. I've been wondering how things are going with you.

In this informal setting, the helping friend responds promptly to the cue for a visit and starts right in expressing concern.

Statements or leads such as those above, which draw out information in a nonthreatening, open, indirect manner can be called "door openers" or "ice breakers." Their purpose is to keep the communication flowing without any judging, confronting, or manipulation. Other such leads are "Tell me more about that", "I'm wondering about . . .", "Seems to me that . . .", and "That sounds really interesting." Minimal verbal statements can also effectively keep the communication flowing as do head nodding, smiling, and affectionate shoulder pats.

You need to be supportive and encouraging in order to establish an effective helping relationship. However, if you confuse re-assurance with support and encouragement, you may aid people to avoid rather than to approach their true concerns. If you are overly reassuring, you are denying the legitimacy of the helpee's concerns and, by doing this, imposing your values and judgments even though you think you are being nice and making someone else "feel better."

You may ask questions when you feel they will augment the communication flow, but it is best to phrase them indirectly and open endedly. Most people ask too many questions to begin with, so it is a good idea for helpers-in-training to limit themselves to as few questions as possible and to concentrate on responsive listening statements. You'd be surprised how often you can turn a question into a statement that will produce more information than the question.

The issue of reluctant clients can affect this first step. There are times when silence is the only way of responsively attending to a reluctant client. This will be further discussed in chapter 8.

Clarification of Presenting Problem

Remember that it may take some time and patience to get to the true problem that is of concern to the helpee. Understandably, most people test out helpers with superficial concerns before they trust them enough to reveal more basic concerns. For example, a woman came in to see me recently and told me that the reason she came was because she was worried about one of her children. As we proceeded to develop a relationship, it became apparent that she was very angry at her husband and really concerned about her marriage. The child, in this case, was the less painful focus of concern and actually helped her to avoid looking at and dealing with her marital relationship. It is important that you actively listen and respond to the helpee in order to avoid being sidetracked by superficial concerns.

It is possible that a helpee will present several different concerns. By using responsive listening techniques, you can aid the helpee in sorting out the different concerns and ranking them according to priority. The following examples show two different approaches to the same initial helpee statement.

Example 1. *Helpee:* I'm really having family problems. My fiancee and I have a mutual uncle and he is close to my parents and me. Her parents have not seen nor spoken to him in fifteen years. They have forbidden her to visit him or come to my house if he is there.

Helper: That's rough. Must make you feel guilty about your relations with your uncle.

Helpee: Yes. The problem is the wedding. My mother insists he come and my fiancee says it's impossible.

Helper: You're really in a bind and you don't know how to get around this.

Helpee: I'm beginning to think we should elope. You know large Italian family weddings; I don't know how we can make everyone happy.

Helper: Let's talk about the different ways we can deal with the wedding invitations.

Example 2. *Helpee:* I'm really having family problems. My fiancee and I have a mutual uncle and he is close to my parents and me. Her parents have not seen nor spoken to him in fifteen years. They have forbidden her to visit him or come to my house if he is there.

Helper: You seem to be upset that your fiancee's parents have such control over her.

Helpee: Yes, I guess they really do.

Helper: It's uncomfortable for you to be in the middle of the two families and for her not to be taking a stand with you.

Helpee: I think her first loyalty should be to me! After all, I'm going to be her husband!

Helper: Sounds to me like you're wondering how she'll react to her parents' pressures after you're married.

Helpee: That's really it.

The helper in the second example was able to clarify the real issue, rather than be sidetracked to an apparent problem. You can see how important it is to take the time to get to the real problem and not to rush too quickly into problem solving. It has been my experience, both as a counselor and with colleagues at meetings, that unless the time is taken to identify clearly the problem and its "ownership," a large amount of problem-solving activity is futile. What I mean by problem ownership is the identification of what person has the problem. One has to feel that they own at least part of the problem before one will invest much energy in the problem-solving process.

Another example illustrating the problem clarification step is the following:

Helpee:	I'm not going to be able to come in for work tomorrow. I know you need me for the inventory, but I just can't make it.
Helper:	Sounds like something is bothering you.
Helpee:	No, not really. I'm going to have to start looking for a place of my own to live.
Helper:	Your present living situation isn't working out.
Helpee:	I'll say! The lady I'm living with is really bitchy and giving me a hard time. I need an apartment of my own, even though I don't know how I'll manage.
Helper:	You seem scared about the financial responsibilities and you seem to be torn between getting a place of your own and putting up with a bad situation.
Helpee:	That's right. I've never been on my own before. I don't know if I can do it. Everything seems to cost so much.
Helper:	Let's see if I can help you plot out what it will cost.

Again, by taking the time really to listen to what the helpee is saying, the helper was able to get to the underlying fear and insecurity, rather than be sidetracked onto the helpee's relationships with the landlady.

Structure/Contract for the Helping Relationship

Once the problem has been clarified and acknowledged by the helpee as one needing some kind of resolution, you can decide whether or not you are able to provide help for this type of problem. If you feel that you are unable to provide this help, you can aid the helpee in obtaining assistance elsewhere, by means of **referral.**

Referrals occur when you make arrangements for someone to see a designated individual (or agency) for a specific purpose. In helping relationships, early referrals are especially important because they can take some time to effect. There may be a waiting period before a referral can take place and during that period you may want to maintain a supporting, encouraging relationship. The helpee may be reluctant to accept a referral and this acceptance (readiness) may become the goal for your helping relationship. If you serve in a helping role in a setting where personal or long-term counseling is not available, you can learn to identify available community resources so that you can quickly make contacts for helpees. An example of a referral follows:

Ms. White, age forty-two, has been employed as a supervisor in the keypunch unit for eight years. She has recently lost a lot of weight and has displayed irritable, irrational behavior with her workers. Her behavior is unusual; for these eight years she has been regarded as one of the most easy going supervisors in the company. The following excerpt occurs at the end of the second session with Ms. Graham, the personnel manager, someone with whom Ms. White has talked before. Ms. White requested these sessions because she felt the need "to talk to someone."

Ms. White: And so, it seems as if my whole world is falling apart. I can't eat, I can't sleep, I can't think.

Ms. Graham: I'm concerned about you. You're really having a difficult time.

Ms. White: I went to the doctor a couple of days ago. He says except for the weight loss and nerves that it's all in my head and I just have to stop worrying. I don't even know what I'm worrying about.

Ms. Graham: Thelma, I'd like to be able to help you, but I really think you need a different kind of help than I can give.

Ms. White: What do you mean? I'm not mental or anything like that.

Ms. Graham: No. I know. But you are having problems that lots of people have at one time or another in their life. And there are people around who are trained to help you. They can help you find out what's worrying you.

Ms. White: I don't know. I don't think I could talk to anyone the way I can to you. And I can't afford much.

Ms. Graham: You can still talk to me. Let me try and find out who in your town can be of help and the cost and so forth. Then we can talk some more about it.

Ms. White: If you really think that's what we should do.

Ms. Graham: Can you come see me tomorrow morning? Around 9:45—just before coffee break? We can talk some more about it then.

In this case, Ms. White is frightened of a referral and Ms. Graham is sensitive to this fear. It is important in a case such as this that the helper take the necessary time to allow the trusting relationship developing with the helpee to be used as a vehicle for helping the client accept a referral. As Ms. Graham knows that Ms. White has received medical clearance, she can take the time to be supportive and effect what she believes will be a satisfactory referral.

It is important for you to learn what you can and what you cannot deal with, to learn who around you can handle what kinds of situations, and to be able to feel good about making a referral.

If, on the other hand, the nature and extent of the problem is such that you feel you can provide help, it is important for you to state clearly to the helpee just what you can do and what you cannot do, what you expect from the helpee, how you perceive his or her expectations of you, and how much time you can devote to this helping relationship. This applies to both formal and informal helping relationships, whatever the setting. This step is often neglected and unhappiness and frustration result on both sides when expectations (which have not been clarified) are unmet.

One way to clarify expectations is to make a contract. A contract can be written or spoken. It is clear, understood by all parties, and is always open to revision. For example, if you say to a helpee that you would like to meet five times and then see how things are, you can always decide to lengthen or shorten that time as long as you both agree. Agreement is the key variable. The terms of the contract can include time of sessions, length of sessions, site of sessions, fees (if applicable), estimate of number of sessions needed, who can or will attend sessions, procedures for changing any of these terms, and helper and helpee expectations. The following example demonstrates this step.

> Marianne, age eighteen, a college freshman, has been referred to the counselor by her residence advisor because of continuing homesickness. The following excerpt occurred at the end of the first session, during which the counselor identified the problem as being one of low self-concept with resulting feelings of inferiority and inadequacy.

> *Counselor:* Our time is almost up, Marianne. I'm wondering how you feel about our talk today.

> *Marianne:* It's been O.K.

> *Counselor:* Would you like to come in again?

> *Marianne:* Yes, I think so. Do you think I should?

> *Counselor:* It's up to you. I do think we can talk some more about what you're doing and feeling.

> *Marianne:* Uh-huh.

> *Counselor:* Why don't we plan on having three more sessions —one hour per week, and then we can see where to go from there. You may want to see about joining a group then or you may want to continue coming in. We can leave that open for now.

> *Marianne:* That sounds O.K. Do I make the appointments with you or the secretary out there?

In this case, the counselor suggests that there is more material to gather and that, in a few weeks, they may have some other options to consider. This kind of structuring provides a frame of reference so that the helpee does not feel caught up in an endless process.

Intensive Exploration of Problems

Using the responsive listening model of communications, you can begin to aid the helpee to look at more aspects, implications, and ramifications of his or her problems. Of course, many new ones will continue to emerge throughout the entire helping process. Again, it is important to know just what the problem is, who has responsibility for the problem(s), and to what extent the helpee is able to effect some problem solving.

The problem is often part of the system in which helpees find themselves. In these cases, helpees are likely to feel very frustrated, hopeless, and helpless. However, the same principles apply in these cases—you try to learn as much as you can about the helpee, the system, the possibilities for change, and what choices do exist. Throughout this period, you are learning more about the thinking process, the feelings, and the behaviors of the helpee both in and out of the helping relationship. You are discovering the client's values, beliefs, attitudes, defense and coping strategies, relationships with others, hopes, ambitions, and aspirations. This is a time when you encourage the helpee to express whatever thoughts or feelings are being experienced, without the fear of being judged or directed into any one particular area. All the while, you are assisting the development of trust, genuineness, and empathy, so that you can create a safe climate in which the helpee feels free to explore his or her own self-awareness.

The following excerpt is from the third counseling session with Marianne and demonstrates some intensive exploration of the problem.

Counselor:	So you've felt for a long time that you couldn't do much on your own.
Marianne:	My mom and Pat [older sister] always did everything for me.
Counselor:	And that made you feel sort of . . .
Marianne:	Dopey. They even would check over my homework every night. You see, Pat got married right after high school and never went on to college. She had been an honor student, and now here she is widowed and back home with a baby.

Counselor:	Seems like you're supposed to make up to your mom and Pat what they didn't have.
Marianne:	They always say they want me to be and have what they didn't have. That's why it was so important for me to come to college.
Counselor:	It was important to you, too?
Marianne:	I don't know. I never thought about what was important to me. I never want to upset my mom, she cries so easily.
Counselor:	And your dad . . .
Marianne:	Oh, he wants whatever my mom wants. He never interferes or anything.
Counselor:	I hear some anger in your voice.
Marianne:	I was just thinking that there have been times when I wish my dad would stick up for me.

The counselor is learning as much as possible about Marianne's background and all the aspects of her feelings of inadequacy. This takes time and skill, but some exploration is necessary before goals and objectives can be established. This is a continuous step that occurs throughout the helping relationship. For many helpers, this is one of the most challenging and exciting steps of a helping relationship. In fact, many relationships end at this step because the act of mutual exploration is in itself therapeutic.

Establishing Possible Goals and Objectives

When the problem(s) has been thoroughly explored, the helper and the helpee can more specifically develop goals and objectives for the relationship. This can be done in a systematic or casual fashion, depending upon the style of the parties in the helping relationship. The important point is that both parties agree to whatever the goals and objectives are. It would certainly not be helpful for the client if the goals met the helper's needs only.

You will find immediate and long-range goals, specific and diffuse goals. For example, a student who is referred to a counselor because he or she faces possible failure in a course may also have family problems. You and this student may choose to work on the more specific, immediate goal—that of passing the course and staying in school—rather than the long-range, more diffuse goal of family problems. These goals are not all necessarily valid or equal and it is up to the helper and the helpee to determine mutually which goals are feasible, given the nature and conditions of the particular helping relationship.

It is possible that the goal of the relationship is to develop the relationship further, so that the helpee's self-concept is enhanced, or to provide a vehicle for self-understanding. That could very well become the goal in the case of Marianne. Or it may be that the goal is to make some kind of decision or to seek some alternative forms of behavior. The point is that both the helper and the helpee need to know why this relationship is occurring and what the goals are. When I ask students what distinguishes a particular session in a counseling center from a friendly talk over the coffee table, they usually reply that helping relationship involves goals and objectives that one does not usually consider in a friendly conversation.

If several different goals and objectives are formulated, it is a good idea to decide which has priority and where the focus will be for how long. Sometimes this falls into a logical sequence, other times helper and helpee arbitrarily decide. The following excerpt illustrates some goal setting at the end of the first session.

Mr. Winsor, age thirty-two, has come to see the adult advisor at the local community college. He wants to take some courses that will give him upward job mobility. He is feeling trapped in a job that will not take him any place.

Counselor:	It's really important for you to see some possibilities of moving ahead.
Mr. Winsor:	Yes. I have a growing family, we're having a hard time making ends meet, and we do want to be out of the city by the time the oldest starts school.
Counselor:	But you're not really sure just what courses you might want to take or what kinds of jobs to aim for.
Mr. Winsor:	At this point, I just want to move . . . up.
Counselor:	It seems to me we ought to find out more about what kinds of work you'd really like and be suited for, rather than just sign up for some courses.
Mr. Winsor:	What do you mean?
Counselor:	Why don't you take our battery of vocational interest and aptitude tests and then we can go over the results and, together, try to decide what would be the best path for you to follow?
Mr. Winsor:	I guess so. Will it take long?
Counselor:	I can set you up for a testing session next week and we can talk before registration.
Mr. Winsor:	I've heard about those tests . . . can't do no harm. I'm game.

It is clear here that the objectives of the relationship became focused on vocational testing and exploration.

Goal setting is also important with children. Like adults, children increase their motivation, which usually results in higher outcomes, by participating in goal setting.

RELATIONSHIP EXERCISES

The following exercises will give you some more practice in developing the communications skills that enhance helping relationships and uncover problems. They will also give you the opportunity to relate to the different steps of the relationship stage. The more you actively participate in process exercises and discuss with others your feelings and reactions to these exercises, the more meaningful the concepts discussed in this chapter become.

Exercise 4-1. For the following client statements, circle the letter of the response that you believe would best facilitate the development of an empathic relationship and lead to clarification of the presenting problem.

(1) "Ms. Smith said you wanted to see me."

    a. Yes, Mary. She tells me you're not getting on very well in that group.

    b. Oh? That's right, I did. Can you tell me what's going on in the steno pool? I understand production is way off.

    c. I have been wanting to talk to you, Mary. How do you feel about the way things are going in the steno pool?

    d. Yes. I want to see if there's any way we can help you feel good here. Can we talk about how things are going in the steno pool?

    e. Ummmm. I want to hear your version of what's going on in the steno pool.

(2) "I'm not going to be able to get through that interview. I know I'll mess it up like all the other times!"

    a. No you won't. Not if you make up your mind not to.

    b. Come on! Have some faith in yourself. Of course you'll do O.K.

    c. You're worried that you'll fall apart once you get in there?

    d. Why don't you talk to some people who've already had their interviews and see if they can clue you in as to what it'll be like.

    e. You feel that because you've had some bad experiences interviewing, this one will be bad, too.

(3) "I don't understand why we're always fighting. We just can't seem to talk about anything anymore."

    a. Tell me about it.

    b. All married people fight sometimes.

    c. It's frightening to be so angry with your husband most of the time. Makes you worry about what's happened to change your relationship.

d. What do you fight about?

e. You probably need a change. How about changing your routine a bit—maybe go out to dinner or to a movie or something that's different.

(4) "I've come to see you because I need help. What do you think I should do about this?"

    a. You seem to want me to tell you what to do.

    b. The first thing is to check out some information. Have you looked into financial aid?

    c. I can't solve your problems for you, you know.

    d. What do you *want* to do?

    e. I don't know. Let's talk some more about it.

(5) "Business has really fallen off. They're talking about laying people off."

    a. You're worried that you may be laid off if things don't start to get better.

    b. I know. I'm worried too. Don't know what will happen.

    c. Yeah, times are rough. Everyday the papers report more layoffs.

    d. Don't worry. I'm sure things are just exaggerated right now.

    e. Don't you think we're all in the same boat?

(6) "I can't decide which high school to go to next year. I'm supposed to go to East, but I can get special permission to go out of district to West."

    a. Sounds like you've been thinking a lot about it.

    b. What are the things you're looking for at each of these schools?

    c. Have you visited each of the schools yet?

    d. It's a hard decision to make. Let's talk about what you feel about each school.

    e. I can see you're discouraged. Tell me more about what needs change.

(7) "My coming to see you really won't help. You can't change anything."

    a. You wish I could make things easier for you.

    b. You're pretty discouraged. You wish there were some way I could change things for you.

    c. Sounds to me like you're not even willing to try.

    d. Maybe there are some things *you* could change!

    e. I can see you're discouraged. Tell me more about what needs change.

(8) "If only I had listened to my dad. He told me this wouldn't work."

    a. Well, you live and you learn. It's not so terrible to make a mistake.

    b. Crying over spilt milk won't help.

    c. It's rough. Tell me why you think it didn't work.

    d. It's sort of scary to think your dad may be right about things. What else may he be right about?

(9) "I don't want to go back to school ever. I'm not learning anything and the teachers are terrible. I want to get a job now."

    a. You know, John, if you don't finish school, you'll be sorry later on and it will be too late.

    b. I know how you feel, but it's pretty difficult getting a job these days.

    c. You really are feeling down about that school. Sounds like you really want to get away from there.

    d. You're not sure what you're getting out of being in school. Seems like a waste of time for you.

    e. I'm wondering what you're doing to help yourself out over there.

(10) "My parents are always on my back. They always want to know where I am, what I'm doing, and whom I'm with. They never leave me alone."

    a. It does seem as if parents worry too much, doesn't it?

    b. You're really upset because it seems to you that your parents don't trust you.

    c. I'm sure they really love you and are just worried. It's so hard these days with teenagers.

    d. Have you ever done anything to give them cause for worry?

    e. It's nice to know they care so much, isn't it?

Remember, you do not want to come across as a judge, an interrogator, or as a disinterested party. It is sometimes difficult for us to communicate warmth and acceptance because we do have immediate reactions to and feelings about the helpee's statements and manner of presentation. Perhaps we've shared a similar experience or problem and we're anxious to pass on how we reacted and coped. There are times when such self-disclosure is facilitative, but in the initial steps of relationship building it is more likely to focus attention on you and off the helpee. Possible answers for the preceding exercise are (1) d, (2) e, (3) c, (4) a, (5) a, (6) a or d, (7) b or e, (8) d, (9) c or d, (10) b. Discuss your answers in small groups and see if you can determine why some answers are more appropriate than others.

Exercise 4-2. Discuss in small groups the following situations. Then, if possible, role play the different possibilities and see if you can share with the other members of your group your feelings and reactions. Give your rationale for accepting or rejecting the listed alternatives and then supply some of your own.

(1) Mary, age ten, comes to you, her girl scout leader, to tell you that two other girl scouts in your troop stole some candy from the local dime store yesterday. She's been with them when they've done that before, too. What would you do and why?

    a. Call in the other two girls and confront them with Mary's report.

    b. Discuss with Mary the morality of shoplifting, tattling, and association with wrong-doers even if you don't misbehave.

    c. Explore with Mary her own concerns about this and what her options are.

(2) Mr. Green comes into your public employment office to insist that he did, in fact, show up for a scheduled job interview, even though the employer claims that he did not show up. What would you do and why?

    a. Tell Mr. Green that you know he has lied and that you can no longer refer him for job interviews.

    b. Ask Mr. Green to tell you what happened and explain to him what you can and cannot do for him and the various options available to him.

    c. Suggest to Mr. Green that he join a vocational counseling group for practice in interviewing.

(3) Tom, age fourteen, comes to your gymnastics class at the local recreation center "stoned." You have been concerned about Tom's erratic participation (despite his steady attendance) in this class for a few weeks. Every time you've asked him what's wrong, he tells you "Nothing. Don't bug me." What would you do and why?

    a. Tell Tom that you want to have him in your class, but he really can't come when he is stoned, as that is not fair to you and the others in the group.

    b. Again, tell him that you're concerned about him and will be available to talk to him about whatever seems to be bothering him whenever he's ready.

    c. Ask him if you can take him home and talk to his parents with him.

(4) You are a store manager in a fashionable suburban shopping center and you have noticed for several weeks that your senior salesperson has consistently been making errors during the nightly audit. You have also noticed that she is irritable and snapping at coworkers over every little thing.

    a. You tell her you've noticed she seems upset and you're concerned. Can she tell you what's going on?

    b. You explain to her that your regional manager is on your back about these errors and you need to know if she needs help at night.

    c. You suggest to her that she seems to be troubled and perhaps needs to talk to someone. You know someone at a local agency that you would be happy to refer her to.

(5) You are a volunteer for a local crafts program for the elderly. One of the gentlemen, Mr. Roberts, appears to be withdrawn and cranky. When you go to talk to him, he tells you that his daughter-in-law is being nasty to him and he is unhappy living with her.

    a. You discuss with him how unsympathetic in-laws often are and sympathize with his position.

    b. You discuss with him the capabilities he has and the options he has for different activities within the community.

    c. You empathize with his loneliness and discuss with him what you and others can offer him in the way of companionship and activities.

Play out as many of these responses as you can and see where they go. Get in touch with your own feelings and values as you identify with both the helper and the helpee. Sharing these in group discussion can be very productive.

Exercise 4-3. Which of the five steps of the relationship stage (initiation/entry, clarification, structure/contract, exploration, possible goals/objectives) is evident in the following examples?

(1) *Helpee:* If I am pregnant, my folks will murder me.

Helper: You're scared of what your parents will do to you.

Helpee: You don't know them! They always are yapping at me and telling me I'm gonna end up just like my sister.

Helper: You don't want to be like your sister.

Helpee: You bet your sweet—I don't! She had to marry Ron when she was in high school and now she's really stuck with two brats and a husband who beats her up.

Helper: That's scary. You seem afraid that you may have gotten yourself into a situation where you can end up the same way.

In this excerpt, the counselor is in step 2, clarification of the problem. She is trying to determine whether possible pregnancy (the presenting symptom), relationship with parents, or fears of being "trapped" is the major issue.

In the following examples, decide yourself and then discuss in pairs or small groups what you've decided. My comments are at the end of the chapter.

(2) *Helper:* There are only two more weeks of school left. Would you like to spend that time working on your shyness in class, so you can start next year off feeling more comfortable?

Helpee: Do you think I'll ever be able to answer out loud in class without getting all messed up?

Helper: There are exercises we can practice that will help you become less nervous.

Helpee: That would really help. If I could learn that, my marks would go up.

(3) *Helpee:* Am I too early?

Helper: No, right on time. Come in and sit down.
Helpee: Over here?

Helper: Fine. Now, tell me about your father-in-law.

Helpee: Yes, I'm so worried about him. You see . . .

	(4)	*Helpee:*	Do you think you can help me find a job?

(4) *Helpee:* Do you think you can help me find a job?

Helper: We can work together on preparing a resume and choosing leads to follow.

Helpee: I don't really know where to start. What do you charge for this?

Helper: Let's set up three sessions to get things rolling. Here's a copy of my fee schedule. There are also some forms for you to fill out.

(5) *Helpee:* I just don't know whether it's best for me and everyone to stay with Joe or to leave.

Helper: You feel a lot of ambivalence about your marriage.

Helpee: Well, I don't want the children to grow up without a father, and he says we can't afford financially to split up. But then, I'm thirty-seven and I hate to think of spending the rest of my life this way. There must be something better for me.

Helper: Let's focus on this ambivalence for awhile. What do you see yourself getting for yourself by staying in this marriage?

Exercise 4-4. The purpose of this exercise is to afford you the opportunity to enact the principles and steps discussed in this chapter. Form new triads, if possible, with people with whom you have not worked and formed relationships. Rotate roles of helper, helpee, and observer and select one or more of the following situations (or choose one of your own) as a presenting problem. Choose whatever setting feels comfortable to you. The helper is to work with the helpee for about one-half hour; the observer uses the rating sheet in appendix A and makes notes about the steps and behaviors of the helper. At the end of the session, take as much time as necessary to fully process so that both the helpee and observer can provide as much specific feedback as possible to the helper. What steps were you able to accomplish? How did you feel? What do you feel you need to work on? This exercise is one that can be used for weeks of training, in or out of class.

(1) You've had a blow-up with your father.
(2) You're never able to get assignments in on time.
(3) You want to lose weight.
(4) Your best friend has moved away.
(5) Your car is in the shop for repairs and you don't know how you'll manage.
(6) You're afraid of flying and you have an upcoming trip to make.
(7) You're shy and have difficulty meeting new people.
(8) You're not sure why you're here.
(9) You have trouble saying "no" to people when they ask you for something.
(10) You don't know what program to pursue.

In this exercise you can experience the power of the helper-helpee interaction. Helping relationships can vary in intensity, depending upon the situation. Important factors to note are the helpee's expectations and feelings of insecurity and anxiety at the beginning of a session, as well as the expectations, feelings, competencies, and skills of the helper. Try to pinpoint these as you work through these exercises.

SUMMARY

In this chapter we have discussed basic conditions (initial contact, duration, applications and forms, facilities, timing, and record keeping) and the five major steps (initiation/entry, clarification of presenting problem, structure/contract for the helping relationship, intensive exploration of problem, and establishing possible goals and objectives) of the first phase of the helping relationship, the relationship stage.

Research has been unable to prove the effectiveness of any one technique over another technique, but studies do show that the effect of a given helping relationship can depend as much on the quality of the relationship as upon the techniques and strategies the helper uses. With this knowledge, we can proceed to the next stage, the strategies stage.

EXERCISE ANSWERS

Exercise 4-3. Excerpt (2) is in the fifth step, setting possible goals and objectives. There is a time limitation here and the helper and helpee choose to use this time focusing on assertive behaviors. Excerpt (3) is the initiation/entry step. Excerpt (4) is the structure/contract step, where fees, time, and specific commitments are discussed. Excerpt (5) is a brief sample of intensive exploration, where the helper and helpee are covering all the aspects and consequences of the helpee's concerns.

REFERENCES AND FURTHER READINGS

Benjamin, A. *The Helping Interview*. Boston: Houghton Mifflin, 1974.

Delaney, D., and Eisenberg, S. *The Counseling Process*. Chicago: Rand McNally, 1972.

Egan, G. *The Skilled Helper: A Model for Systematic Helping and Interpersonal Relating*. Monterey, Ca.: Brooks/Cole, 1975.

CHAPTER 5

HELPING
THEORY

Now that we have covered the steps involved in the relationship stage, we can begin to look ahead to the application of strategies. In order to provide a framework for understanding how to apply counseling skills and strategies, however, we must review the major formal theories of helping. This overview will cover their theoretical assumptions, their pertinent views of the helping relationship, their significant strategies, and their implications for helpers. Before studying the major scientifically based theories, we will explore your own internally based values and needs that comprise your "personal" theory. Your personal theory will undoubtedly affect the manner in which you conceptualize and accept or reject the formal theories of helping.

WHY THEORY?

You may now be asking yourself why we should bother exploring behavioral theories when we are learning about practical skills to apply in the context of unique helping situations. Perhaps you are asking this question because you are uncomfortable with what might imply an ivory tower approach to a down-to-earth situation. Furthermore, the term "theory" is somewhat threatening to many of us, possibly because it implies some kind of rigidity or need to justify our positions.

First, let me point out that we each already have our personal views or assumptions that form a "theory-of-use" about human behavior. By theory-of-use I mean those beliefs and assumptions that operate in our day-to-day living. Our personal theories do exist and affect our actions. Whether or not we are able to express them or are even aware of them, they affect our behavior, especially in our interpersonal relationships. We each possess values, beliefs, and attitudes as well as philosophical concepts that influence the way we live and affect our approaches to working with people. Our personal theories have been influenced by our ethnic, socioeconomic, and familial backgrounds; biological factors; sex; past experiences; exposure to different schools of thought; the people with whom we deal and study; and opportunities. Our personality and temperament also influence our personal theory, as does our degree of self-awareness. Each of you will become more aware of your personal theory of helping as you think about it and as you explore helping situations.

Regardless of what the theory is, we need to understand its content because it affects our actions and reactions in dealing with the people we are helping. Unless we acknowledge our personal theoretical base, we may "help" people more to apply our theory than to satisfy a helpee's needs.

We should acknowledge that an ability to formulate a conceptual understanding of human behavior is important for anyone working with people. The issues that we must grapple with as helpers, whether through study of formal theories solely, through experiential learning, or through some integration of both types of learning, include how personality is formed, how personality is developed, why people behave as they do, what motivates people, how to motivate people, how people think, how people learn, if there are patterns in human development, the impact of groups on individual behavior, and how behavior can be changed.

We all have theories about these questions, although we often are not able to express these thoughts as theories until we have given the matter a great deal of thought. Nevertheless, our behavior and attitudes in interpersonal relationships are affected by our beliefs about these issues; and helpers who are aware of their beliefs and have consciously grappled with these questions are aware of the influence of their own theoretical views on their perceptions, attitudes, and behaviors toward helpees. For example, if we believe that by changing behavior we can change attitudes and feelings, we are more likely to adopt action-oriented counseling strategies focusing on behavioral changes in a formal counseling relationship than if we believe that only through the development of self-awareness will behavior change. In the latter case, we are more likely to adopt an approach utilizing verbal techniques to develop insight. Likewise, an understanding of basic learning theory will enable us as helpers to be aware of and consciously utilize our potential as a model in a helping relationship.

Thus, knowledge of theory and its application is essential if we are to help effectively in a "practical" field. Each helper, however, develops a personal style of helping that is consistent with his or her personal theory. For example, how important to you is a personal relationship in helping and how can you create the kind of helping relationship that is consistent with your personal theory? We can each answer this question differently and still be effective in our own way.

Unfortunately, there is all too little consistency between what people involved in human behavior fields say they believe as theory and what they actually practice. If we can become more aware of our own personal theory, we will be able to see how it relates to formal theory and to our own helping practices. In order to start thinking about some of your theoretical assumptions, ask yourself the following questions:

1. What are human beings? Are they good or bad? Are they born that way? Are they controlled or controlling? What motivates them?

2. How do human beings learn? Are there different kinds of learning?

3. How do personality traits develop? Are they inherent or learned? Are certain personality categories distinct from others in behavior?

4. Can people change? How do they change? Does something external cause someone to change or does it come from within?

5. What is social deviance? Who decides what is deviance? What can or should be done about deviance? What behaviors (in myself and others) do I find acceptable and unacceptable? Are these deviant?

Try answering these questions in your own words, from your own frame of reference. You may be surprised that you do have answers for each of these questions! Compare them to other persons' answers. Your answers are not right or wrong, and today's answers could—and probably will—change as you continue to learn and become more aware of your own views and feelings.

How open are you to different viewpoints? Openmindedness will affect your flexibility and adaptability, which, in turn, will affect the range of people with whom you're able to work and the settings in which you feel comfortable.

See what you can accept and reject now from the following necessarily brief overview of the major theoretical views of helping. You may see some of your present assumptions reflected in the theories discussed in the following pages. Your assumptions may change by the time you finish using this book.

THEORIES OF HELPING

Here we will review the relevant primary aspects of major theories of helping by considering underlying theoretical assumptions, their views of the helping relationship, and their major approaches to helping. Suggested further readings for each of the major theoretical viewpoints appear at the end of the chapter. Specific strategies applying these theories will be explored in chapters 6 and 7.

Psychoanalytic

The psychoanalytic (Freudian) approach has the longest history of any of the presently used theories. Freud is recognized for his great insight in developing procedures for treating disturbed persons based upon his observations and conceptualizations of mental and emotional processes. Many other theories trace back ultimately to his.

Theoretical Assumptions Freud's view of human beings is negative in that he perceived them as being inherently selfish, impulsive, and irrational. Psychoanalysis, the strategy that applies this view, is based on a dynamic theory of personality that is also deterministic (predetermined by biological variables). Psychoanalytic personality theory includes the following concepts:

1. the **id,** representing the primitive, selfish aspect of humans demanding immediate gratification by increasing pleasure and reducing tension

2. the **ego,** attempting reality orientation by mediating (thinking, perceiving, and deciding) between the aggressive id, the moralistic superego, and the external world

3. the **superego,** representing the internalization (conscience) of parental, societal, and cultural injunctions

Behavior is considered to be the product of interaction between these three systems and can occur consciously (with awareness) or unconsciously (without awareness).

Libido is stored in the id. Survival instincts include life instincts such as hunger and sex and death instincts such as aggression and hostility. **Neurosis** occurs when the superego imposes guilt upon the ego to limit impulses of the id, resulting in **defense mechanisms** (such as **repression, projection, denial, compensation, intellectualization**) that actually obscure the true nature of the intrapsychic conflict.

Freud also put forth **psychosexual stages** from birth through adolescence. These stages are critical in their impact on personality development. These stages are the **oral stage** (first year or so of life when baby receives pleasure from sucking), the **anal stage** (around the second and third years of life where child receives pleasure from stimulation of anal erogenous zone), the **phallic stage** (next few years when child receives pleasure from stimulation of genital region), the **latency stage** (from around nine to twelve years, when child appears to lose interest in sexual fantasies and genital stimulation), and the **genital stage** (occurs at puberty, when adolescent begins to focus his or her concerns and gratifications on others rather than on the self. According to the Freudian School, neuroses can be traced to fixation at any one of these psychosexual stages.

The following are the major psychoanalytic constructs:

1. Human behavior is determined by unconscious forces.

2. Sex drives are the principal determinants of behavior.

3. Adult behavior is greatly influenced by early childhood development.

4. There is a fixed quantity of libido stored in the id.

5. Problems arise from intrapsychic conflict caused by the past history resulting in defense mechanisms using an inappropriate amount of libido.

Major Approaches to Helping The purpose of psychoanalytical treatment is to make the patient conscious of unconscious material and to restructure the personality to attain a healthy balance of energy. It is a **directive therapy** within an interview format using such techniques as interpretation, dream analysis, **free** (stream of consciousness) **association, transference, recall,** and **projective techniques**. It is a costly form of treatment, usually taking several years.

View of Helping Relationship Psychoanalytic treatment postulates a directive, authoritarian relationship between the helper and the helpee. The relationship is not a reciprocal one; the helper is an expert authority figure and remains detached, objective, and completely neutral. Transference, a special part of this relationship, occurs when the patient revives attitudes originally present in the parent-child relationship and directs these attitudes toward the therapist. For example, the patient may see the therapist as his father with his father's attributes and feelings and, therefore, be able to work through his unresolved conflicts with his father by means of this transference relationship.

Implications for Helpers   This form of treatment requires the helper to undergo many years of rigorous training, so it is not directly relevant for counselors and helpers in other than traditional medical settings. However, it does have important implications for nonpsychoanalytic helpers. Helpers need to recognize that there are motivating forces within people that are not wholly conscious, how people defend themselves from internal and external threats with defense mechanisms, the significance of early childhood experiences, and the possible implications of the concept of transference upon any relationship.

Phenomenological / HumAnistic

The phenomenological theories of helping focus on the uniqueness of each person's internal perspective. The emphases are on the here and now, rather than what was or what will be, and on how the person perceives and feels about himself and his environment, rather than on the person's adjustment to prevailing cultural norms. The two most widely utilized approaches are the "client-centered" theory developed by Carl Rogers and the "Gestalt" theory advanced by Fritz Perls.

The **client-centered** approach, established during the 1930s and 1940s, was largely a reaction to the rigidity of the psychoanalytic school that dominated the helping professions in this country during that period.

Theoretical Assumptions   Contrary to the psychoanalytic view, the client-centered theory assumes that human beings are rational, good, and capable of assuming responsibility for themselves and making their own choices that can lead to independence, self-actualization, and autonomy. Further, people are constructive, cooperative, trustworthy, realistic, and social. The theory does admit that negative emotions such as hate and anger exist, but they exist mainly as responses to frustrated needs for love, security, and a feeling of belonging, which are basic human needs. This is a "self" theory, based on a belief that people act in accordance with their **self-concept** and that their self-concept is heavily influenced by their experience with others. It is phenomenological in that it is concerned with the person's perception of his or her self and situation, not the helper's or the outside world's perception of the person. This theory is not concerned with causes of behavior or with changing behavior; rather it focuses on the individual's current experiences, feelings, and interactions.

The following are the major client-centered constructs:

1.   Self-concept is our perceptions of ourself based on our interactions with others.

2. The phenomenal field is the individual's reality and consists of the self-concept and the individual's perceptions of his or her world.

3. Individuals behave in whatever ways will enhance their self-concept.

4. Problems arise out of incongruencies between the self-concept and life experiences that become threatening to persons and cause them to utilize defenses such as the denial or distortion of experiences, which lead to disorganization and pain.

5. Only by receiving unconditional positive regard (acceptance) by a significant other can persons be open to their experiences and develop more congruence between self-concept and behavior.

Major Approaches to Helping The foundation of client-centered therapy is to create an empathic relationship between therapist and client that will allow the client to experience spontaneity, genuineness, and here-and-now feelings. The goals of this therapy are self-actualization and complete self-realization. This therapy requires full participation on the part of both therapist and client. Major verbal techniques employed by the helper are minimal verbal leads such as "mm-mm," "I see," and "Yes" (connoting acceptance); reflection (a verbal statement mirroring the client's statement); clarification (which explores and develops a client's statement); summarization (which synthesizes a number of client statements); and confrontation (a verbal statement that non-judgmentally encounters a client statement).

View of Helping Relationship More than in any other helping approach, the client-centered theory focuses on the relationship between helper and helpee, which is nondirective and emphasizes the communication of respect, understanding, and acceptance by the helper. The goal is an affective, warm relationship that reduces the helpee's anxiety and removes any threat to create a climate freeing the helpee for experiencing, expressing, and exploring his or her feelings. The helper is presented as an equal, a coworker of the helpee, not an expert or authority. And the client experiences the helping relationship as one that allows him or her to take responsibility for determining goals and for taking action toward these goals.

Implications for Helpers Because relationships more than techniques are emphasized in client-centered therapy, counselors' selves or being are more important than their acts or doing. Thus, the helper is with the helpee on the helpee's level, from the helpee's frame of reference; encourages the helpee to continue to develop his or her own self-awareness at the same time that the helper continues to develop his or her self-awareness and ability to elicit feelings in order to facilitate growth and responsibility in clients; and focuses more on process than content of verbal behavior.

The *Gestalt* approach to helping is based upon the perceptual learning theory developed by Kurt Koffka, Wolfgang Koehler, and Max Wertheimer, although the application of this theory to therapy approach was developed by Fritz Perls in the late 1940s. Gestalt is a German word meaning the "whole." All human behaviors and experiences are organized into gestalts, into patterns in which the whole is greater than the sum of its parts. Like client-centered therapy, this is a phenomenological approach in that it focuses on the present, the client's perspective, and the here and now and is not concerned with original causes. Its concern is with increasing understanding and emotional and physical awareness of and by the client. Thus, Gestalt therapy is experiential (doing and acting out, not just talking), existential (people can make choices and be self-responsible), and experimental (trying out new expressions of feelings).

Theoretical Assumptions　The emphasis in Gestalt theory is on the whole person (mind and body are the same, not separate) and this theory regards the self as a total organism as it responds to the environment. Human experience is organized into succeeding gestalts and everything we are and do is related to everything else we are and do. Only the how of the present is considered legitimate material for discussion, not the why and when, the past, or the future. Conflict arises from an impasse (inconsistency) between the organism and its environment, which results in avoidance of contact, denying, negating, covering up a present experience rather than accepting it, and emphasizing what is not present rather than what is present. The individual must become aware of his or her mind and body, must develop awareness, acceptance, wholeness, and responsibility in order to achieve **organismic** balance. Feelings are considered energy. A person gets into trouble by not expressing feelings and accumulating unfinished business, which results in tension and somatic difficulties, thus not providing closure to concerns.

The major constructs of this theory are the following:

1.　Maturity (wholeness) occurs when persons are able to be self-supported rather than environment-supported, when they are able to mobilize and utilize their own resources rather than manipulate others.

2.　Awareness reduces avoidance behavior.

3.　Change occurs when people assume responsibility for themselves, when they give closure to unfinished business (unfinished business occurs when people refuse to act in the present).

4. Focus of therapy is on the individual's current feelings and thoughts; on exploring all the sensations, fantasies, perceptions, and dreams; and on encouraging the individual to take the responsibility for them and to own them.

5. The individual is encouraged to trust his or her intuitive senses rather than adjust to prevailing society.

Major Approaches to Helping Gestalt therapy utilizes a workshop approach to helping with one-to-one relations being developed within a group setting, although the techniques can be applied on an individual basis. It is a process of self-discovery of feelings and senses with the goal of developing awareness, examining this awareness in detail, and reintegrating the client and his or her environment so that the client is self-responsible. Thus, the goal is to interrelate mental activity, feelings, bodily sensations, and actions. Body language and awareness of body language are as important as awareness of verbal language.

The methodology of Gestalt therapy takes the form of the therapist acting as a catalyst alternately to direct and frustrate clients so they may develop awareness of their whole (gestalt). Vehicles for expression include acting out exercises and games, with playing out of conflicts in the present through exaggeration and role reversals. The Gestalt therapist refuses to allow clients to avoid present experiences by intellectualizing (talking about), escaping into the past, or daydreaming about the future. The therapist's interventions involve asking "what" and "how" questions (never why!) to help expand the individual's sense of responsibility (owning the problem) and awareness and to make the implicit explicit by exaggeration of behavior.

Like client-centered therapy, there is no interpretation in this approach; unlike client-centered therapy, the Gestalt approach is directive in that the therapist is like the director of a play. Therapists ask clients to engage in certain role playing or acting out exercises and direct them to focus on certain details and feelings.

Use of rules and games is a major technique, designed to encourage and facilitate present, responsible living. Some of the Gestalt rules are

1. Use the phrase "here and now" to focus on the present and on people who are here.

2. Use more direct language, such as changing the word "it" to "I" or the phrase "I can't" to "I won't."

3. Allow no gossiping. The client cannot talk about people who are not present but can talk directly to the person by role playing.

4. Insist that clients own their own feelings, thoughts, and actions by using "my" and "I" and "I take responsibility for. . . ."

5. Direct the client to take action instead of imagining and thinking.

Games such as "Dialogue," "I take responsibility," and "Reversals" encourage present-oriented and responsibility-oriented verbal styles. In these games clients deal with an absent member by role playing, take both roles in a dialogue, play all the roles including inanimate objects from a dream, and so forth.

View of the Helping Relationship   The therapist is involved in a learning situation with clients and has the skill to teach them how to learn about themselves and become aware of how they function. The focus in Gestalt therapy is on both verbal and nonverbal techniques. Warmth and empathy are not emphasized as in client-centered helping relationships; but unless the client has faith in the therapist's **potency** (ability and skill to help), it is unlikely that Gestalt therapy could be effective, as the client would resist the therapist's suggestions and directions to carry out specific exercises. The Gestalt therapist is confrontative and frustrating. For example, the therapist often asks if the client can "stay with this feeling," which is frustrating for the client who wants to avoid that particular feeling. In this way, the Gestalt therapist encourages the client to analyze and reintegrate the unpleasant feeling with his or her whole self.

Implications for Helpers   There are several concepts in Gestalt theory that are important for helpers. Without extensive training in Gestalt methods we can emphasize body language (nonverbal) as well as verbal language and attempt to integrate these into a whole. We can emphasize clients' responsibility for their feelings, thoughts, and actions in the here and now; use techniques to encourage clients' self-awareness and self-reliance; and recognize the effect of "unfinished business" on current functioning.

Behavioral

Unlike the psychoanalytic and phenomenological approaches, which were developed from clinical practice, the behavioral approaches to helping were developed in psychological laboratories. The ethos of behavioral approaches arose from the inability of scientists to measure and evaluate the outcomes of psychoanalytic and phenomenological approaches to helping and from a need to predict and measure outcomes of helping based upon specific, observable, objective, and measurable variables (i.e., overt cognitive, motor, and emotional behavior). We cannot see, therefore cannot measure, feelings or thoughts; so we must only concern ourselves with behavior in order to be truly accountable as helpers.

Theoretical Assumptions   Behavior is determined by its immediate consequences in the environment. Therefore, it is learned from situational factors, not from within the organism (cf., psychoanalytical theory). All behavior is learned and, thus, can be unlearned. Difficulties occur when learned, maladaptive behavior results in anxiety; the anxiety is learned as a contingency of the learned maladaptive behavior. This view assumes that people have no control of their behavior from within, no self-determinism: all behavior is determined by environmental variables. The human being is viewed as an organism capable of being manipulated. Values, feelings, and thoughts are ignored; only concrete, observable behaviors are considered.

The major constructs of this theory are the following:

1. All behavior is caused by the environment (stimuli).

2. Behavior is shaped and maintained by its consequences (responses).

3. Behavior that is reinforced is more likely to recur than behavior that is not reinforced.

4. Positive reinforcement has more conditioning potency than negative reinforcement.

5. Reinforcement must follow immediately after the behavior has occurred.

6. Reinforcement may be either concrete or social.

7. Behavior can be extinguished by the absence of reinforcement.

8. Behaviors may be shaped by reinforcing successive approximations of the desired behavior.

Major Approaches to Helping   The behavioral helping approaches are specifically directive and controlled. The helper identifies unsuitable stimulus-response bonds (causes and effects of the target behavior(s) and arranges to interfere with or to **extinguish** these unsuitable bonds. The helper then helps to set up conditions for teaching new, more desirable stimulus-response bonds so that more appropriate behaviors will be learned. The four general approaches are (1) imitative learning (modeling), which teaches new behaviors by actual or simulated (video or audio tape) performing of desired behaviors by models; (2) cognitive learning, which teaches new behavior by role playing rehearsals, verbal instructions, or **contingency contracts** between helper and helpee that spell out clearly what the helpee is to do and what the consequence or reinforcement of this behavior will be; (3) emotional learning, such as **implosive therapy** (massive, exaggerated exposure to highly unpleasant stimuli in imaginal form to extinguish associated anxiety) or "systematic desensitization" (conterconditioning to reduce anxiety by pairing negative events with complete physical relaxation, a positive event to extinguish the negative quality) or "covert sensitization" (the pairing of anxiety-producing stimuli with those that have pleasant associations); and (4) **operant conditioning,** whereby selected behaviors are immediately reinforced and where systematic schedules of reinforcement have been consciously determined in advance.

View of Helping Relationship   The direct helping relationship is not considered important in this approach. In fact, the helper often serves as a consultant and does not have direct contact with the helpee, except perhaps for initial observation. There are even cassette tapes available for some of the more specific techniques.

The human relationship is not considered a variable in changing behavior unless, for some reason, the helper has tremendous reinforcement value to the helpee. The helper is more of a behavioral engineer: objective, detached, and professional. Where there is verbal contact, the helper is highly trained to use systematically concrete, verbal reinforcement. The helper is also highly trained in observational and evaluation skills. Because of the focus on observable, overt behavior, the behavioral helper is able to determine what interventions have been effective and when to terminate by noting the presence or absence of specific target behaviors.

Implications for Helpers   Because the behavioral approaches are specific and relatively open to measurement evaluation, they have helped to move counseling and helping from the "art" end of the continuum toward the "science" end. Focusing on behavioral outcomes appears to mitigate dependency relationships and results in short-term treatment. As helpers we can focus on observable behavior (rather than talk about feelings and thoughts, which are difficult to measure); utilize techniques that enable us to evaluate the results of our interventions; specify goals, strategies, and outcomes of helping and thus be more accountable and avoid running the risk of imposing our subjective values and attitudes upon the helpees; focus on what the helpee is doing and can do as opposed to what the helpee cannot or should not do, thereby emphasizing the positive rather than the negative aspects of individual behaviors; and deal only with observable behaviors and avoid risking questionable interpretations of subjective data.

Cognitive-Behavioral

Cognitive-behavioral approaches to helping deal with rationality, with the thinking processes, and with problem solving. They are instructive, directive, and verbally oriented (as opposed to an approach like Gestalt, which utilizes body movement). Many of the vocational counseling approaches fall into this domain, with an emphasis upon testing, synthesis of a variety of collected data, and rational decision making. The major philosophical assumption of these theories is that by changing people's thinking, one can change their belief system, which, in turn, changes their behavior. The two major approaches in this area are Rational-Emotive-Therapy (RET) and Reality therapy (RT).

Rational-Emotive-Therapy was developed by Albert Ellis in the middle 1950s and is based upon his belief that people need to change their way of thinking (cognitive restructuring) to correct faulty (irrational) thinking.

Theoretical Assumptions   Ellis believes that people must take full responsibility for themselves and their own fates. Although there are biological and environmental influences, people intervene between those inputs and their emotional outputs and are, therefore, largely controlling what they feel and do. People are born rational in an irrational world, but they teach themselves to become more and more irrational as they incorporate the world's irrational ideas into their own belief systems.

Ellis postulates an A-B-C theory: A = the activating experience that the client wrongly believes causes C = consequences; B = the client's belief systems, which is the intervening variable really causing C. It is B, the client's belief system, that needs to be restructured. There are twelve irrational ideas (see chapter 6) one keeps repeating to oneself that cause faulty thinking. The following example demonstrates faulty thinking.

> Because it would be highly preferable if I were outstandingly competent, I absolutely should and must be. It is awful when I am not and I am therefore a worthless individual. Because it is highly desirable that others treat me considerately and fairly, they absolutely should and must and they are rotten people who deserve to be utterly damned when they do not. And, because it is preferable that I experience pleasure rather than pain, the world absolutely should arrange this and life is horrible and I can't bear it when the world doesn't.

Ellis claims that these are the kinds of things we tell ourselves that make us upset. We can learn to tell ourselves different messages.

The major constructs of this theory are:

1. Problems are caused by irrational beliefs that have dysfunctional consequences.

2. People are capable of changing their belief systems by learning how to refute these irrational beliefs.

Major Approaches to Helping This is a teaching approach to helping. By direct instruction, giving information, teaching imaging techniques, and assigning behavioral homework, the therapist helps change the helpee's irrational belief system. Thus, the technique is both cognitive (teaching) and behavioral (role playing, homework assignments). RET techniques are designed to change behavior, to change thinking which, in turn, will help the client to feel better. Clients are taught to understand themselves, to understand others, to react differently, and to change their basic personality patterns and their basic philosophic assumptions by correcting their faulty thinking.

View of Helping Relationship The helping relationship is cognitive and directive in that helpers exhort, frustrate, and command that the helpees parse out their thoughts and learn to restructure rationally their belief systems. The helping relationship depends on the potency of helpers and on their ability to communicate their power to helpees, not on warm, empathic, reciprocal relationships.

Implications for Helpers This approach has many implications for dealing with the cognitive domain and helping to integrate this domain with the behavioral and affective domains. Helpers should try to recognize the overlapping and interrelation of reason and emotion; recognize client responsibility for declaring and reassessing their own belief systems; and utilize a methodology that quickly exposes the relationship of feelings, thoughts, and behavior.

Reality therapy, like Rational-Emotive-Therapy, is rational, logical, and learning oriented. Reality therapy explores the values and behavioral choices of the client, exposing inconsistencies and enforcing one's responsibility for one's choices.

Theoretical Assumptions According to the theory of Reality therapy, people have two basic psychological needs: the need to love and be loved and the need to feel worthwhile to themselves and to others. The theory is interpersonal in that one needs to be involved with other people in order to meet these two needs. The goal of Reality therapy is to assist people to become more responsible by making responsible choices (involving consistency between value system and behavior) and to meet these two basic psychological needs without depriving other people of their ability to fulfill their needs. People are seen as capable of assuming responsibility for themselves and capable of rational thought and behavior. They have no excuse for not exercising these attributes.

Major Approaches to Helping　Reality therapy involves a candid, human relationship during which helpers teach helpees to accept responsibility for themselves by analyzing inconsistencies among their goals, values, and behaviors. Reality therapy is a direct approach, dealing with the present. It is based upon five principles: (1) helpers encourage clients to make value judgments about their own behaviors, (2) helpers encourage helpees to make plans aimed at some desired goals, (3) helpers ask helpees to commit themselves to these plans, (4) helpers ask helpees to make no excuses if they fail to keep these commitments or contracts and helpers refuse to listen to or accept excuses for these failures, and (5) helpers will never reject or punish helpees.

The Reality therapist encourages, suggests alternatives, praises positive behavior, confronts inconsistencies openly and directly, and cares enough about the helpees to reject behaviors that prohibit them from meeting their basic psychological needs. Helpers are concerned about present behavior, what helpees are currently doing, and what the consequences of alternative choices might be. They refuse to engage in self-defeating conversations about negative experiences and symptoms.

View of Helping Relationship　The relationship between the Reality therapist and the client is crucial; it must be a warm, honest, personal involvement. Through this relationship, the client learns to feel loved by the therapist, learns to love the therapist, and learns to feel worthwhile because the therapist focuses on what the client is doing, on the client's approach behaviors rather than on avoidance behaviors. (This process is similar to the psychoanalytic concept of transference, although it is not acknowledged as such.) This relationship differs from the client-centered relationship in one major aspect: the helping relationship in Reality therapy is indeed judgmental in that the Reality therapist judges the value of the client's behavior in terms of the therapist's perceptions of reality. For example, if the client persists in self-defeating behavior, the therapist may say "that behavior is really crazy because it will keep you from getting what you say you really want."

Implications for Helpers　The major implication for helpers is that the honest, intense involvement of the helper and the helpee are required for success. Helpers must examine the inconsistencies between the ways people act and their values and needs, focus on action (what the clients are doing) rather than on what they are thinking or feeling, and insist upon clients assuming responsibility for their choices and the consequences of these choices.

Transactional-Communicative

Transactional Analysis (TA), developed by Eric Berne, is an approach that falls midway between the phenomenological and the cognitive approaches. It focuses upon reality, is logical and learning oriented as are the cognitive-behavioral approaches, and utilizes many of the same techniques as Gestalt therapy, emphasizing the client's perspective. However, its goal is more cognitive than that of Gestalt therapy in that it strives for intellectual awareness as well as emotional awareness.

Theoretical Assumptions   This system divides the personality into the parent, the adult, and the child. These are different from the psychoanalytic ego states (superego, ego, id) in that the TA **ego states** are observable, conscious, and segregated from each other. The parent ego state consists of "tapes" developed from original interactions with parents and societal models, of all the rules and caring the person has ever experienced. The adult ego state is in touch with the outside world, with logic, is computing and information giving, and is responsible for solving problems and incorporating facts and data from without. The child ego state is in touch with all the feelings, with what's going on within the person.

The healthy individual is able to function appropriately in each of these ego states and is conscious of which ego state he or she is functioning in. One is aware of one's interpersonal relationship patterns and how one structures time (by withdrawal, rituals, procedures, pastimes, games, or intimacy) and one is encouraged to learn how to achieve genuine intimacy by recognizing one's manipulative styles and becoming aware of one's **scripts** (early childhood decisions that determine roles one will play in later life) and **sweatshirts** (messages that people advertise, usually without awareness, such as "kick me"). People are seen as capable of assuming self-responsibility and of being able to overcome negative parental or cultural influences. People need strokes (responses from other people) in order to grow and live and they are taught how to assume responsibility for both obtaining and giving these necessary strokes.

The transactional analysts believe that there are four major lifestyle positions:

1.   "I'm not O.K., you're O.K.", the position into which we are

all born and which results in the need to learn that we are O.K. This is a position of the child.

2. "I'm O.K., you're not O.K.", the position children see their parents or adults with a strong need to control occupying. This is the parent position.

3. "I'm not O.K., you're not O.K.", the position whereby a person has no confidence in himself or anyone around him. This is a position of the child.

4. "I'm O.K., you're O.K.", when the individual is able to feel confident about herself or himself and others and to feel capable without needing to control and manipulate others. This is the adult position.

TA is oriented to the present, although it acknowledges the past and helps plan for the future.

Major Approaches to Helping   The goals of TA are to match intentions with behavior and to integrate feelings, thoughts, and behavior by (1) examining and up-dating the parent, (2) freeing the child from its not O.K. position, (3) teaching the adult to function without being contaminated by the parent or child, and (4) developing intellectual and emotional awareness, thereby improving transactions. The client is taught the principles of TA instructionally, via diagrams, lectures, demonstrations, and readings. One learns to recognize one's and other people's games, **rackets,** parallel and crossed interactions, use of strokes (reinforcements), scripts, and counterscripts.

Thus, TA examines relationships by analyzing communications. Both content and process are emphasized and Gestalt techniques (e.g., role playing and dialogues) are the major methodology in addition to the verbal analysis of transactions and relationships. TA is a contract therapy in that each transaction between the therapist and client aims toward establishing a contract (whereby the client agrees to perform a specific behavior that will benefit all three of the client's ego states and will resolve a conflict or unfinished business) and obtaining commitment to that contract.

View of Helping Relationship   The helping relationship is directive in that the transactional analyst is a leader who gives clues and hunches and shares fantasies with the client in order to activate the client's adult. There is no advice giving, no diagnosis, no "why" questioning. The helper can help the client by emanating **protection** (it's safe for you with me), **permission** (you can be you with me; you can feel and behave as you want), and **potency** (I am capable, have the power of curing you). Like Gestalt therapy, TA is typically a group approach to helping.

Implications for Helpers TA provides a comprehensive, teachable model that is appropriate for all age groups and that provides a nontechnical vocabulary and concepts for understanding interpersonal relationships. In addition, helpers focus on communications styles and messages and on effective ways to teach better communications behaviors; integrate aspects of behavioral, reality, and Gestalt therapies; provide short-term, flexible helping that deals equally with the affective, cognitive, and behavioral domains.

Eclectic

Most helpers utilize assumptions, concepts, and techniques from a variety of different viewpoints and, therefore, have an eclectic approach to helping. This approach requires some flexibility and versatility on the part of the helper as it is not a pure approach based on a single theoretical construct. A helper who uses an eclectic approach must always strive to be consistent and comprehensive in integrating the different approaches. An eclectic approach requires heightened self-awareness so that helpers understand why certain viewpoints and approaches appeal to them and why some do not.

The eclectic approach presupposes that helpers are continuously open to and searching for more effective techniques and this implies that helpers are actively involved in continuous professional training. It is no longer considered a "cop out" to declare yourself eclectic in human relations. Still, in some circles, it is probably more prestigious to claim allegiance to a specific school of thought.

Arnold Lazarus is perhaps the most articulate spokesman for an eclectic view. He describes a flexible, personalistic approach to helping where the helper is able to use many techniques to fit the treatment to the needs and individual characteristics of each client. If we want to provide effective human services for a broad population, we must be able to respond to the variety of needs they present. Adherence to a single theoretical view could meet the helper's needs more than the helpee's.

SUMMARY OF MAJOR THEORIES

The major theories briefly reviewed in this chapter are compared in table 5-1, which tabulates the similarities and differences of these approaches as well as the domains they fall into.

Table 5-1 *Comparison of Major Theories*

	Psychoanalytical	Phenomenological Client-Centered	Gestalt	Behavioral	Cognitive-Behavioral	Transactional-Communicative
Major Assumptions	1. Man has no free will 2. Behavior determined by biological and environmental factors 3. Neurosis stems from repressed infantile conflicts	1. Man has free will 2. Locus of behavioral determinism internal 3. Neurosis stems from incongruence between self-concept and environment	1. Man has free will 2. Organism works as whole within environment 3. Neurosis stems from impasse between organism and environment	1. Man has no free will 2. Behavior caused by environment and shaped by consequences 3. Neurosis results from maladaptive learning	1. Man has free will 2. Behavior determined by logical thinking and responsibility 3. Neurosis stems from irrational thinking and irresponsible choices	1. Man has free will 2. Man can choose his own behavior 3. Neurosis stems from ego state contamination and exclusion
Therapy Process	1. Directive 2. Diagnosis and past experience important 3. Verbal 4. Transference in relationship important	1. Non-directive 2. Here-and-now experience important 3. Verbal 4. Empathic relationship important	1. Directive 2. Here-and-now verbal and body awareness important 3. Verbal and nonverbal 4. Honest, trusting and, supportive confrontative relationship	1. Directive 2. Present behavior and reinforcement history important 3. Verbal and activities 4. Analytical, conditioning relationship	1. Directive 2. Present behavior, thinking, and values important 3. Verbal and activities 4. Instructional, involved relationship	1. Nondirective 2. Early script, present games, and transactions important 3. Verbal and nonverbal 4. Potent, protective, and permissive relationship
Requisite Therapist Behaviors	1. Therapist neutral, benign, objective 2. Interprets resistances and unconscious material 3. No contracts	1. Therapist honest, congruent, empathic, nonjudgmental, capable of unconditional positive regard 2. Ability to communicate above 3. No contracts	1. Therapist honest, open, confrontative but basically supportive 2. Provides experience via verbal and nonverbal games 3. No contracts	1. Therapist analytical, objective, observational, evaluative 2. Analyzes goals, directs strategies, evaluates, provides positive reinforcement, arranges environmental contingencies 3. Explicit contracts	1. Therapist involved and judgmental and confronts illogical thinking and irresponsibility 2. Rejects illogical thinking and irresponsible behavior 3. Explicit contracts	1. Therapist analyzes games, scripts, and transactions, and ego states 2. Provides experience via verbal and nonverbal games 3. Explicit contracts
Domain	Affective/Cognitive	Affective	Affective	Behavioral	Cognitive/Behavioral	Affective/Cognitive/Behavioral

1.   The psychoanalytical approach emphasizes unconscious causes of behavior and early childhood experiences; it focuses more on content than process.

2.   The phenomenological approach emphasizes process more than content and stresses the helping relationship as a vehicle for change. This helping relationship provides a climate in which clients can explore their own feelings, thoughts, and behaviors to achieve both insight and behavioral change. They also focus on the present, as opposed to the past.

3.   The behavioral approaches emphasize environmental consequences of behavior as determining behavior, the learning of new behaviors, and the extinctions of maladaptive behaviors. The emphasis is upon identifying dysfunctional behaviors, planning new behaviors, and systematically arranging valued reinforcements for new desired behaviors.

4.   The cognitive-behavioral approaches are concerned with teaching new ways of thinking and exploring and examining discrepancies between values and behaviors. They also function in the present, rather than in the past.

5.   Transactional-communicative approaches focus upon relationships (via analyses of communications) and lifestyles of clients and aims toward the integration of feelings, thoughts, and actions.

Perhaps the reason that we have so many different approaches to helping is that we continue to have great diversity among people and their problems. No single theory answers all questions or satisfies all conditions. As helpers find themselves utilizing approaches and viewpoints that are consistent with their personal theories and their personalities, there are bound to be offshoots of major approaches and a continuous search for refining existing approaches and creating new approaches.

An example of a nontraditional offshoot of major approaches is the social systems approach based on sociological, anthropological, and organizational psychological theories. This approach deals with the identification of systemwide problems rather than individual problems. Thus, the client is a system, such as a hospital, school, or correctional institution rather than an individual within a system. Strategies derived from this approach include advocacy and change-agentry. Human relations skills are essential in applying these strategies because effective relationships between helpers and individuals within the system are crucial.

I hope that this overview of major helping theories will both heighten your interest in these theories and help you understand your own theoretical framework. A reading list at the end of the chapter will help you get started in further exploration of these views and approaches.

SUMMARY

In this chapter, we've reviewed the need for developing your awareness of your personal theory of helping. We then briefly summarized the major theories—psychoanalytical, phenomenological, behavioral, cognitive-behavioral, transactional-communicative, and eclectic—that can help you place your own personal theory in perspective. The summary of major theories highlighted their similarities and differences. These theories provide the framework for understanding the strategies presented in the following chapter.

REFERENCES AND FURTHER READINGS

General Theory

Brammer, L., and Shostrom, E. *Therapeutic Psychology: [An Approach to Actualization Counseling and Therapy.]* Englewood Cliffs, N.J.: Prentice-Hall, 1968.
Shoben, E. "The Counselor's Theory as a Personnel Trait." *Personnel and Guidance Journal* 40 (1962): 617 - 622.

Psychoanalytic

Alexander, F. *Fundamentals of Psychoanalysis.* New York: Norton, 1963.
Freud, A. *The Ego and the Mechanisms of Defense.* New York: International Universities Press, 1946.
Freud, S. *An Outline of Psychoanalysis.* New York: Norton, 1949.

Phenomenological

Client-Centered:
Carkhuff, R., and Berenson, B. *Beyond Counseling and Therapy.* New York: Holt, Rinehart, and Winston, 1967.
Combs, A.; Avila, D.; and Purkey, W. *Helping Relationships: [Basic Concepts for the Helping Process.]* Boston: Allyn and Bacon, 1971.
Rogers, C. *Client-centered Therapy.* Boston: Houghton Mifflin, 1951.
———. *On Becoming a Person.* Boston: Houghton Mifflin, 1961.
Rogers, C., and Dymond, R. *Psychotherapy and Personality Change.* Chicago: University of Chicago Press, 1954.

Gestalt:

Fagan, J., and Shepherd I., eds. *Gestalt Therapy Now*. Palo Alto, Ca.: Science and Behavior Books, 1970.

Koffka, K. *Principles of Gestalt Psychology*. New York: Harcourt, Brace, 1935.

Perls, F. *Gestalt Therapy Verbatim*. Lafayette, Ca.: Real People Press, 1969.

Perls, F.; Hefferline, R.; and Goodman, P. *Gestalt Therapy*. New York: Dell, 1951.

Behavioral

Bandura, A. *Principles of Behavior Modification*. New York: Holt, Rinehart, and Winston, 1969.

Krasner, L., and Ullman, L., eds. *Research in Behavior Modification*. New York: Holt, Rinehart, and Winston, 1965.

Krumboltz, J., ed. *Revolution in Counseling: [Implication of Behavioral Sciences.]* Boston: Houghton Mifflin, 1966.

Wolpe, J. *Psychotherapy by Reciprocal Inhibition*. Palo Alto, Ca.: Stanford University Press, 1958.

Wolpe, J.; Salter, A.; and Reyna, L. *The Conditioning Therapies: [The Challenge of Psychotherapy.]* New York: Holt, Rinehart, and Winston, 1964.

Cognitive-Behavioral

Ellis, A. "The No Cop-Out Therapy." *Psychology Today* 7 (1973): 56 - 62.

Ellis, A. *Reason and Emotion in Psychotherapy*. New York: Lyle Stuart, 1962.

Ellis, A., and Harper, R. *A Guide to Rational Living*. Englewood Cliffs, N.J.: Prentice-Hall, 1961.

Glasser, W. *Reality Therapy*. New York: Harper and Row, 1965.

Williamson, E. *Vocational Counseling: [Some Historical, Philosophical and Theoretical Perspectives.]* New York: McGraw-Hill, 1965.

Transactional-Communicative

Berne, E. *Games People Play*. New York: Grove Press, 1964.

———. *Transactional Analysis in Psychotherapy*. New York: Grove Press, 1961.

———. *What do you Say After You Say Hello?* New York: Bantam Books, 1972.

Harris, T. *I'm O.K., You're O.K.* New York: Harper and Row, 1967.

Eclectic

Lazarus, A. *Behavior Therapy and Beyond*. New York: McGraw-Hill, 1971.

CHAPTER 6

INTRODUCTION
TO
STRATEGIES

During the transition between stage 1 (relationship) and stage 2 (strategies), the goals and objectives of the helping relationship are initially explored, then focused on specific helping requirements, and finally agreed to by the parties involved. Before this subprocess can be successfully concluded, it is essential to define meaningfully the problem(s) to be solved and the nature of the help to be generated.

When the problem itself is known, it is then possible to choose an appropriate strategy or combination of strategies to be utilized and the approaches for accomplishing these strategies. Variables of time, timing, setting, and the nature of the presenting problem will affect both how this transitionary period is handled and the resulting strategies.

CLASSES OF STRATEGIES

Categories of helping problems can be described primarily as being part of "affective," "cognitive," or "behavioral" spheres or domains. The relationships of these spheres with various strategies, techniques, and formal theories are illustrated in figure 6-1.

Affective problems are those dealing with self-awareness and awareness of others' feelings (e.g., feelings of inadequacy, inferiority, or not being in touch with what and how you and others are feeling). For these kinds of problems, more experiential strategies

DOMAIN

	AFFECTIVE	COGNITIVE	BEHAVIORAL
PROBLEM AREA:	Awareness (Feeling)	Understanding (Thinking)	Acting (Doing)
CLASS OF HELPING STRATEGY:	Phenomenological (Perceptual)	Rational	Behavioral
REPRESENTATIVE TECHNIQUES:	Gestalt Experiments Responsive Listening Imagery Sensory Awareness	Free Association Dream Analysis Interpretation Decision Making	Assertiveness Training Reinforcement Contracts Modeling Systematic Desensitization Cognitive Restructuring Reality Therapy Contracting
	Psychoanalytic ◄-----------►	Transactional Analysis -----------►	
	Transactional-Communicative -----►		
THEORETICAL FRAMEWORK:	Client-Centered Gestalt	Psychoanalytic	Behavioral Reality Therapy Rational-Emotive Therapy
	◄----- Transactional Analysis -----►		

Figure 6-1 *Relationships of Problems, Strategies, and Techniques in the Different Problem Areas*

focusing on imagery, sensory awareness, and verbal and nonverbal expressions of feeling are effective.

Cognitive problems involve thinking (e.g., decision making and problem solving). People who always seem to end up with the wrong decision or who are afraid to make decisions or who refuse to accept responsibility for their actions can use help in this area. The didactic (instructional) strategies, which focus on step-by-step verbal processing of decision making, analyzing, and problem solving, are effective here.

Behavioral problems concern actions (e.g., stopping smoking or some other habit, learning to be more assertive, or changing self-defeating behavior into behavior that elicits more rewards). Behavioral strategies involve verbal and action-oriented instruction that arrange environmental rewards and elicit behavior change.

These classes of problems and strategies are not always discrete. They may overlap, coincide, or exist alone. The nature of the problem(s), the nature of the helping relations and situation, and the competence and skill of the helper affect the choice of strategies.

In speaking of strategies in this helping relationship context, we are talking about overall approaches to achieving general or long-term goals. The strategies incorporate approaches that are applications of theories or models (described in chapter 5) that apply in certain situations or for certain classes of problems. The techniques are specific applications of the approaches envisioned as the foundation of the respective strategical problem-solving theories and models. Certain strategies and corresponding approaches do lend themselves more readily to different kinds of situations. Although certain techniques are specific for particular strategies, other techniques lend themselves to broader application.

There are times when the nature of the problem requiring help falls clearly into the cognitive, affective, or behavioral domain and the range of strategies to be selected is apparent. For example, if the presenting problem is chronic tardiness, a behavioral problem, the strategy may be behavioral and the techniques may be contracting with or without some cognitive restructuring. Often, however, the presenting problem is in a different domain than the underlying problem.

For example, a client was once referred to me by another counselor for the specific behavioral counseling technique called "systematic desensitization." This client was unable to swallow solid foods; medical examinations were unable to find any organic cause for this condition. After several sessions of establishing a relationship and attempting to meet the client's expectations for systematic desensitization (which will be described later in this chapter), it became apparent that her suffering was rooted more in the affective domain than in the behavioral domain. She was unable to express any anger toward anyone and she had accumulated a great deal of anger, due to a recent broken engagement. She was losing weight rapidly and was endangering her own health—she was eating only liquified foods.

It required many sessions of phenomenological client-centered and Gestalt strategies before this client was able to acknowledge her own feelings and begin to express them appropriately. Eventually, she began to be able to swallow solid foods and to improve her interpersonal relationships. This is an example of the underlying problem (expression of anger) requiring a strategy quite different from the presenting problem (inability to swallow).

STRATEGIES

The following sections will provide you with a brief overview of strategies and techniques in each of the three primary domains, affective, cognitive, and behavioral. Please note that some of these strategies are appropriate for more advanced audiences than beginning professionals and paraprofessionals. This introduction to the strategies will give you some ideas of where your interests and inclinations lie and perhaps will give you some directions for further study. Each section includes examples and exercises, and a reading list is at the end of the chapter. As you work through some of these exercises, see which ones are more comfortable for you and seem to make more sense for you.

Affective Strategies

Rationale   The theoretical rationales for affective strategies come from Carl Rogers's client-centered therapy and the Gestalt theory underlying Gestalt therapy. The prime focus is upon self-awareness and experiencing feelings (see chapter 5).

Techniques   Rogerian client-centered therapy has contributed the basis for responsive listening communication skills (chapters 4 and 5). The helper, by communicating empathy, honesty, genuineness, and acceptance of the helpee is able to create a non-threatening climate in which helpers can explore their own feelings, thoughts, and behavior and gain some understanding of themselves and their world. In order for this technique to be effective, the helpee must be able to perceive these feelings and attitudes of the helper. The technique of responsive listening may suffice as the sole approach in a helping relationship. We have concentrated on these techniques in chapters 2, 3, and 4.

Gestalt strategies specifically focus on awareness. Many helpers with theoretical orientations other than Gestalt nevertheless utilize Gestalt strategies to help clients achieve this awareness. The purpose of Gestalt strategies is to reintegrate attention and awareness so that helpees can take responsibility for the "what" and "how" of their present behaviors.

The verbal techniques of Gestalt strategies are aimed at keeping the helpee in constant contact with what is going on at the very minute. These rules are followed:

1.   Communication between helper and helpee remains in the "now" through the use of the present tense and emphasis is on what is happening now. Questions such as "What are you feeling now?" and "Are you aware that . . . ?" are used.

2.   The words "I" and "thou" are used to personalize and direct communication toward, not at, the listener.

3.   The word "I" is used so that the helpee assumes more responsibility for his or her own behavior by substituting "I" for "it" (i.e., instead of "The noise in the dormitory kept me from doing my homework" substitute "I did not do my homework").

4.   Pursuing the "what" and "how" instead of the "why" (e.g., "What are you aware of now?" and "What are you experiencing now?" instead of "Why do you feel . . . ?") helps lead the client away from endless explanations, speculations, and intepretations.

5.   No gossiping. This promotes feelings and encourages the helpee to deal directly with people. If the people he or she is discussing are not present, the client is encouraged to talk directly with them using the **empty seat** or some other device.

6.   Changing questions into statements helps prevent manipulative games and encourages the helpee to take responsibility for and deal directly with issues.

These rules are based on the following guidelines (Levitsky and Perls, 1970):

1.   Live now; be concerned with the present rather than with the past or future.

We spend too much time daydreaming about the past or present and this distracts and detracts our energies and awareness from right now.

2.   Live here and deal with what is present rather than what is absent.

Another avoidance strategy we use is to focus on what is missing rather than on what we have, on who is missing rather than who is here.

3. Stop imagining and experience the real.

Imagining takes us away from what is and blocks our experiencing and awareness. We sometimes lose sight of what is real for us.

4. Stop unnecessary thinking and taste, see, and feel.

When was the last time, for example, that you ate an orange without thinking about the concept of orange but just sensing every feeling, taste, and smell? We have allowed thinking to block out our senses and we need to take the time to get back in touch with our senses.

5. Express rather than manipulate, explain, justify, or judge.

Learn to express directly, to ask for what you want, to accept yourself and others for what they are, not for their verbal competencies.

6. Expand your awareness by giving in to unpleasantness and pain as well as pleasure.

True awareness includes negative experiences as well as pleasurable ones and if we use our energies to block out the negative, we will also lose some of the sensing of the positive.

7. Accept no "should" or "ought" other than your own and follow no idol.

The words "should" and "ought" have caused more difficulties than just about any other words in the English language. We must assume responsibility for our rules and mores and our own behaviors.

8. Take full responsibility for your actions, feelings, and thoughts.

This is the essence of maturity in Gestalt thought. We must stop blaming others and situations and take full advantage of our autonomy and the choices that do exist within any situation.

9. Surrender to being you as you are.

Accept yourself for who you are and what you are and not what you or others think you should be.

The following excerpt is an example of the application of a Gestalt strategy.

> *Helpee:* I'm upset with my fiance because he decided where we would live next year without talking it over with me. We're going to Des Moines, and that's over a thousand miles away!

Helper:	You feel angry because he is making important decisions without consulting you.
Helpee:	Well, yes. I don't want to go so far away. My mother lives all alone here and we're very close. If I go so far away, I won't be able to see her and she needs me.
Helper:	Are you aware that your right hand is tightly clenched?
Helpee:	Oh . . . yes, I guess I'm more upset than I realized.
Helper:	Let's try something to see if we can find out what this is all about. How about letting your right hand be the Pam who doesn't want to go away from your mother and your left hand be the Pam who wants to go with your fiance. See if you can have your two hands talk to each other.
Helpee:	Well, I'll try. (shaking right fist) Listen, you, you know you're afraid to leave your mother . . . she won't be able to manage without you and you don't know really if you can get along without her.
Helper:	Now be the other Pam.
Helpee:	Come on, now. I'm a big girl and I certainly can make it on my own. Besides, I love Ron and I want to marry him and that means I go where he goes.
Helper:	See if you can talk directly to your other hand. Tell her what you feel.
Helpee:	(still the Pam who wants to go) I'm annoyed at you for always getting in my way. You're a scaredy cat and you always foul things up by getting angry when you don't want to do something. (now the right-hand Pam who doesn't want to go) I don't want to go. I've never been that far away before.
Helper:	What are you feeling now, Pam?
Helpee:	I'm feeling scared, but also a little bit excited about the possibilities of a new life.

This short dialoguing experiment helped Pam become aware of her true feelings and the real issues she is struggling with. Although there is reason for Pam to deal with and work through her feelings about her fiance, it became clear that the underlying problems dealt with Pam's dependence-independence from her mother.

The technique demonstrated above is called the dialogue game. It can take place between two aspects of the helpee or between the helpee and another person with whom he or she is experiencing some kind of continued conflict. Other techniques involve the use of imagery and sensory awareness, focusing on the relationship between verbal and nonverbal behavior ("You say you are angry; yet you are smiling."), acting out fantasies (playing all the live roles and environmental parts in the fantasy), repeating and exaggerating your verbal or nonverbal behaviors ("Can you stay with that feeling? Exaggerate your leg swing and repeat what you just said in a louder voice . . . louder . . . louder."), playing out projected roles by doing to others what one does to oneself, and completing unfinished business through active role playing.

Important Gestalt questions include "What are you experiencing now?", "Where are you now?", "What do you want to do?", and "What are you doing now?" Helpees are encouraged to use "I" messages by completing such statements as "I am aware that . . .", "Now I feel that . . .", and "I notice that . . ." The goals of the affective strategies are to develop feelings and self-awareness, utilizing techniques of responsive listening and Gestalt experiments. The focus is on the present and the here and now.

Problems Strategies utilizing responsive listening and focusing upon the development of a genuine, empathic relationship are appropriate for individuals who are unable to express their feelings and are unable to have close, meaningful personal relationships with family or friends. The technique of responsive listening may suffice as the sole approach in a helping relationship with the goal being the development of self-concept in the helpee. If a helpee who has difficulties with interpersonal relationships is able to develop an honest, close, meaningful relationship with the helper, the experience in itself is irreversible in that once having attained this type of relationship with someone, the chances are higher that one will be able to transfer this new type of relating to others. If a close relationship has never been experienced, the chances for this transfer would not exist. This approach is also appropriate for informal and short-term relationships, where the mere happening of someone listening to and understanding one's concerns is helpful in and of itself.

Gestalt techniques are particularly effective for people who lack awareness of the "how" and "what" of their present behavior, people who refuse to take responsibility for themselves and their lives, people who interact rigidly and in a ritualized manner with their environment, people who dwell on past unfinished business or on future rehearsing, and people who seem split in two because they deny or exclude part of themselves. Gestalt techniques are also particularly effective with children, who are more in touch with their fantasies and imagination than older people. These techniques are not generally effective with the people who do not want to develop awareness of their feelings, for people who need information in order to make immediate decisions cognitively, for people who have experienced sudden crisis, and for those who are unable to imagine and fantasize sufficiently to participate in the games and experiments.

Exercises　In order to use Gestalt techniques effectively it is important for you to have actually participated in Gestalt games and experiments in order to develop some confidence in your own capacities for self-awareness and the taking of responsibility. (We will not review the responsive listening techniques because we have done so in chapter 4.)

Try some of the following exercises to see how you feel about Gestalt techniques. You may wonder whether or not people you are helping would think you were crazy for using these techniques, but you will find that if you have an effective, trusting, helping relationship, helpees are usually willing to engage in different, novel kinds of techniques. Actually, some of the communications skills exercises in chapter 4 are Gestalt exercises, so you already have tried some.

Exercise 6-1.　An effective beginning Gestalt exercise involves a group sitting in a circle and each person beginning a three-minute monologue with "Now I am aware that. . . ." Try to get in touch with as much of yourself in the here and now as you can. Personalize pronouns and begin each sentence with "I" in order to focus on your self-awareness. For example, "Now I am aware that I am sitting in a hard chair with a pillow at my back, my legs are crossed and I am typing this manuscript. My fingers are deftly moving over the keyboard, my eyes are on the draft, my shoulders are sort of slumped . . . and so forth." (This exercise may also be performed in dyads.)

Exercise 6-2.　Fantasy is very much a Gestalt technique. Each person in a small group is asked to think of a place where he or she feels especially comfortable, to visualize all the details of those surroundings, to get in touch with the sights, smells, and noises as well as the thoughts and feelings associated with this special place. Then, each person takes turns relating his or her scene in the present tense, personalizing pronouns. Other people in the group may ask "what" and "how" questions and may also ask the person sharing the fantasy to act out different aspects of it, playing out the animate and inanimate roles. For example, if I describe a scene at the beach, I may be asked to be the water, to be the sand, to be the sun.

Exercise 6-3.　Shuttling is an extension of exercise 6-2. Spend some time in your special place and then shuttle to the here and now and get in touch with the details of where you are right now, the sights, smells, noises, and other people. Then return to your special place. Shuttle back and forth between your real and fantasy sites with several minutes spent in each place. How hard is this shuttling? What do you feel? Where do you want to be? What have you become aware of?

Exercise 6-4. Dialoguing is a useful Gestalt technique. Imagine that one of your parents is sitting facing you. Describe this scene as precisely as you can, relating the emerging feelings as you face this parent. Then begin to talk aloud to this parent, using the first and second persons ("I" and "you"). Say whatever comes to your mind. Stay with the feelings that are emerging and switch seats when you choose and be your parent talking back to you. Go back and forth between your seat and your parent's seat until you feel as if you are ready to stop. If possible, share your feelings with your group and see if you have learned something about your feelings and relationship with this parent. If you are having a difficult time getting started, begin in your parent role introducing you. Tell who you are and how you feel about your offspring, you.

Cognitive Strategies

Rationale   Here the emphasis is on rationality, on our thinking processes and our understanding of ourselves and our world. The theoretical foundations are information and decision-making systems.

Techniques   Decision-making techniques fall into this realm because decisions are cognitive processes. It is important to help people learn decision-making skills so that they will have more freedom and control over their entire life. We make decisions from the moment we get up in the morning to the moment we retire.

Although there are different models for decision making, the basic process recommended for helping relationships consists of the following steps:

1.   State the problem clearly.

Be sure that you have identified the problem that is causing difficulty. In order for problem solving to be effective, the correct problem must be accurately identified.

2.   Identify and accept ownership of the problem.

Unless the decision maker believes that he or she has a problem and has some power to effect a decision, the decision-making process is futile. People do not invest legitimate energy into decision making unless they have a stake in the outcome.

3.   Propose every possible alternative to the problem **(brainstorming).**

Often we are limited when considering options. Brainstorming enables every possible option to be considered, without evaluation. It gives us more to choose from.

4. Evaluate each proposed alternative in terms of implementation realities and hypothesized consequences (values clarification).

Here we have the opportunity to evaluate each of the alternatives proposed in step 3. Some we will automatically discard because they are either impractical or because they violate our value system. Before discarding any item, however, we try to hypothesize its consequences.

5. Reassess the final list of alternatives, their consequences, and the risks involved.

We review our final list and for each alternative we review the steps involved and the likely consequences. We may further eliminate some alternatives in this step.

6. Decide to implement one or more alternative.

Based on our previous assessments, we choose one or more alternative. We may even list some back-up alternatives.

7. Determine how and when to implement the plan.

Here we spell out exactly what is needed to implement this decision, who needs to do what, when, where, what materials are required, and so forth. Decisions are often not carried through because of failure to work through this step.

8. Generalize to other situations.

This may or may not be an immediate step, but it involves the effect that this decision and process can have on other situations.

9. Evaluate the implementation.

This is a crucial step in order to determine whether the implementation plan was satisfactory and whether the choice was satisfactory. Too often we blame a choice as being poor when, in fact, it was the implementation that was poor or lacking.

Helpers can aid this process by clarifying, providing information, and suggesting alternatives in the brainstorming step. In instances such as vocational and educational planning, the use of information from tests may be utilized in the decision-making process. The gathering and synthesizing of pertinent information is a valuable tool in cognitive decision making.

In addition to test interpretation and dissemination of appropriate information, helpers can use values clarification exercises, observation, and didactic teaching to aid the helpee in learning to understand and to apply data obtained from tests, written and verbal information, and observation. This data can help people clarify and explicate their own values, attitudes, and beliefs as well as their assets and liabilities. It is the helpee who makes the final decision. The helper provides invaluable inputs. An excerpt of this kind of helping follows.

Helpee: I'm having a hard time figuring out how to deal with the tardiness in my department.

Helper: It's frustrating, isn't it? Sounds like you're being held accountable for it.

Helpee: Oh, yes. As department head, I get landed on when the boss calls up in the morning and the girls aren't there to answer the phones and give him the information he wants.

Helper: So it becomes your problem. What kinds of things have you thought about doing?

Helpee: Oh, I don't know . . . docking people's pay, sending notes up to personnel to be put in their files, making people make up lost time, rescheduling.

Helper: Sounds like you have thought of some options. Let's jot them down. Can you think of any others?

Helpee: I don't know. I suppose I could just ignore it and see what happens.

Helper: Have you thought about holding a department meeting and discussing it there? Maybe you could get some more ideas from your staff.

Helpee: Um . . . I don't know. We never seem to get anywhere when we discuss these kinds of issues.

Helper: Um. Maybe if you told them that your problem is that you're being held responsible for their tardiness . . . Anything else we can put down as possible options?

Helpee: Wait a minute. I think before I really can consider different possibilities, I ought to see what my own staff has to say. Sort of put the shoe where it fits.

In this particular excerpt the decision-making process is not completed but, rather, the helpee decides to get some more information before making a final decision. This is indeed appropriate, as sometimes decisions are made too quickly, before all the necessary data is collected.

Problems Cognitive decision-making strategies are effective for educational and vocational planning and for problem solving and decision making in just about any life situation. There are some categories of decisions where more cognitive information is needed and there are some categories of decisions where information about attitudes and beliefs is required.

Exercises The following exercises will help you to recognize how you make everyday decisions in your life and how inputs from another person(s) can help.

Exercise 6-5. The purpose of this exercise is to get you in touch with your own decision making. Think back over the past forty-eight hours and write down every decision you have made (such as what time you got up yesterday morning, what you had for breakfast, what you wore, when you brushed your teeth). See how many decisions you've made in this time span and then go over your list and classify your decisions according to the following code: A = major decisions; B = commonplace, but not everyday, decisions; C = routine, everyday, taken-for-granted decisions. What does your list look like? Compare it with others.

Exercise 6-6. In small groups, take a few minutes to jot down all the variables that went in your decision to be where you are right now, in class, on a job, or wherever. See if you can go back to the very beginning of your decision making and identify the problem clarification point. Share with your group and note similarities and differences.

Exercise 6-7. Divide into groups of six. Pick a problem that you can all agree to as being a problem in your setting (e.g., too much noise in the cafeteria, inadequacy of parking places, etc.). Try to decide what to do by going through the first seven steps of the decision-making process. Share your learning with each other.

Affective-Cognitive Strategies

Rationale The theoretical basis for affective-cognitive strategies is developmental psychoanalytical theory, where the goals are to bring unconscious material into the conscious realm and to restructure personality by achieving insight (awareness and understanding).

Techniques The major techniques of psychoanalytic helpers are free association, dream analysis, and interpretation. These are verbal techniques that allow helpees to proceed at their own pace to develop a transference relationship with the helper and work through unconscious conflicts. The purpose of free association and dream analysis is to allow the helpees to be gradually drawn into deep, unconscious material.

Problems Psychoanalytic techniques are in order for people who have deep-seated problems requiring restructuring of the personality. Unless you pursue psychoanalytic training, it is unlikely that you will have the opportunity to do more than provide a supporting relationship to this type of helpee as a psychiatric aide.

Exercise   The following exercise will help you experience free association and what it can mean to and for you.

Exercise 6-8:   In pairs or small groups take ten minutes for each person to look at a list of words (such as the colors red, blue, black, pink, white) and say whatever comes to mind as a result of the stimulus word. After each person has taken ten minutes for this task, each can share reactions and new learning. Other members of the group can then ask some questions and share their reactions.

Cognitive-Behavioral Strategies

Rationale   Cognitive-behavioral strategies are approaches that deal with both the thinking and the behaving processes. They are based on the premise that faulty thinking must be changed before effective behavior change can occur. The theoretical bases come from Ellis' Rational-Emotive-Therapy and Glasser's Reality therapy as well as from behavioral theory (see chapter 5). Rationality and responsibility are key concepts in these approaches.

Techniques   Cognitive-behavioral techniques are largely verbal and involve homework outside of the helping relationship to facilitate the transference of new thinking into action behavior.
The Rational-Emotive-Therapy model has contributed an effective strategy entitled "cognitive restructuring," which means correcting faulty thinking with new, rational thinking. This strategy includes techniques of didactic teaching, persuading and confronting, and assigning behavioral homework. The purpose of cognitive restructuring is to aid helpees to control their emotions by telling themselves more rational and less self-defeating sentences, rather than telling themselves the crazy things that emanate from the following list of irrational ideas abstracted from the work of Albert Ellis (1962).

1.   It is a dire necessity for me to be loved or approved by everyone for everything I do.

2.   Certain acts are wrong and evil and people who perform these acts should be severely punished.

3.   It is terrible, horrible, and catastrophic when things are not the way I would like them to be.

4. Much human unhappiness is externally caused and is forced on one by outside people and events.

5. If something is or may be dangerous or fearsome, one should be terribly concerned about it.

6. It is easier to avoid than to face life difficulties and self-responsibilities.

7. One needs something other or stronger or greater than oneself on which to rely.

8. One should be thoroughly competent, adequate, intelligent, and achieving in all possible respects.

9. Because something once strongly affected one's life, it should indefinitely affect it.

10. What other people do is vitally important to our existence and we should make great efforts to change them in the direction we would like them to be changed.

11. Human happiness can be achieved by inertia and inaction.

12. One has virtually no control over one's emotions and one cannot help feeling certain things.

The helper continually unmasks helpees' faulty thinking by bringing these thoughts (statements helpees say over and over to themselves) to their attention, showing them how these thoughts are maintaining their disturbance, demonstrating the a-b-c-d-e links, and teaching helpees how to rethink and reverbalize these and similar sentences in a more logical, self-helping way. Thus helpers directly contradict and deny the faulty statements that helpees repeat to themselves and they demand that the helpees become involved in some kind of activity (homework) that will act as a "counter-propagandist" force against the faulty belief system.

In the a-b-c-d-e system a stands for activating event, b stands for belief system, c stands for consequences, d stands for disputing irrational ideas, and e stands for new emotional consequence or effect. The following excerpt demonstrates this.

> *Helpee:* I'm really upset. I just did a job for a person and it didn't come out right. I can't stand it when things don't go right and I just don't understand how it happened. It really is terrible!
>
> *Helper:* Wow, you seem to believe that everything should always go right and that if it doesn't, you're no good. You're really doing a job on yourself.

Helpee: Well, I don't understand when things don't turn out right and I've done the right thing. I'm really upset.

Helper: I know you're upset. But you're upset because of what you're thinking about a job not coming out right, because you believe that everything should go right and if it doesn't, you're no good. Let me draw you something. See this a? That's the activating event, the job that didn't come out right. The b is your belief that everything should go right and if it doesn't, you're no good. The c is the result of b, your feeling upset. Come on now, what kinds of things do you think you're telling yourself in b that are resulting in your feeling upset?

Helpee: I'm not sure. I guess I'm telling myself that I should always do well and that it's terrible when I'm not perfect.

Helper: That's really crazy. How about telling yourself that you did the best you could and that it's O.K. when everything does not always work out and you don't have to be perfect?

The homework in this particular case may consist of the helpee practicing new sentences, such as those suggested by the helper in the preceding excerpt, every time he or she begins to feel upset when things don't go well. Helpees report back on their homework assignments. In conformance with Ellis' approach, the following kinds of rational ideas are taught:

1. It is not a dire necessity for one to receive love or approval from all significant others. One can concentrate on loving rather than being loved.

2. It would be better not to determine self-worth by external competence, adequacy, and achievement, but to focus on self-respect and winning approval for performance.

3. Wrongdoers ought not to be blamed or punished, but should be considered merely stupid or ignorant or emotionally disturbed.

4. All human unhappiness is caused or sustained by the view one takes of things rather than the things themselves.

5. If something is dangerous, one should face it and try to make it nondangerous and not catastrophize over it.

6. The only way to solve difficult problems is to face them squarely.

7.   It is usually far better to stand on one's own feet and gain faith in oneself and one's ability to meet difficult circumstances of living.

8.   One should accept oneself as imperfect with general human limitations and specific fallibilities.

9.   One should learn from one's past experiences but not be overly attached to or prejudiced by them.

10.   Other people's deficiencies and weaknesses are largely their problems and putting pressure on them to change is unlikely to help them do so.

11.   Humans are usually happiest when they are actively and vitally absorbed in fulfilling pursuits outside themselves.

12.   One has enormous control over one's emotions if one chooses to work at learning new, right kinds of sentences.

Needless to say, pointing out "faulty" thinking once is not likely to result in permanent behavior change. Rather, the helper must keep fighting and pounding away at the faulty belief system, time and again. Helpers must insist upon the completion of homework assignments that will demonstrate some behavior change.

The following is an excerpt from a Rational-Emotive-Therapy training session:

Mr. Whittier is sixty-six years old, retired, and widowed. He is living alone, in the same apartment he's been in for forty years. He has three grown sons who live in other towns. He's been referred to a counselor because of continued moping and self-pity.

Mr. Whittier:	I'm all alone now. The boys, they've gone off and they don't really bother with me now. I suppose I should move to a smaller apartment, but all the memories are there. Where have all the years gone to?
Helper:	Mr. Whittier, you seem to think that your boys should be more attentive to you.
Mr. Whittier:	Yes . . . why not? What are children for? We all had some good years together.
Helper:	It certainly would be nice if your boys did pay more attention to you, but the fact that they don't doesn't mean you have to stop living, you know.
Mr. Whittier:	What do you mean?

Helper:	You keep acting as if you can't live without them. You go around here telling everyone how terrible it is that your sons don't write more, don't visit and call more. But you are healthy and you are living and things don't always have to be the way you want them to be.
Mr. Whittier:	What kind of talk is this? Things *don't* always have to be the way I want them to be . . . um . . . let me think.
Helper:	Isn't that what you keep on telling yourself?
Mr. Whittier:	(long pause) Maybe, maybe, young lady, you have something.
Helper:	Let me help you think it out. There are some new sentences you can learn to say over and over to yourself every time you feel yourself getting upset with your sons. If, instead of telling yourself over and over again how terrible it is that your boys don't call, write, and visit more, you could learn to say instead, it's too bad those boys don't call, visit, write more—we could have good times together—but I'm making friends of my own here at the center and I'm going to manage and live anyway. . . .

In this case the helper had gotten to know Mr. Whittier over several years at the community center, so she felt comfortable confronting him with his irrational thinking.

Reality therapy provides another form of techniques in the cognitive-behavioral domain. Involvement between the helper and the helpee is crucial to Reality therapy techniques, which involve seven steps:

1. Get involved; be personal and communicate "I care about you" by words and actions.

2. Stay in the here and now; avoid references to the past and avoid feelings. What the person does with them is more important than the feelings themselves.

3. Evaluate behavior; ask the helpee to evaluate his or her own behavior and ask "Is what you did appropriate?"; "Is it helping you . . . others?" If the client cannot evaluate his or her behavior to your satisfaction, it is necessary to return to step 1. The helpees must decide whether or not to change their behaviors.

4. Plan to change behavior; ask "What do you think would be a better way to do things?" Help the client formulate a plan. Let the client choose, offering suggestions, but not providing the plan. The

plan should be minimal, specific ("How and when will you do this?"), positive rather than negative or punitive, and have a high probability of success.

5.   Contract to seal the plan. If necessary, write out a contract and have the helpee sign it. Follow through with a check on how it is going and support success. This contract is between the helper and the helpee.

6.   Accept no excuses for failure to fulfill the plan. If the contract is not fulfilled, ask "When will you do this?" not "Why didn't you do this?" If unsuccessful, follow through with the natural consequences of not having followed the plan and then go back and make a new plan.

7.   The helpee should know and be involved with making the rules. Use the natural consequences (results when the rules are broken), not punishment.

A helper using Reality therapy techniques will become very involved with the helpee, who can then begin to evaluate his or her own behavior and see what is unrealistic. Helpers confront clients with reality and ask them again and again to decide whether or not they wish to take the responsible path. They are then asked to make specific plans and to take responsibility for implementing them. Helpers can reject unrealistic behavior but still accept helpees and maintain respect for them. Helpers will teach helpees better ways to fulfill their needs without hurting themselves and others. Helpees assume responsibility for their behavior, work in the present, learn to deal with the morality of their behavior, and learn more effective ways of behaving. An example of this approach follows:

> *Helpee:*   I don't want to finish school. I hate the teachers, I can't learn anything from them, and it's no use going back there.
>
> *Helper:*   What's going on in school? What are you doing?
>
> *Helpee:*   I'm always getting sent to the office. My English teacher is a real nag. She picks on me for everything and I know she has it in for me.
>
> *Helper:*   What are *you* doing?
>
> *Helpee:*   Nothing much. I just sit there . . . sometimes I mess around a little.
>
> *Helper:*   What's "messing around"?
>
> *Helpee:*   Oh, you know, talking to other guys, fooling around. . . .
>
> *Helper:*   Do you think this is appropriate behavior?

Helpee:	Aw, I don't know. Most of the guys do it.
Helper:	Let me ask you something. If you don't go back to school, what will you do?
Helpee:	I'll get a job. I want to go up north and work at a ski resort. I can be an instructor.
Helper:	You think you can get that kind of job without a high school diploma?
Helpee:	I think so . . . I don't know. Why would a ski instructor need a high school diploma?
Helper:	Well, it might help. It will certainly give you more choices for the rest of your life.
Helpee:	I'm sick of school. I don't really want to go back.
Helper:	It's up to you to decide what you want to do. I think you should think about what you're doing and whether or not it is going to get you what you want in this world.

This excerpt shows that steps 2 and 3 have been implemented (step 1 had been started in previous sessions). This is a teaching strategy that deals directly with choices of the helpee. The basic philosophy is that the helpee can decide whether or not to be troubled.

Note that these cognitive-behavioral techniques include evaluation and judgment on the part of the helper, who labels the helpee's thinking and behavior as "rational," "irrational," "responsible," or "irresponsible." The helper's value system is not arbitrarily imposed upon helpees, but emphasis is placed upon examining and evaluating the helpee's values. In other words, helpers challenge helpees but do not punish them or reject them for not having the "right" values or beliefs. This does differ, however, from the phenomenological strategies, which are nonjudgmental and nonevaluative.

Problems These approaches have been used with a wide variety of the population, in schools, hospitals, industry, and correctional institutions. The Rational-Emotive-Therapy approach might not be effective with helpees who are not intelligent enough to follow a rational analysis or for those people who are so caught up in emotion that they cannot attend to this logical procedure. The Reality therapy approaches involve much straightforward common sense and have been used with a broad spectrum of the population.

Exercises The following exercises will provide you with opportunities to question your own belief system and to design a Reality therapy contract.

Exercise 6-9. In triads share the last strong negative feeling each of you has experienced. Describe the circumstances and help each other to parse out the irrational thinking via the a-b-c-d-e system. Which of the twelve ideas does the faulty belief system come from? What kinds of new sentences can you teach yourself to refute the old sentences you've been telling yourself? Prepare a homework assignment for yourself and report back to your triad in one week.

Exercise 6-10. In groups of six, reverse roles such as masculine-feminine, supervisor-supervisee, black-white (dependent upon the makeup of your group). As a group, role play a scene using your new roles and then discuss the assumptions and conceptions you've become aware of as you've role played an unfamiliar role and perceived others playing a role familiar to you. What irrational beliefs have you uncovered? What do they mean to you?

Exercise 6-11. In small groups construct a Reality therapy contract for at least one member of the group in accordance with the seven steps previously discussed. Stick to specific behaviors and identify the logical consequences of meeting and not meeting the contract. What did you find functional or dysfunctional for you in this process?

Behavioral Strategies

Rationale   These approaches are based on learning theory (see chapter 5) and focus upon specific, observable behaviors as opposed to feelings and thoughts. The objectives of these strategies are to alter inappropriate behaviors and to teach appropriate behaviors. The assumption is that a change in behavior results in changes in feelings and thoughts and that helpers can only evaluate their effectiveness by observing concrete, specific behavior changes.

Techniques   The many behavioral techniques require some prerequisite skills of the helper. Some of these skills are the following:

1. understanding of the concepts and principles of reinforcement, punishment, extinction, discrimination, shaping, successive approximation, and schedules of reinforcement

2. ability to identify specific target behaviors that the helpee wishes to change

3. ability to identify and assess the conditions preceding the helpee's target behavior

4. ability to collect baseline data on the frequency and severity of target behavior

5. ability to identify and assess those conditions that result from the target behavior and maintain (reinforce) it

6. ability to determine reinforcements that are meaningful for the helpee

7. ability to determine feasible and meaningful schedules of reinforcement

8. sufficient knowledge of theoretical framework, design, and application of different behavioral strategies

9. ability to evaluate outcomes of behavioral strategies

It is beyond the scope of this book to teach you the above skills, but you will find readings at the end of this chapter that cover this material. Behavioral strategies are being taught to teachers and parents and are increasingly being used in business, schools, and health organizations. Many paraprofessionals and beginning professionals are assisting in the implementation of these strategies. Some important behavioral techniques that we will discuss are modeling, contracting, **assertiveness training,** and systematic desensitization.

Modeling is based on the principle that people learn to behave in new ways by imitating the behavior, values, attitudes, and beliefs of significant others. Modeling may be used through role playing, the use of media, and individual and group counseling relationships. Remember that the helper is a model, a very powerful model, in a helping relationship. An example of role playing modeling follows.

Helpee:	I always have a hard time at those dorm parties. I'm never able to go up and start a conversation with someone I don't know.
Helper:	Um. Let's role play. I'll be a stranger at a party and you be standing by the wall with a beer.
Helpee:	O.K. (rearranges self) Ummmmm . . . hot, isn't it?
Helper:	Yeh.
Helpee:	Lots of people here. Oh darn! See, I can't do it; it just goes nowhere.
Helper:	O.K. Now let's reverse roles and see what happens. Hi, there. Some crowd here . . . it's difficult getting around. You struck me as someone interesting to talk to.
Helpee:	I did? Oh, well, thanks. That's nice.
Helper:	I was wondering what you're thinking about all this (gestures around the room).

> *Helpee:* I see what you did. You asked broader questions and I asked dumb ones that didn't need answering.
>
> *Helper:* That's one thing. What were you feeling when we did this?

In modeling, it is important for the helper to be aware of his or her modeling influence on the helpee and of those positive and negative models in other aspects of the helpee's life. Sometimes we arrange for people to work or study together or in small groups, having definite models in mind. By the same token, we sometimes break up existing groups or cliques because of the effect of negative models.

Contracting is based on theories of reinforcement, which state that reinforced (rewarded) behavior tends to be repeated. A behavioral contract is a specific agreement between the helper and the helpee that breaks down the target behavior into its smallest parts and provides for systematic reinforcement upon the performance of the behavior.

Contracts may be informal (i.e., "If you do x, I will do y") or formal (written statements of specific behavior to be performed, the specific reward to be granted, and the specific responsibilities and conditions for implementing and monitoring the contract).

Contracts should follow the rules proposed by Homme (1970) in that they (1) use reward liberally and immediately following performance, (2) are clearly understood by all parties, and (3) are expressed in positive terms, meaning what one is to do, not what one is not to do.

Here is an example of a formal contract drawn up between a residence advisor and a college student in a dormitory. The problem was that the student was in danger of failing a chemistry course due to his falling behind with homework assignments and his low test scores. Tom, Mary Beth, and Len agreed to participate on these terms.

> If Tom reads one chapter of his chemistry text and completes the problems at the end of the chapter with 75 percent accuracy by 9:30 each evening, he will meet Mary Beth in the lounge for coffee between 10 and 11 PM. Len will be available to correct the problems at 9:30 PM. If Tom does not meet these terms, he will stay in his room the rest of the evening and not meet with Mary Beth. This contract will be reviewed after two weeks.

Like Reality therapy contracts, there is no punishment or rejection for an individual not meeting the terms of the contract; however, the reinforcement is only given after performance of the target behavior and it is important that this reinforcement not be available outside the terms of the contract. Contracts must be positive and within the realm of possibility. The target behavior is broken down into its smallest component parts and an appropriate amount of reinforcement is administered for each small component behavior performed. For example, Tom may be far enough behind in his chemistry to warrant reading two chapters per night; but the contract begins with one chapter because Len and Tom know that Tom can definitely meet those terms. When the contract is reviewed, the terms may change.

The use of contracts in a helping relationship has the advantage of specifying in positive terms exactly what is expected from the helpees and what they will receive for these performances. Contracts enable some movement and growth in problem areas that result in higher self-esteem and permit attention then to be turned to other areas of concern. Contracts are ethical as long as they do not specify performance of immoral behavior (in which case it would be bribery) and as long as all involved parties agree to the terms.

Assertiveness training also belongs to the cognitive domain as it might involve changing helpees' belief systems by teaching them that they do have the right to stand up for their own rights, as long as they do not harm someone else in the process. This is a technique that reduces anxiety by teaching and practicing responses that will help people say what they want to say.

Experience shows that assertive expression tends to inhibit anxiety. In assertiveness training, it is important to differentiate between assertiveness and aggressiveness (the latter impinges upon someone else's rights). Methods of assertiveness training can involve role playing (successive approximations, a little bit at a time, leading to a totally assertive response), modeling from media, and verbal instructions and illustrations.

An example of assertiveness training involves a twenty-five-year-old divorcee:

> *Helpee:* I've been in a terrible state all day. Since I've left Russ, my parents have really been on my back. My dad called last night and announced they're coming up this weekend and now I have to change all my plans. I've been unable to concentrate on anything all day.

> *Helper:* Sounds to me like you're really uptight about this. You were unable to tell your parents that this weekend was inconvenient for you.

> *Helpee:* Yes. I never can tell them what I feel. They get so upset and carry on so. But I hate myself for getting into this state.

Helper:	I wonder what would happen if you called your dad tonight and told him you'd like to see him, but this weekend is inconvenient for you and you'll let him know when he can come up.
Helpee:	I wish I could do that. I'd love it. I don't think I can.
Helper:	Let's rehearse and see what happens. (They then role played the same scene over and over, with the helper playing both roles at different times for modeling purposes. After the fifth rehearsal, the helpee reported that she felt less anxious.)

The next day the helpee reported that she had phoned her father and she felt relieved that she had been able to take this step. You will note that her assertive responses did not contain a "you're no good, you have no right to interfere in my life" kind of message. She sent an "I message," communicating her interest in seeing him, but letting him know, clearly and firmly, that she has her own life to lead and will let him know when it is all right for him to come up. As she continues to practice this kind of behavior, she will come to change her belief system and really believe that she has the right to her own life.

Systematic desensitization involves breaking down anxiety-response behaviors and exposing the helpee to the imagery of these behaviors while in a state of deep physical relaxation. The theory is that anxiety responses have been **conditioned** (learned) and can be counterconditioned (unlearned). One way to do this is to pair the anxiety response with an incompatible state, in this case, a physiological state of relaxation, which inhibits anxiety. The anxiety stimulus eventually loses its potency and the helpee no longer needs to expend energy on this anxiety response. It is unlikely that many human service workers will actually apply complete systematic desensitization; but the first stage, that of inducing deep muscle relaxation, is often helpful in and of itself and is easy to learn to apply.

It usually takes two to three sessions to effectively teach relaxation, a technique involved in systematic desensitization. In between sessions, helpees are asked to practice these skills at least once per day. Helpees are taught to contract (tense) and then relax specific muscle groups for several minutes at a time until they learn to monitor their own relaxation.

Before beginning this training, the helper explains the process to the helpee. The helper explains that it is impossible to be both tense and relaxed at the same time and that once helpees learn relaxation, they can use this training whenever they are tense. This is skill learning and requires continuous practice in order to be effective.

The helpee is seated in a comfortable chair that supports all body muscles. Eyes are closed (the helpee is asked to remove eyeglasses or contact lenses), the head is supported by the chair or wall, arms are on the armrests of the chair, legs are uncrossed and firmly on the floor. Relaxation training commences after the helper demonstrates to the helpee the tensing and relaxing of each muscle group. It is a good idea to darken the room and reduce interfering noises. The following is an example of relaxation instructions (I am indebted to Flora Hummel, R.N., for introducing me to this technique):

Close your eyes now, lean back and just get comfortable. Think about your body and what you're feeling now . . . now I want you to raise your hands and clench your fists as tightly as you can . . . feel those muscles pulling . . . tighter, now . . . O.K. 1 . . . 2 . . . 3 . . . 4 . . . now relax and let your hands fall into your lap. Now let's do that again . . . tighten those hands . . . 1 . . . 2 . . . 3 . . . 4 . . . now let them relax again . . . now raise your forearms and pull those muscles as tightly as you can . . . 1 . . . 2 . . . 3 . . . 4 . . . relax and let them fall into your lap . . . attend to the different feelings you get from relaxed and tense muscles . . . now let's do those muscles again . . . 1 . . . 2 . . . 3 . . . 4 . . . relax . . . feel your arms getting heavier as they become more relaxed . . . now pull in on your upper arm muscles by raising your arms and flexing those muscles . . . harder, now . . . that's right . . . 1 . . . 2 . . . 3 . . . 4 . . . relax . . . your arms feel heavier and warm feelings are spreading down through your fingertips . . . now let's do that again . . . 1 . . . 2 . . . 3 . . . 4 . . . relax . . . we'll concentrate on your head muscles now . . . let your arms continue to grow heavier and relax more while you think about your head muscles . . . now raise your eyebrows and wrinkle up your forehead as much as you can . . . tighter . . . hold it . . . 1 . . . 2 . . . 3 . . . 4 . . . now relax, and feel that tension slipping out over your head, right over the top . . . let's do that again . . . hold it, 1 . . . 2 . . . 3 . . . 4 . . . relax . . . now scrunch up your eyes and feel them get as tight as possible . . . 1 . . . 2 . . . 3 . . . 4 . . . now do that again . . . 1 . . . 2 . . . 3 . . . 4 . . . relax and feel your eyelids getting heavier as everything gets darker . . . now scrunch up your nose as tight as you can . . . hold it . . . 1 . . . 2 . . . 3 . . . 4 . . . now relax . . . do it again . . . 1 . . . 2 . . . 3 . . . 4 . . . that's right, now relax and feel your breathing get clearer and easier . . . now stretch your mouth in an ear-to-ear grin and pull on your lip, jaw, and cheek muscles . . . come on, you can pull tighter than that . . . hold it, . . . 1 . . . 2 . . . 3 . . . 4 . . . now relax . . . let your jaw hang loosely and your head lean right into the back of the chair . . . do that again . . . 1 . . . 2 . . . 3 . . . 4 . . . that's right, now relax . . . now think back over your arm muscles and let your head rest heavier and heavier . . . you're getting more and more relaxed and all you're thinking about is your muscles getting more and more relaxed . . . now pull in your neck and throat muscles . . . feel that tension . . . hold it . . . 1 . . . 2 . . . 3 . . . 4 . . . now pull in your neck and throat muscles . . . feel that tension . . .

hold it . . . 1 . . . 2 . . . 3 . . . 4 . . . relax . . . let your neck and head slump into the chair . . . how about repeating that . . . 1 . . . 2 . . . 3 . . . 4 . . . relax and feel your neck get looser and looser . . . now raise your shoulders and pull those muscles tightly . . . hold it . . . 1 . . . 2 . . . 3 . . . 4 . . . that's right, now relax and let those shoulders slump . . . let those warm, tingly, relaxed feelings connect up from your shoulders down your arms . . . that's right . . . repeat that . . . 1 . . . 2 . . . 3 . . . 4 . . . relax . . . feel those relaxed feelings getting deeper and deeper . . . now tighten up your upper back muscles by arching it as much as you can . . . 1 . . . 2 . . . 3 . . . 4 . . . relax . . . slump down into your chair . . . do it again and tighten your chest muscles at the same time . . . 1 . . . 2 . . . 3 . . . 4 . . . relax . . . take a couple of minutes to feel more relaxed and go over your arm muscles and your head muscles . . . if any group of muscles start to tighten up, pull them in, contract them and then relax them, like a rubber band . . . now pull your tummy muscles in as tightly as you can and feel that tension . . . hold them . . . 1 . . . 2 . . . 3 . . . 4 . . . relax . . . feel your stomach get looser . . . repeat that . . . 1 . . . 2 . . . 3 . . . 4 . . . relax . . . breathe deeply and slowly and with each breath in, feel more relaxed and with each breath out feel that relaxation spreading throughout your body . . . now tighten your buttocks and hold them tight . . . 1 . . . 2 . . . 3 . . . 4 . . . relax . . . now do that again . . . 1 . . . 2 . . . 3 . . . 4 . . . relax and sink deeper and deeper into the chair . . . now we'll work on your leg muscles . . . tighten your thigh muscles . . . 1 . . . 2 . . . 3 . . . 4 . . . relax . . . do that again . . . 1 . . . 2 . . . 3 . . . 4 . . . feel your legs getting heavier and the warm, relaxed feelings spreading down . . . now tighten up your calves by pointing your toes away from your head . . . 1 . . . 2 . . . 3 . . . 4 . . . relax . . . repeat . . . 1 . . . 2 . . . 3 . . . 4 . . . that's right . . . the warm tingly feelings are spreading down your legs . . . now crunch up your toes and tighten those feet muscles . . . 1 . . . 2 . . . 3 . . . 4 . . . relax . . . now do that again . . . 1 . . . 2 . . . 3 . . . 4 . . . fine . . . now think back over all the muscle groups we've relaxed and see if they can become more and more relaxed . . . that's right . . . the arms . . . your head . . . your shoulders . . . back . . . stomach . . . buttocks . . . legs . . . take a few minutes to really get in touch with these warm, tingly feelings . . . . now I'm going to count to 20 very slowly and when I use an odd number, breathe in and when I use an even one, breathe out (counts to 20 very slowly). (At this time desensitization is about to begin or, if relaxation is being used alone, after several moments, you count slowly to 10 and ask the helpee to open his or her eyes and slowly stretch.)

If desensitization follows, it is in this relaxed state that the helper asks the helpee to call different scenes to mind: a neutral scene (like a blank screen), which does not arouse any feeling; a comfortable scene (like sitting in front of a fireplace or by the ocean), which arouses only comfortable feelings; or an item from a desensitization hierarchy, which can arouse anxiety. Anxiety scenes are first introduced for ten seconds, then followed by a neutral or pleasurable scene and more relaxation concentration, then for twenty seconds and after more pleasurable scenes, for forty seconds. If anxiety occurs, the helpee signals the helper and the hierarchy scenes are lowered. An item is considered successfully passed when the subject can imagine it for three forty-second periods without experiencing any anxiety.

A hierarchy is constructed during the first two relaxation training sessions used for desensitization. This hierarchy is a series of statements that help the client vividly imagine an experience that helps recall actual stimuli. A sample of an anxiety hierarchy used for test desensitization follows (number one causes least anxiety; number thirteen, the most):

1. walking to class
2. professor announces examination is two weeks away
3. copying classmate's notes for missed class
4. obtaining references to study with
5. discussing class with friends
6. studying the week of the exam
7. studying the night before the exam
8. waking up the morning of the exam
9. walking to the classroom
10. the exam is being handed out—you receive a copy
11. while trying to think of answer to an exam question you notice everyone around you writing quickly
12. you come to a question you don't know the answer to
13. professor announces that forty minutes remain; you have one and a half hours work to do

When the cause of anxiety is something that can actually be tested out in the helping relationship, you can validate the desensitization by real life experience after it has occurred symbolically. For example, I once treated a client who had a phobia for driving. After successfully reducing her anxiety by an imagined hierarchy, we entered my car and found that she was able to drive for the first time in eighteen years by utilizing relaxation to reduce her anxiety.

Problems Behavioral strategies are effective with a wide population and have proven to be especially effective with people who have difficulty with verbal strategies. These are action strategies that usually are shorter term than some of the other types of strategies.

In particular, modeling is effective for those who are unsure of themselves and need specific teaching examples. Contracting is helpful for retarded as well as "normal" populations and is particularly effective in families and organizations where the reinforcements can be immediately provided and monitored. Assertiveness training is helpful for shy, inhibited people; this technique has been used in womens' consciousness-raising groups. Systematic desensitization is helpful for those with phobic behaviors, such as fear of flying and fear of the water.

Exercises The following exercises will give you some experience with the previously described behavioral techniques.

Exercise 6-12. The purpose of this exercise is to check your ability to identify behavioral statements. Which of the following statements are behavioral (i.e., objective, concrete, observable)?

(1) That child is no good—he's stubborn and fresh.
(2) Johnny never sits down at his desk. He's always up walking around.
(3) I feel so guilty when I think of him all alone.
(4) Ms. Leonard always comes late to the board meetings.
(5) Ms. Leonard really isn't interested in this organization.
(6) Pam is so spoiled—she's always whining and complaining.
(7) My husband doesn't appreciate me.
(8) He's lazy just like his father.
(9) He never seems to get anything done on time.
(10) I had a boring day today.
(11) I cleaned the house all day.
(12) She really is a good mother.
(13) My secretary is the fastest typist I've ever seen.
(14) He belongs to a gang.
(15) Gangs are roaming the streets at night.

Answers. (2), (4), the second part of (6), (11), (13), and (15) are all behavioral statements. The others are subjective conclusions, attitudes, and evaluations.

Exercise 6-13. Individually, write down the five behaviors that you think an effective helper ought to possess. Then, in small groups, arrive at one list based on the small group's concensus. Then small groups can share their lists. Do the lists all contain behaviors or did some attitudes and evaluations show up?

Exercise 6-14. Modeling: Who are the most influential role models in your life? What are their most important characteristics, in your opinion? Discuss these questions in small groups and see if you can draw up a list of effective model characteristics. Compare the lists among the small groups.

Exercise 6-15. Reinforcement: In triads or small groups, discuss what is reinforcing to each of you in your life. See if you can identify the major social (from people, such as smile, gesture, visiting) and concrete (things, such as money, gifts, purchases) reinforcers that operate in your life at home, your life at work, and your leisure life. See if they differ in the different settings. As you discuss different peoples' reinforcers, you will see that different people have different kinds of reinforcers and that what is reinforcing for one person may or may not be for another person.

Exercise 6-16. Reinforcement: Put yourself in some familiar setting, either at home, work, or school, and see if you can determine what kinds of reinforcements you give to others and to yourself, both social and concrete. For example, when I am at home and complete a housekeeping task I dislike, I usually reward myself by talking to a friend on the phone or having a cup of coffee with a neighbor. Share your responses in small groups.

Exercise 6-17. Contracting: In pairs, draw up contracts for each of you, listing your partner as monitor. This contract may be between you and your partner or between you and someone else. Select a target behavior (like losing x pounds or getting to class on time), use a time limit, and write out what you will do, when you will do it, and what you will receive for your performance. For example, "If I lose two pounds between today and next Thursday, I will buy myself a new shirt." It is essential that the reinforcement be something that is meaningful to the helpee, not to the helper.

Exercise 6-18. Assertiveness training: For each of the following situations, which response is the most assertive? (Answers are at the end of the chapter.)

(1) Your mother telephones you long distance and wants to know why she hasn't received a letter from you all week.

   a. "It's hard for you to realize that I'm grown up now. I'll write when I can."
   b. "I'm sorry, ma, I've just been too busy. I'll write tonight."
   c. "Oh, mom, please stop bugging me. I'm not a baby, you know."

(2) A co-worker asks you to get him coffee. This is the umpteenth time and you do not want to do it.

   a. "I guess so, since I'm going down there anyway."
   b. "Why can't you get your own coffee?"
   c. "I'd really feel better about our relationship if you would stop asking me to get your coffee."

(3) Someone pushes in front of you at the box office line.

   a. "Who do you think you are?"
   b. "I'm ahead of you in this line. Please move."
   c. "Some people really have a nerve!"

(4) Your boss asks you at the last minute to stay late to work on a report. You know it is not an emergency and this is the third time this has happened this month.

   a. "O.K. You're the boss."

b. "But we're having company tonight and I promised Marge I'd pick up some ice."

c. "I do have other plans tonight and I'm afraid it's too late for me to change them."

(5) Your friend wants to borrow your car. Last time this happened, you promised your husband you wouldn't do it again.

a. "I wish I could, but Jim made me promise not to lend out the car."

b. "I'd like to help out, but Jim and I have agreed that we can be more accountable about the car if we don't let others drive it."

c. "Oh dear, I think I'll need it when you want it."

(6) The sales clerk tells you that the store does not accept returns or exchanges. If the merchandise is defective, you'll have to deal directly with the manufacturer.

a. "That's ridiculous. I'm going to call the Better Business Bureau."

b. "I insist that you refund my money and I'm not budging until you do."

c. "I'd like to see your manager, please. I intend to straighten this out here and now."

(7) Your doctor tells you that there is nothing wrong with you, but he would like you to have some tests made anyway.

a. "Before I have any tests, I'd like to know the reasons, costs, and just what's involved."

b. "But why do I need these tests if there's nothing wrong with me?"

c. "Is this another example of useless tests I keep reading about?"

(8) Your friend pleads with you to go out to dinner and you want to stay home alone and relax, after a hard week.

a. "I have a headache, so I want to go to bed early."

b. "I'd really like to be alone tonight and relax. Some other time."

c. "Well, why don't you come over here and we'll fix something to eat?"

(9) A neighbor calls you to complain about your son being a bully. This has happened before with this particular neighbor and you have checked it out and determined that it is your neighbor's problem, not yours.

a. "I'm sorry. Thanks for letting me know about this. I'll talk to him."

b. "You really ought to find out about your own kids before you complain about mine."

c. "I'd appreciate it if you check out both sides of the situation, as will I."

(10) You've been sitting in the restaurant for over an hour and you still have not been served, even though you ordered an hour ago and told the waiter you have a curtain time to make.

    a. "Waiter! What's taking so long? I told you I have to be at the theater in half an hour."

    b. "Waiter! Curtain time is in thirty minutes. I expect to have finished eating by then."

    c. "Waiter! Will you please hurry? The service around here is terrible."

Exercise 6-19. Assertiveness training: Arrange a line of seven or eight people, such as at a grocery checkout counter, at the box office of a movie, or waiting to get on a bus. Ask one person at a time not in the line to try and break in and push ahead. See how each of you react and then discuss this as a group. The purposes of these last two exercises is to help you become aware of your own assertive behaviors or lack of them. In smaller groups, identify situations that require assertive (not aggressive) behaviors and role play these situations in as many ways as you can.

Exercise 6-20. Relaxation: Using the relaxation training example in this chapter, see if you can relax one or more in your group. Allow several seconds for each set of ellipses. Keep your voice soft and soothing and be careful not to rush. Experience the role of the relaxer as well as the relaxee and share your feelings and reactions.

Multimodality Strategies

Rationale Cutting across the affective, cognitive, and behavioral domains are Transactional Analysis and other eclectic approaches. These approaches draw upon many of the theoretical bases of the other approaches.

Transactional Analysis (TA) involves the analysis of communications and the structural analysis of personality via script and game analyses. The purpose is to change behavior by experiencing intellectual and emotional awareness.

Techniques Analysis of games and scripts, identification of ego states, and analysis of communication patterns and different transactions are TA techniques. Transactional Analysis utilizes Gestalt experiments and games in order to achieve these ends. It is a contractual and reinforcement strategy. The vocabulary and concepts of TA must be mastered in order for these techniques to be used. Helpers explain this vocabulary and these concepts to the helpee, usually assigning some reading material for teaching purposes.

The following is an excerpt from a TA counseling session.

Helpee: I'm unhappy in my marriage. My husband is always picking on me and nagging me. I feel so low.

Helper: Stay with that low feeling. Your voice has dropped, too. You sound like a scared little girl.

Helpee: I guess I am scared. It just seems as if all we do is fight these days.

Helper: Your husband is relating to you out of his critical parent state and you're responding by feeling low and scared in your child ego state. What does that mean to you? Sounds like you're getting something out of it.

Helpee: I guess I at least get his attention that way. It's just that I never seem to do anything right for him. The meat is too well done, the laundry isn't picked up on time, the kids aren't well behaved.

Helper: This scared feeling is familiar to you.

Helpee: Yes, all my life I've been scared.

Helper: I have a hunch that when you were a kid you were told you could never do anything right.

Helpee: My mother was always criticizing me. How did you know that?

Helper: So you learned how to be scared and play "stupid." You and your husband have a real game going there. It looks something like this (figure 6-2).

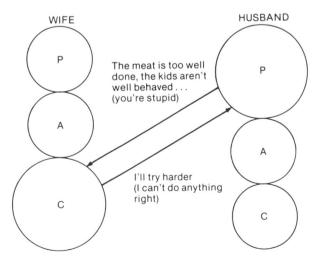

Figure 6-2   *Transactional Analysis*

This excerpt shows the identification of ego states, the racket feeling of being scared, and is just getting into identification of the game. The husband and wife are involved in a parent-child game where the husband occupies an "I'm O.K., you're not O.K." position and the wife occupies an "I'm not O.K., you're O.K." position. The helper is just getting to the early childhood decision that resulted in the script to do everything wrong and feel not O.K. about it.

Helpers use all three of their ego states to help clients activate their adult ego state as the executive of the personality. Helpers use their nurturing parent ego state to provide protection, caring, and permission; their adult ego state to provide skill and expertise in helping; and their child ego state to provide fun and intuition.

A major technique of TA is called reparenting, which occurs when the old critical parent ego state is replaced with a new nurturing ego state that allows for rescripting (changing those early childhood decisions). One way helpers can identify ego states is to have the helpee, by means of a Gestalt dialogue, role play the different ego states interacting with each other.

Problems TA is particularly effective for persons with interpersonal difficulties and with persons who seem to function inadequately (perhaps because of ego state **exclusion** or **contamination**). There are materials that can be used with young children listed at the end of this chapter. As the helpee must be able to understand the vocabulary and concepts of TA, it would probably not be effective with retarded populations.

Exercises The following exercises illustrate some of the TA principles.

Exercise 6-21. In small groups, role play some two-person dialogues and see if you can identify which ego state is operating in each participant. Note tone of voice, choice of words, body posture, facial expression, gestures, etc. The nurturing parent ego state is loving, caring, supportive, and rescuing and consists of caresses, tender smiles, and loving words. The critical parent ego state includes values, prescriptions, injunctions, frowns, pointing finger, punishments, and words such as "do," "don't," "should," and "ought to." The adult ego state is like a computer; it provides information, asks "what," "when," and "where" questions, lacks feelings, and is entirely objective, with a level, clear tone of voice. The child ego state is spontaneous, intuitive, angry, defiant, and complacent. It giggles, cries, scowls, gestures obscenely, sulks, and uses words like "golly," "gee whiz," "I can't," and "oh boy." Suggestions for role plays are (1) a dialogue between parents at the dinner table about their seventeen-year-old daughter's hours, (2) a dialogue between physician and patient, (3) a dialogue between welfare worker and client, and (4) a dialogue between boss and employee.

Exercise 6-22. In small groups see if you can identify games that you have played. Games are unstraight ways that your not O.K. child uses to get stroked (reinforced) and avoid responsibilities. Common games are "Stupid," "If it weren't for you," "Kick Me," and "Harried." What kinds of games do students play? Teachers? Parents? Helpers?

Exercise 6-23. Brainstorm in small groups ways that you can make your home, work setting, or the setting you are now in for training more O.K. How can you give yourself and others more positive strokes? Share with your group three things you like about yourself and then after everyone has shared, each person can take responsibility for giving at least one stroke (positive only!) to one person in the group, based on what has happened today in your group. The purpose of this is to learn how to give and receive strokes, to take responsibility for what makes you feel O.K.

The following exercise serves as a review of the criteria on which to base your choice of approach. Remember, the more strategies you can learn and utilize effectively, the wider the variety of problem-solving situations you can help with.

Exercise 6-24. Based on your reading and understanding of this chapter and your review of chapter 5, circle the letter of the strategy you would consider *most* appropriate for each of the following cases. In small groups, discuss your reasons for your selections. Remember, there are no hard and fast rules, except for some very specific cases and even then, more than one strategy can be applied. Possible answers are discussed at the end of the chapter.

(1) Lisa, age eighteen, is deathly afraid of flying. She is unable to identify the source of this fear, but she is concerned because her fiance has accepted an out-of-town job and she is expected to fly in to see him once a month for the next year.

　　a. client-centered therapy
　　b. Rational-Emotive-Therapy
　　c. systematic desensitization
　　d. Reality therapy
　　e. Gestalt therapy
　　f. Transactional Analysis

(2) Ms. Carleton is feeling anxious because her supervisor has unexpectedly left and the new supervisor hasn't arrived yet. She was very close to her old supervisor and doesn't know anything about the new one. Her work is suffering and she is scared.

　　a. client-centered therapy
　　b. Rational-Emotive-Therapy
　　c. assertiveness training
　　d. Reality therapy
　　e. Gestalt therapy
　　f. Transactional Analysis

(3) Mr. Wright, age forty-five, married with three children, was just told he'd have to take a 20 percent salary cut in order to keep his job. The firm for which he works has been having difficulty for several months. As Mr. Wright's living costs have risen considerably due to inflation, he does not think he can manage on this reduced salary.

a. client-centered therapy
b. Rational-Emotive-Therapy
c. decision-making therapy
d. Reality therapy
e. Gestalt therapy
f. systematic desensitization

(4) Susie, age thirteen, is causing her mother great distress because of her low marks and fresh conduct at school and at home. Her mother has come for help because she is "at the end of her rope" and doesn't know what to do.

a. client-centered therapy
b. Rational-Emotive-Therapy
c. contract therapy (behavioral)
d. Reality therapy
e. Gestalt therapy
f. Transactional Analysis

(5) Phyllis, a thirty-four-year-old divorcee, is unable to pay child care costs for her son on her salary. However, if she quits work, she won't have any income, as her ex-husband is out of work and can't help out at all. She doesn't know what to do and she is very depressed.

a. client-centered therapy
b. Rational-Emotive-Therapy
c. assertiveness training
d. Reality therapy
e. Gestalt therapy
f. Transactional Analysis

(6) Sandra's father has told her that she must quit college and get a job. He does not believe that women should go to college and he is worried that he won't be able to provide tuition for Sandra's younger brother, who is a junior in high school. Sandra has been an average student, is in her sophomore year at school, and, while she wants to stay in school, she sees no way that she can disobey her dad.

a. client-centered therapy
b. Rational-Emotive-Therapy
c. assertiveness training
d. Reality therapy
e. Gestalt therapy
f. Transactional Analysis

(7)   Mr. Brown feels that his boss is constantly criticizing him in front of others in the office. He works in a small office, can't really get out of sight of his boss, and has become increasingly nervous and distraught.

   a. client-centered therapy
   b. Rational-Emotive-Therapy
   c. assertiveness training
   d. Gestalt therapy
   e. Reality therapy
   f. Transactional Analysis

(8)   Martha, age fifteen, is very angry with her mother. She says her mother is unfair, too punitive, and not at all understanding. Martha's marks in school have dropped considerably this year and she is much moodier than previously.

   a. psychoanalysis
   b. client-centered therapy
   c. Rational-Emotive-Therapy
   d. assertiveness training
   e. Reality therapy
   f. Gestalt therapy

(9)   Tom, age fourteen, comes for help because he is scared. Several of his friends were involved in a house break-in over the weekend and although he didn't go in the house, he was outside waiting for his friends to come out. Everybody in town is talking about the vandalism this gang did in this house and Tom is afraid he'll be implicated sooner or later.

   a. psychoanalysis
   b. Reality therapy
   c. Rational-Emotive-Therapy
   d. client-centered therapy
   e. Gestalt therapy
   f. systematic desensitization

(10)   Mary Lou, age twenty-three, is distressed because another love affair has just ended. She feels very sorry for herself and resents that this always happens to her. "Every time I get close to or begin to get close to someone, he leaves me."

   a. psychoanalysis
   b. Rational-Emotive-Therapy
   c. modeling
   d. Reality therapy
   e. Gestalt therapy
   f. Transactional Analysis

(11)   Larry, age twenty-two, is very angry and bitter because he did not get into graduate school. He feels he had to settle for second best in college, too. Larry says, "I never get what I want. I always end up with second best."

a. psychoanalysis
b. Rational-Emotive-Therapy
c. Reality therapy
d. client-centered therapy
e. Transactional Analysis

(12) Marianne, age thirty-two, is severely depressed and has not eaten or slept more than a few hours in days. She has a long history of illnesses and a high amount of absenteeism from work. She doesn't know what's bothering her and just wants to be left alone.

a. psychoanalysis
b. client-centered therapy
c. Reality therapy
d. systematic desensitization
e. Gestalt therapy
f. Transactional Analysis

(13) Max, age eighteen, has been accepted into the four colleges to which he applied. Although he is overjoyed, he is stymied over which one to attend and he has become increasingly nervous and irritable as the deadline approaches.

a. Reality therapy
b. decision-making therapy
c. client-centered therapy
d. Rational-Emotive-Therapy
e. assertiveness training
f. Gestalt therapy

(14) Ms. Wolfe is the divorced mother of three young children. She's come for help because she can't manage her children and is always losing her temper and slapping them. She feels that 100 percent of her time and energy is devoted to motherhood and that she has no time for herself.

a. contracting
b. Rational-Emotive-Therapy
c. psychoanalysis
d. systematic desensitization
e. Transactional Analysis
f. client-centered therapy

(15) Mr. Winters has recently been released from a mental hospital. He is having trouble finding work. He is very nervous and always lets others get ahead of him in employment lines.

a. Rational-Emotive-Therapy
b. assertiveness training
c. Transactional Analysis
d. modeling
e. client-centered therapy
f. Gestalt therapy

SUMMARY

The brief overview of strategies suggests the skills and some of the criteria necessary for selection of strategies. It must be emphasized that this is only an initial exposure to the different strategies. Helpers modify and adjust various combinations of effective strategies according to their own personalities and preferences and the needs of the helpee.

Again I want to reiterate that there is no *one* strategy to fit any particular problem. As the last exercise shows, some strategies appear to be more effective than others for each of the situations presented, but a skillful helper could effectively adopt many of the possible strategies for any one problem. The only effective way I know of choosing strategies is to learn from your own and others' experiences to risk whatever seems right to you at the particular moment.

EXERCISE ANSWERS

Exercise 6-18. (1)a; (2)c; (3)b; (4)c; (5)b; (6)c; (7)a; (8)b; (9)c; (10)b.

Exercise 6-24. Possible Answers

(1) Systematic desensitization has been proven to be effective with phobias. One can utilize client-centered therapy at the same time.

(2) I would opt for client-centered therapy here, involving the client in a relationship that would reduce her anxiety.

(3) Some decision-making and/or Reality therapy would be helpful here, examining all the options and values involved so that Mr. Wright can accept responsibility for taking the cut or looking for a new job.

(4) Teaching the mother how to use behavioral contracts may clear up some of the hassling that is occurring at home. We don't know enough to know what the problem is or whose problem it is, but if Susie becomes the client, Reality therapy may be helpful and if the mother remains the client, TA can be helpful.

(5) Except for assertiveness training, any of the other strategies could be appropriate in this case. Client-centered therapy could help her feel better about herself, RET could get her in touch with her irrational ideas, RT could help her with choosing responsible behavior, and

Gestalt and TA could enhance her emotional and intellectual awareness.

(6) Assertiveness training could help Sandra deal with her father; RET could help her examine her belief system about families, authority, and education; and RT could help her make responsible choices.

(7) Assertiveness training along with some Rational-Emotive-Therapy could be effective here.

(8) In cases such as this, I have found a combination of client-centered therapy and Gestalt therapy to increase insight and self-concept.

(9) Reality therapy and client-centered therapy can be helpful here, the former to help Tom evaluate his own behavior and the latter to help him feel good about himself.

(10) Psychoanalysis or Transactional Analysis could be helpful here to enable Mary Lou to gain some insight into patterns of relating.

(11) Again, psychoanalysis or Transactional Analysis could be helpful here. I'd opt for the TA, as it sounds as if Larry has made an early decision never to make it.

(12) Psychoanalysis could be helpful here if this has been going on for a long time. Reality therapy could be effective, too, in forcing Marianne to assume some responsibility for her behaviors.

(13) Decision-making therapy is the obvious choice here.

(14) Some RET might help here. It sounds as if Ms. Wolfe has some "crazy" ideas about motherhood. Some contracting principles could help her in child management and some TA could give her insight into where she's coming from.

(15) Some client-centered therapy could help him gain self-confidence. Assertiveness training would also be useful.

These answers are only suggestions and are open to your discussion.

REFERENCES AND FURTHER READINGS

Psychoanalytic

Blocher, D. *Development Counseling*. New York: Ronald, 1966.
Bordin, E. *Psychological Counseling*. New York: Appleton-Century-Crofts, 1968.
Freud, S. *An Outline of Psychoanalysis*. New York: Norton, 1949.

Holzman, P. *Psychoanalysis and Psychopathology*. New York: McGraw-Hill, 1970.

Phenomenological

Client-Centered:

Carkhuff, R., and Truax, C. *Toward Counseling and Psychotherapy: [Training and Practice.]* Chicago: Aldine, 1967.

Patterson, C. *Relationship Counseling and Psychotherapy*. New York: Harper and Row, 1974.

Rogers, C., ed. *The Therapeutic Relationship and Its Impact*. Madison: University of Wisconsin Press, 1967.

———. *Client-centered Therapy*. Boston: Houghton Mifflin, 1951.

Gestalt:

Fagan, J., and Shepherd, I., eds. *Gestalt Therapy Now*. Palo Alto, Ca.: Science and Behavior Books, 1970.

Levitsky, A., and Perls, F. "The Rules and Games of Gestalt Therapy." In Fagan and Shepherd, eds. *Gestalt Therapy Now*, pp. 140 - 150. New York: Harper and Row, 1970.

Passons, W. *Gestalt Approaches in Counseling*. New York: Holt, Rinehart, and Winston, 1975.

Perls, F. *The Gestalt Approach and Eye Witness to Therapy*. Palo Alto, Ca.: Science and Behavior Books, 1973.

Polster, I., and Polster, M. *Gestalt Therapy Integrated*. New York: Brunner Mazel, 1973.

Behavioral

Alberti, R., and Emmons, M. *Your Perfect Right*. Los Angeles, Ca.: Impact, 1970.

Homme, L. *Use of Contingency Contracting in the Classroom*. Illinois: Research Press, 1970.

Krumboltz, J., and Krumboltz, H. *Changing Children's Behavior*. Englewood Cliffs, N.J.: Prentice-Hall, 1972.

Krumboltz, J., and Thoreson, C. *Behavioral Counseling*. New York: Holt, Rinehart, and Winston, 1969.

Ullman, L., and Krasner, L. *Case Studies in Behavior Modification*. New York: Holt, Rinehart, and Winston, 1965.

Wolpe, J. *The Practice of Behavior Therapy*. New York: Pergamon Press, 1969.

Cognitive-Behavioral

Ellis, A. *Reason And Emotion in Psychotherapy*. New York: Lyle Stuart, 1962.

Glasser, W. *Reality Therapy*. New York: Harper and Row, 1965.

Transactional-Communicative

Freed, A. *TA for Kids*. Sacramento, Ca.: Jalmar, 1972.

———. *TA for Tots*. Sacramento, Ca.: Jalmar, 1972.

James, M., and Jongeward, D. *Born to Win*. Reading, Ma.: Addison-Wesley, 1971.

———. *Games for Winning*. Reading, Ma.: Addison-Wesley, 1973.

Shepard, M., and Lee, M. *Games Analysts Play*. New York: Berkley-Medalion, 1970.

CHAPTER 7

APPLYING
STRATEGIES

In this chapter we will examine the six steps in applying strategies during this stage of the helping relationship. We will then look at another application of strategies, namely crisis intervention, which, while requiring the same communications skills for establishing a relationship, is directed more toward meeting the needs of specific emergency situations. We will conclude this chapter with some case studies, which will take you through the steps of both the relationship stage and the strategies stage.

STEPS

The six steps of the strategies stage are (1) acceptance of defined goals and objectives, (2) planning strategies, (3) using strategies, (4) evaluating strategies, (5) termination, and (6) follow-up.

The boundary line between the first (relationship) and the second (strategies) stages is not distinct. You will know when you are in this transition when you are able to focus on identifiable problems, when you find yourself thinking, "O.K., now that we know what the trouble is, what can we do about it?" Remember that you do not want to rush into the strategies stage until you have clearly ascertained and developed the problem and until you have agreement from the helpee that he or she wants to do something about it.

Acceptance of Defined Goals and Objectives

It is necessary that the helping relationship focus on areas of concern to the helpee, not those concerns that the helper thinks the helpee ought to work on. This may become a serious issue in some organizational settings, where there may be conflict between organizational policies, which you may represent as the helper, and the needs of the helpee. For example, if you are working in a correctional institution and an inmate who is causing some disruption and is seen as a "troublemaker" who "must be changed" is sent to you, you may find that you and this inmate have different objectives. Yours may be, of institutional necessity, to help the inmate conform to the system whereas the inmate's objectives may be to disrupt and get whatever attention results from the disruption. No one can tell you how to handle this kind of conflict, but you really have to think it out and come to a decision with which you are comfortable.

Remember that in order to be of help, you must have a strong helping relationship and that this involves identifying goals and objectives that are accepted by all involved parties. Strategies will not be effective if a strong helping relationship does not exist.

The following examples illustrate negative outcomes when this step is not attended to.

Mary and Tom entered counseling with an accredited marriage counselor for intensive sex therapy. Their objective was to improve their sexual relationship. The counselor felt that he needed to explore the dynamics of their marital relationship, as he believed the underlying problems in the marital relationship were maintaining the sexual dysfunctioning. When Mary and Tom achieved success through some behavioral sexual therapy, they wished to terminate the therapy. They became upset when the counselor suggested they remain in treatment for more intensive marriage counseling. The point is that the helper and the helpees had not clarified the nature and extent of the problem and treatment. Thus, what began as an effective helping relationship ended with confusion and misunderstanding on both sides.

John went to a vocational counselor for tests to help him make a career decision. He was very disturbed when the counselor tried to get him to talk about his personal feelings and lifestyle instead of presenting him with factual results of his interest and aptitude tests. After the third session, he quit and decided to go elsewhere. This is another example where the nature of the problem and approach were not fully clarified.

Ms. Conn agreed to have Sara, age 8, work with a volunteer aide for individualized help. Ms. Conn thought that Sara would receive some academic skills help on reading and arithmetic. The aide was told by the classroom teacher that her objective was to "develop a relationship with Sara to improve her self-concept." The aide played games with

Sara and took her for walks. Sara's social skills improved and she seemed happier in her class, but her mother became angry when she found out that academic tutoring was not occurring and insisted that this relationship terminate. This is still another example when objectives of a helping relationship were not clarified.

Exercise 7-1. Using the preceding three examples, discuss in small groups how you could handle these three cases in a different manner. See if you can act out different approaches and share your feelings and reactions. How can you be sure that the helpee really accepts goals and objectives and is not just trying to please you?

Here is an excerpt illustrating this step:

Lauren was referred to a counselor in May of her senior year in high school. The presenting problems were promiscuity and possible pregnancy (which did not materialize). In the first three sessions, the counselor discovered that Lauren had a very low self-concept, received little, if any, positive feelings from her parents (who were divorced), had no close girl friends despite her popularity and was, in fact, quite the opposite of her outward image of a beautiful, talented, bright "model" teenager. Lauren has just expressed some concerns about going away to college in the fall.

> *Counselor:* You're wondering if you're going to be able to find the kind of friends and relationships you want there without getting into trouble.
>
> *Lauren:* I'm not sure I'll be able to handle difficult situations when they come up. I always get messed up.
>
> *Counselor:* You really don't think much of yourself, do you?
>
> *Lauren:* (laughs nervously) I know . . . it's just that sometimes I try to think so much, I get awfully confused.
>
> *Counselor:* Well, we have eight weeks left before you leave, and we've agreed to meet weekly. How about if we focus on talking about your concerns and situations as they come up and see if we can help you to feel better about yourself before you go away.
>
> *Lauren:* I'm already feeling better since I've been coming in here. I do want to make it on my own next year.

In this case, the counselor and Lauren decided that the major goal would be to increase Lauren's self-confidence and to afford her the opportunity to receive empathy and support from the counselor.

Planning Strategies

Here we go through a phase similar to the decision-making process in that we think of all the possible options and then select the most effective strategy or combination of strategies. The client's participation in this decision making increases the possibilities for successful outcomes. We carefully explain to the helpee the approaches we are considering, their rationale, possible consequences, time and activities involved, and any other pertinent information. If the helpee seems to be resistant to some strategies, we discuss the resistance and then decide together whether to hold off or tentatively to try it out. Some strategies may seem threatening at first but become less so as the helping relationship develops. For example, I often use Gestalt techniques and unless the relationship is well established and the client trusts me and my professional ability, a common response to the suggestion that we engage in a particular Gestalt dialogue or role play is "That's silly; I can't do that." Sometimes helpees become scared away because they do not understand what is going on and strategies have not been adequately explained. If you explain different techniques in a tentative way, the helpee can refuse without losing dignity or self-respect. Thus, timing and your manner of introducing alternative approaches are important variables, as illustrated in the following example.

> *Helper:* We seem to agree that one of the immediate problems you want to work on is to be able to say "no" to people, to see if we can find some other ways for you to feel good about yourself so you won't always have to buy friendship.
>
> *Helpee:* Yeah. My way certainly hasn't worked either.
>
> *Helper:* Evelyn, I wonder if we can do some role playing and practice what you might say to Benny the next time he calls you.
>
> *Helpee:* Sure. What do you mean?
>
> *Helper:* Well, I'll be Benny, and I've called you to have you come up for the weekend. Now what do you really want to say to me?

Here the helper has left the helpee an outlet. The relationship is such that the helpee knows she will not be rejected if she does not go along, but because she believes that the helper knows what she is doing, she is willing to go along and try something new.

Another example can be drawn from the case of Lauren:

Counselor:	Lauren, in addition to talking about you and what's happening in your life, I'd like to ask you to keep a diary. If each night you'll write down all the things that happened that day to make you feel good about yourself, it would be helpful.
Lauren:	I don't know if there'll be any, but I'm willing to try.
Counselor:	We can go over your list when you come in. It might help us both to find out what pleases you. To get started, I'd like you to draw up a list of all the things you like about yourself. You don't have to show it to anyone and you can bring it in next week.
Lauren:	O.K.

The purpose of this "homework assignment" is to help Lauren focus on positive aspects of herself. It also provides some continuity between sessions.

Exercise 7-2. How would you plan strategies for the above two excerpts? Role play the scenes out and create your own cases that you can act out. Discuss in small groups the criteria and reasons for your selections. Remember that there is not just one technique for any one problem. There are times when helpers try something that both parties agree to and it doesn't work very well. If the relationship is effective, no one need lose face and the planning strategies step can be repeated.

Using Strategies

A particular strategy or combination of strategies may be used for short-term or long-term goals. The helper may spontaneously decide to change strategies and this is fine, as long as the helpee knows what is going on and agrees to the change. Often, your intuition sparks appropriate selection of strategies midway through this step. For example, several years ago I was utilizing systematic desensitization with a college physical education student who had a phobic reaction to balloons and who was finding that she needed to be able to tolerate being in the same room with balloons for school affairs. She was an excellent candidate for systematic desensitization and responded beautifully. One day, after a successful session, while she was still relaxed, I asked her to engage in some Gestalt dialogues with balloons. She was equally responsive to this technique and we both learned some important information about her aversion to balloons. I also learned that relaxation facilitates Gestalt dialoguing.

As you gain experience, your self-confidence in the use of strategies increases and you feel more comfortable trying out new techniques. However, do not be afraid to let the helpee know if you are trying something you have not used before. You can say something like "I have a new idea of what we may try and I'm not sure how it will work. Let's try it out and see if it works." Perhaps you can arrange for some supervision or consultation from someone more experienced with a particular strategy. Pretending to be an expert when you're not can backfire and even if it doesn't, it is of questionable ethics. On the other hand, if you restrict yourself to the familiar and comfortable, you won't be able to extend your capabilities. However, for both your and the helpee's benefits, any significant move into new strategies should be accomplished carefully and under the guidance or supervision of someone who is qualified in that particular area.

The amount of time available for a helping relationship is important in the use of strategies. By this I mean both the amount of time for each session and for the entire relationship. It is impossible to say how much of the entire helping relationship is devoted to using strategies—it may be a little, it may be the bulk. It depends on many other variables, the most important being the nature of the problem and your setting. Some strategies can be used in a shorter time span than others; behavioral strategies are relatively short-term, whereas psychoanalytic and client-centered strategies can last indefinitely. It seems that those strategies that lean toward the behavioral domain are more specifically evaluated and easier to limit to a time frame, whereas those strategies that lean toward the affective domain take a longer time for application.

Strategies provide for learning. Coupled with a strong helping relationship, they can powerfully expedite the helpee's feeling, thought, or behavior changes.

Exercise 7-3. The purpose of this exercise is to give you some limited experience in planning and using strategies. In triads, rotate the roles of helper, helpee, and observer. You can choose your settings and circumstances, but assume that both helper and helpee have agreed to one of the following goals for the helping relationship. After selecting an objective, role play it as far as you can. What strategies would you want to use? How would you want to use it?

Agreed upon objectives:

(1) to learn how to make friends of the opposite sex

(2) to get homework assignments in on time and regularly

(3) to learn to get along better with the boss

(4) to decide whether or not to have a baby

(5) to try and control anger when things don't go your way

Assume that you already have an effective relationship. Discuss your choice and use of strategies in small groups.

Evaluating Strategies

Evaluation (judging the effectiveness) is on-going from the beginning of the use of strategies. If at any time both the helper and the helpee feel that the strategies are not effective, it is necessary to review and reassess the situation. However, sometimes it takes a while for something to work and a sensitive helper knows when to apply evaluation criteria.

Evaluation has always been difficult because, except for behavioral strategies, we do not always have observable criteria. Actual behavior changes are the best criteria for evaluating strategies. These behavior changes can be reflections of feeling and thinking changes. If we do not look for behavior changes, we may be fooled by some people who say they feel good because they want to please us. You can always tell if something has been effective by looking at actual behavior. This behavior change does not just occur within the helping relationship; it is also generalized to other situations in the helpee's life. The helpee may report these changes or you may receive feedback from significant others, such as a supervisor, parent, spouse, or teacher. Here again, the effectiveness of the helping relationship is important. You and the helpee can objectively seek criteria for evaluating helping and you can both validate these criteria, rather than to take effectiveness for granted. Time is important because it is realistic to expect some ups and downs during the course of a helping relationship and new behaviors, attitudes, and thoughts take time to become stable.

Based upon the evaluation, the helper may decide to utilize another strategy, work on some other objectives and goals, or terminate. The helpee participates in determining which of these outcomes is selected. The following example demonstrates this step.

> Dr. J. is fifty-two-year-old dentist who came for help when his twenty-two-year-old son dropped out and joined a religious cult. Terribly distressed, Dr. J. didn't understand what went wrong and how this could have happened to his family. The counselor has been utilizing Rational-Emotive techniques and assigning homework to Dr. J. to dispute his irrational ideas. This excerpt is from the ninth session.

Helper:		I'm wondering how things are going at home for you now.
Helpee:		They're beginning to change. Every time I start to think or say that my wife or one of the kids *should* be or do something, I catch myself and shudder at that awful word "should."
Helper:		And what happens?
Helpee:		I don't get so angry anymore. I keep telling myself that everyone doesn't have to be perfect all the time and neither do I. Also, things don't always have to go my way. I'm beginning to believe it.
Helper:		(laughs) Good. You're learning.
Helpee:		Well, my wife says things are much pleasanter and we don't have so much quarreling at the dinner table.

In this case, the helper was checking up on the effectiveness of some strategies and, in addition to learning whether the strategy was working, gaining some insights into future directions of this helping relationship.

Exercise 7-4. The purpose of this exercise is to familiarize you with evaluative criteria. For the following objectives of helping relationships, pick out what you think would be appropriate evaluative criteria. Answers are at the end of the chapter. Discuss your answers and reasons in small groups.

(1) Objective: learning to get along better with coworkers

      Criteria: a. fewer complaints from supervisor
               b. positive report from helpee
               c. your observation of friendlier relationships in department
               d. your observation of helpee in cafeteria engaged in friendly relations with coworkers

(2) Objective: feeling less depressed

      Criteria: a. client improves appearance
               b. client reports feeling better
               c. client reports more involvement in activities
               d. client doesn't cry as much

(3) Objective: increasing self-understanding

      Criteria: a. client reports feeling better
               b. client wants to continue sessions
               c. client talks in sessions with more assurance and confidence
               d. client reports better interpersonal relationships

(4)   Objective: learning to make friends of opposite sex

　　　　Criteria: a. client talks about going to singles' bar
　　　　　　　　　b. client reports making date for tonight
　　　　　　　　　c. client asks if your receptionist is single
　　　　　　　　　d. client says he has struck up conversation with a
　　　　　　　　　　　girl in his class

(5)   Objective: improving marital happiness

　　　　Criteria: a. husband says wife doesn't nag so much anymore
　　　　　　　　　b. clients report they spend more time together
　　　　　　　　　c. clients say their communications are good during
　　　　　　　　　　　counseling sessions
　　　　　　　　　d. clients report they try but never complete home-
　　　　　　　　　　　work exercises

Termination

Evaluation of the results or progress of the application of strategies may lead to termination of the helping relationship. There are three kinds of termination that can occur:

1.　When both the helper and the helpee feel that all objectives have been reached. This is a positive termination, albeit one involving loss and sadness of a meaningful relationship. Sad feelings usually occur in both the helper and the helpee and both may experience some separation anxiety, where they feel sad about the impending loss of a significant other. These feelings can be explored and shared so that both the helper and the helpee can leave each other feeling a real sense of growth and satisfaction that comes from the achievement of objectives. It is important for both parties to have some notice of when the last meeting will occur and to leave enough time to discuss these feelings.

2.　When the helper initiates termination before the objectives have been achieved. This happens often in schools when terms end or in settings where personnel changes frequently and rapidly. In these cases it is essential that the helper let the helpee know in advance of the impending termination and that they both fully explore the feelings aroused by this necessity. The helpee often feels angry and rejected and the helper often feels guilty and uncomfortable. Ideally, the helper effects a positive referral before termination occurs. If you've had an effective relationship with the helpee, it will be that much easier for him or her to work effectively with someone else.

3.　When the helpee terminates a relationship prematurely. The helpee may feel relieved to get away from a threatening situation and the helper may feel useless and inadequate. It is important for the helper really to listen and try to determine whose problem this premature termination is; it might be the helpee's problem if he or she is refusing to work further and chooses avoidance over approach. On the other hand, it might be the helper's problem in that he or she has been unable to develop an effective helping relationship or has selected an inappropriate strategy.

In any of these three kinds of termination, helpers can provide positive support to the helpee concerning his or her decisions and behavior changes while making sure there are no other major concerns at the moment and communicating interest in being of help should there be such need in the future.

Some helpers spread out termination over several weeks. They may lengthen the time between sessions, such as reducing weekly sessions to bi-weekly sessions, then monthly sessions, then one every three months. This has the effect of reducing anxiety and providing follow-up and evaluation while maintaining necessary support. On the other hand, you want to be aware of the possibility of the helpee's dependency needs prolonging the helping relationship. You may need to set some limits in order to avoid reinforcing these dependency needs.

The same conditions that are necessary for the initial contact (encouragement, warmth, focusing on the helpee's needs) are necessary for the final contact. It is allright for you to share your true feelings with helpees and let them know that you will miss them, too. The following is an excerpt from the end of the final session with Lauren.

Helper: You've come a long way this summer.

Helpee: I feel so *good* about myself and I'm looking forward to college. Did I tell you I got the name of my roommate?

Helper: No, but that does make it more real. You're looking forward to making new friends and a new life.

Helpee: I think everything's going to be fine. If I need to, can I come see you?

Helper: Of course, you know how to reach me. Listen, you've worked through some tough situations this summer. We both know you can do it.

Helpee: Yes, that's true. I'm going to miss you.

Helper: I'm going to miss you, too. Let me know how you're doing, O.K.?

Helpee: Sure thing.

The helper leaves the door open, in case the helpee wants to come back at any time and feels free in expressing sadness at the end of the relationship.

Exercise 7-5. Pick someone you feel particularly close to as a partner, someone you have shared with. In pairs, find some place where you can spend some time together and role play helper and helpee roles, with each of you having the opportunity to play each role. Pretend this is the last time you will meet together and see how effectively you can share your real feelings and concerns. What does this remind you of? How do you usually cope with separation anxiety? After you have processed this, join with another pair and continue to process.

Exercise 7-6. This is a Gestalt exercise to get you in touch with feelings of separation anxiety. Take something out of your purse or pocket that is very necessary to you (your wallet, your car or house keys). Put that article under your chair, lean back, and close your eyes. Now imagine that you are not going to retrieve that article and that you need it. Let yourself get in touch with the panicky feelings that emerge. Process this after several minutes of imagining in the same manner as exercise 7-5.

Follow-up

Follow-up is checking to see how the helpee is doing with respect to whatever the problem was sometime after termination has occurred. This is a step that many helpers do not utilize. However, some work settings require formal follow-up by mail or telephone. In other work settings where follow-up is not required, many helpers informally do their own follow-up by dropping in on former helpees to say "hello" and see how everything is or by dropping them a note or by a telephone call.

Here again, the helper must distinguish between genuine follow-up and extension of a helpee's or helper's possible dependency. The purpose of follow-up is to evaluate long-term effects of helping strategies and your effectiveness as a helper. Occasionally follow-up will result in additional helping; in most cases, however, it serves as a genuine evaluating point for both the helper and the helpee. It is a form of recognition that both parties can appreciate, in that it can communicate genuine caring and interest.

I generally telephone former clients six months to a year after termination to let them know I've been thinking of them and am wondering how they are. I leave enough telephone time for them to fill me in on developments in their life and I check to see if they have been able to use what they learned from the helping relationship in other aspects of their lives.

Now that we've briefly discussed each of the steps of the strategies stage of the helping relationship, we'll do an exercise reviewing all six of them before going on to our discussion of crisis intervention.

Exercise 7-7. The purpose of this exercise is for you to recognize the different steps of the strategies stage. From which step do you think each of the following was excerpted? The answers are at the end of the chapter.

(1) *Helper:* Hello, Mr. Witkins. This is Mr. ____ calling. How are you?

Helpee: Oh! . . . I'm fine, thank you. How are you?

Helper: I guess you're surprised to hear from me. I've been thinking about you and was wondering how everything is going.

Helpee: Well, everything is real O.K. I've been working since March and I really like it . . . in the accounting office of _____ Associates. The hours and pay are better than the last job and I'm home to help out more after supper with the kids.

Helper: You and Ms. Witkins getting out together more now?

Helpee: Oh, yes. We make a point of going out alone once a week. And we're beginning to have company in now, too. Things really have been better since I found the new job. And I have to thank you for seeing me through that rough period.

Helper: Well, I'm glad I called. Hope things continue to go well for you. Regards to your wife.

Helpee: Thanks. Appreciate your calling.

(2) *Helpee:* I'm really in a bind. There's no place for the old man to go. We can't afford a home and Jim's brother is out of the country and I'm just stuck, that's all.

Helper: Let's focus on what we can do to make this situation tolerable for you and your family. Since, as you say, your father-in-law's residing with you is a given. . . .

Helpee: Yes, I need to learn not to react so much, not to get so upset every time he says or does anything. I know it's not good for Jim and the children, but I just can't help myself.

Helper: O.K. We'll focus on the home situation before we think about your ideas of getting a job.

(3)	*Helper:*	How'd you do on your last math test?
	Helpee:	I passed it! And my homework assignments are O.K.
	Helper:	Do you feel you're meeting the terms of the contract?
	Helpee:	There was one day I didn't do my work. I just went without watching TV. I didn't like that, though, because the next day my friend Jeff told me I missed a great game.
	Helper:	What are you going to do about that?
	Helpee:	I'm not going to miss anymore.
(4)	*Helper:*	It sounds to me like somebody once told you when you were a kid that it's not O.K. to cry.
	Helpee:	I never cry. Yes, I remember something happened when I was very little, around four or maybe even three.
	Helper:	I'd like to try a role play with you that may get us in touch with that early decision. O.K.?
	Helpee:	Sure.
	Helper:	Now be that little girl and tell me what happened.
	Helpee:	I left my doll carriage on the driveway and my dad ran over it when he came home that night.
	Helper:	Go on.
	Helpee:	I cried . . . and he came up to me and hit me . . . and he said I'll show you what happens to little girls who leave their doll carriage on the driveway and cry. And he took the doll off the driveway—it was a raggedy type of doll—and he tore her apart and threw her away.
	Helper:	And you decided never to cry again.
	Helpee:	(crying) Poor little girl.
	Helper:	(throwing her a large cushion) This is your dad. Be that little girl and tell him what you want to tell him.
(5)	*Helper:*	We have only two more sessions together. I'm wondering how you feel about that.
	Helpee:	Well in a way I'm glad and in a way I'm not sure. I think I'm doing much better. I don't get stoned

> anymore. But every now and then, I get scared . . . and lonely. I think I'll take your suggestion and join that group you were telling me about.

Helper: We can use the next two sessions to talk more about that, if you'd like.

(6) *Helper:* What often works in cases like yours is what we call systematic desensitization. Have you ever heard of it?

Helpee: No.

Helper: It's a form of counterconditioning. I can teach you how to relax each of your muscle groups and, when you're able to master that, we begin to imagine all aspects of flying while you're relaxed. It's impossible to be anxious and relaxed at the same time and this is a technique that can be used whenever you're anxious. I have a paper you can read about it.

Helpee: How long does it take?

Helper: It usually takes about three sessions for relaxation, and then somewhere between ten and fifteen sessions for desensitization. I often use other strategies along with desensitization, but we can see as we go along.

Helpee: I'm willing to try.

CRISIS INTERVENTION

Crisis intervention can be defined as those skills and strategies that helpers use when an unexpected happening of potentially harmful proportions occurs. This can happen at any time during or outside of a helping relationship. Crises are not usually predictable or expected. Crisis intervention is what takes place after a traumatic occurrence and it may range from just being available for immediate contact or support to initiating intensive treatment or therapy. It is usually an approach to helping relationships that is distinct and separate from the model developed in this text, although the same communications skills are used.

Kinds of Crises

Crises can be precipitated by such occurrences as bad drug trips, an alcoholic binge, rape, suicide threats or attempts, acute bereavement over the loss of a significant other, shock reaction to bad news, loss of job, psychotic episodes, discovery of an unwanted pregnancy, a severe marital fight, abandonment, or learning that you or an intimate has a terminal illness. Although these examples of crisis are not necessarily equivalent in terms of severity or magnitude, they may all produce equal amounts of stress and "psychological disequilibrium." A person's perceptions and judgments of the crisis are what helpers work with, not the actual event itself. How a person responds and reacts to crisis depends on past learning and experiences (how one has reacted to meeting minor crises throughout childhood and adolescence), lifestyles, and life philosophy.

For example, a volunteer rape counselor reported that she had two married women in their forties with similar educational and socioeconomic backgrounds report for crisis counseling the same night. The situations were so alike that the police suspected the assailant was the same in both cases. One victim collapsed hysterically and required intensive care and counseling, missing work for two weeks. The other victim required factual information about police and court procedures before driving herself home (twenty miles), having a drink with her husband while she related the details of her assault, going to bed, and reporting for work the next morning. Neither reaction is "better" or "more normal" than the other. These two women had different histories, philosophies, and coping and defense mechanisms. They needed different amounts of time and types of help in working through their feelings about this crisis.

Who Deals with Crises?

Police, friends, pastors, family, or physicians are usually the first to be alerted to a crisis. They, in turn, usually bring in the counselor or human services worker to help in direct problem solving and working through the feelings associated with the crisis.

Crisis intervention is considered a legitimate human service these days and two types are prevalent: (1) hot lines, drop-in centers, and crisis clinics where victims can come in person or telephone twenty-four hours a day and (2) outreach counseling, where helpers go to the victim to provide immediate support and comfort as soon as they are notified of the crisis. Crisis intervention settings are usually staffed by volunteers who undergo intensive, short-term, on-the-job training. They may or may not be supervised by professional helpers.

Hot lines, Drop-in Centers, Crisis Clinics Helpers working through hot lines, drop-in centers, and crisis clinics, deal with suicide, drug, runaway, rape, alcoholic, and abortion crises, to name a few, and the helpers are taught specialized knowledge about these issues. For example, a drug counselor knows the names of commonly used drugs, the effects of these drugs and the duration of these effects, and how to help the user with a bad trip. The suicide counselor knows how to recognize suicide threats, has studied factual information and statistics (as separate from myth) about suicide, and is aware of different interventions, such as providing a network of supporters for the victim during the crisis, helping the victim and his or her family to change behaviors to alleviate the crisis, and helping the victim gain a different perspective of the crisis and situation precipitating suicide.

In these settings, helpers sometimes only get one or two shots at working with the victim. Therefore they must be skillful at establishing empathic relationships and providing accurate information and alternative options to the victims, all within a short period of time. Contact is important—whether over the telephone or in person. This contact does not know the boundaries of time and may involve helpers working overtime or continuing contact by telephone or by effecting immediate referrals.

Outreach Counseling The outreach form of crisis intervention occurs when the helpers go to the crisis victim rather than wait for the victim to come to them. This is a relatively new concept in human services and is based on the "visiting nurse" concept, where primary care is taken to the client in the client's own setting. The advantage of this is that the helper is able to see the victim in a familiar habitat and to draw upon immediate available resources, such as family and neighbors. In addition, the helper is able to provide direct assistance in immediate problem solving (e.g., what to do with the children in the case of a parental accident, talk down a drug victim on a bad trip in a familiar setting, or arrange for immediate medical care).

Outreach counseling usually involves more time and cost than other types of counseling and perhaps this is why so little of it exists. The time that the outreach worker spends traveling to and from clients is time not used for helping.

The outreach counselor feels comfortable in different settings and is not bound by the clock or site. Some are on twenty-four-hour call and think nothing of accompanying clients to the welfare or employment office or obtaining legal, educational, and health care. They engage in recreational and leisure time activities with clients, know how to break up fights, deal with implosive violence, and have learned to establish trusting relationships in the most suspicious climates. Research (as limited as it is) has shown that the best outreach counselors are those recruited from and trained within the communities where they will work. They are in touch with the mores and lifestyles of their neighbors and can more easily overcome distrust and suspicion.

Outreach counseling requires unlimited patience and dedication. Crisis intervention is only one part of outreach counseling, which occurs throughout the community—on the streets, in pubs, houses, schools, centers, on playgrounds. This is an action type of counseling that requires active participation in the life of the community. In addition, empathic listening skills are crucial for establishing and maintaining relationships within the community.

Skills for Crisis Intervention

In crises, helpers' abilities to remain calm in an emergency, to use common sense, and to project self-confidence are important. Helpers rely greatly on their responsive listening communications skills both to get at the nature of the crisis and its stressful ramifications and also to communicate comfort, support, and respect to the helpee.

In addition to responsive listening, physical gestures such as holding hands, putting an arm around someone's shoulders, and holding someone close communicate caring and concern. Except in the case of loss, it is important to differentiate between empathy and sympathy, as the latter can impede recovery from a crisis by fostering prolonged dependence. One way to do this is to focus on what can be done about the crisis rather than repeating over and over again the details of the actual crisis situation. In other words, focusing on action rather than talking about what happened is more conducive to recovery from a crisis after the initial ventilation period, during which the crisis victim describes in great detail the actual crisis. Focusing on the helpee's past and current strengths and positive experiences helps to emphasize the positive rather than the negative and encourages helpees' faith in their capacities to recover.

At the same time that the helpers are communicating comfort, support, and respect to crisis victims, they may need to take some kind of direct action. They may physically have to prevent someone from hurting him or herself or others; seek medical help; actively recruit networks of family, friends, or neighbors to stay with the helpee until the crisis has passed; arrange for some kind of immediate placement (e.g., in a hospital or shelter); talk to people involved in the crisis situation to alleviate the cause of stress for the victim; or arrange for burial and insurance benefits. Crisis victims are often unable to take these actions themselves and need to feel they can depend on others for a short while.

The dependency of a crisis victim on the crisis helper is accepted by the helper until such time that the victim is ready for a referral or for taking over for him or herself. The counselor may need to keep in contact with and share information with others involved with the helpee in order to reach this stage of readiness and to provide other supportive people for the crisis victim.

Reactions to crises involving loss, such as divorce and death, have distinct stages, as noted by Krantzler (1973) and Kubler-Ross (1969). The initial reaction is one of shock and denial. The feeling is "this can happen to others, but not to *me*." Helpers provide empathic support during this stage. As the denial fades, anger results and helpers often receive some of the fallout from this anger. Acceptance and then coping occur when the helpee can remobilize coping strengths and resources and begin to plan and implement action leading to recovery.

Another skill utilized by crisis workers in certain types of situations is that of confrontation, where the helper faces the helpee with discrepancies or ramifications of the crisis situation in order to stimulate immediate action of some kind. An example of this is when a helper said to a remorseful alcoholic who had beaten his wife while on a binge: "It's hard for you to control your temper when you drink. Now your wife is in the hospital and she is thinking about pressing charges. In any case, she says she'll take the children and leave this time. It seems to me that you have to decide what you want to do about your drinking. If you want to keep your family, you'll have to deal with it. Let's go over the options you have." In a sense, this helper is telling the helpee to "shape up or ship out." Often a kind of "shock treatment" confrontation such as this is necessary to help get someone off dead center and begin to move in some direction.

In crisis situations, time is often a crucial variable and helpers do not have the luxury of waiting to build up long-term helping relationships before attempting problem solving. Therefore, confrontation sometimes occurs earlier in crisis intervention than in other forms of helping. However, it is possible to be empathic and confronting at the same time; one's tone of voice, body posture, and facial expressions can differentiate between a hostile confrontation and a constructive one. A constructive confrontation is not merely critical; it includes acknowledgment of the helpee's strengths and ability to choose a course of action. When using confrontation, it is vital that you do so for the helpee's benefit, not to let off your own steam, prove your superiority, or impose your will. In other words, the confrontation can be assertive rather than aggressive and be in line with your helping objectives.

Knowledge

In addition to the knowledge required about specific types of crises (e.g., drugs, alcohol, child abuse, suicide), human services workers involved in crisis intervention need to become thoroughly familiar with the sociological, economic, and cultural characteristics of the community in which they are working and the available resource within the community. Knowledge about the community, resources and available services are needed to effect significant referrals, especially when time is of the essence. Following are two examples of crisis intervention.

> Betty, a nineteen-year-old university student, came to see me unexpectedly. I had met her once, when she accompanied her roommate to my office; but I had had no direct contact with her. She was in obvious distress and incoherently blurted out that she had some pills and was seriously thinking about taking them because she "didn't want to live anymore." I immediately notified my secretary to hold all calls and appointments and spent the next couple of hours talking with her. She told me that her fiance and brother had been killed in an automobile accident six weeks before and that she just couldn't get over it. She didn't feel she had anything to live for. She cried . . . I held her . . . we went over her loss and her anger at being left alone over and over again. Finally, when she was completely exhausted, I asked her if she thought we could work together to find some meaning in her life. When she tearfully agreed, I pushed for some commitment: would she give me the pills and promise not to do anything to herself until I could see her the next day at 3:30? I asked her to look me in the eye and promise that much. It took some time for her to be able to do that. I then suggested that it might be helpful for her to have some friends help her. She said that she had friends here, including her roommate, but she had tried to keep her grief from them. I secured permission from her to telephone her roommate and to arrange for constant companionship until our next appointment. This was arranged to everyone's satisfaction. The next day, Betty felt that the crisis was over and that we could begin to meet regularly to work this through without fear of suicide. Whether or not Betty's threats were legitimate is not important. I would never ignore such a threat nor discount it and I do not leave clients until I have secured commitment that they will not harm themselves.

> Phil, nineteen years old, came into a neighborhood drop-in center obviously distraught. He had smoked something "very strong" and was terrified by his reactions. He was experiencing a lot of disconnectedness and fear. His eyes were watery and he kept looking around as if he expected someone to pounce on him. The helper, who had some experience in drug counseling, sat with Phil and talked quietly. He explained to Phil that his reaction was temporary; that it was due to the drug, not to some incipient insanity; that many people experience the same reactions; and that, in fact, these reactions are positive and thrilling for some. In a calm, soothing tone, the helper talked with Phil for over an hour, until Phil became calmer. Then he was given a cool drink and allowed to rest until he felt better. Several hours later Phil felt well enough to go home by himself. Note that there was no moralizing, punishing, or judging. The helper communicated empathy and demonstrated calm, confident behavior.

CASE STUDIES

Two brief case studies will now be presented to show how counseling progresses through the relationship and strategies stages. These two case studies have been selected to illustrate different types of strategies. The names and identifying information have been changed to protect the clients' identities.

Case of Ms. S.

General Description and Presenting Information: Ms. S., age forty-eight, was referred to this counselor by her counselor at an outpatient clinic of a state hospital because her counselor was leaving the state. Ms. S. had been in and out of treatment for ten years, although she had never been hospitalized. She was diagnosed as being depressed with phobic reactions. For ten years, she had refused to leave her home except with her husband, a truck route driver for a large baking firm. Thus, all her marketing, shopping, and errands were done with her husband, who worked an early shift and was home by 4 PM. Ms. S. lived in a lower-middle-class neighborhood with her mother (age eighty-two), her husband (age fifty-two), and her twenty-two-year-old retarded son. At this particular time, a crisis had arisen because Mr. S. was being transferred to another route, which would involve him in work all day and not leave time for marketing at Ms. S.'s favorite small markets.

Session I: Mr. S. drove Ms. S. to the session and arrived a few minutes late. He waited outside in the car. Ms. S. apologized for being late, took a while to get comfortable, and then sat primly with her hands folded on her lap. As she seemed to expect to be questioned and as I already had background information, I asked her to tell me about what she had been doing all day. **(Initiation/Entry)** Very slowly, she told me about her sewing, her cleaning, and the time her son and mother took. Her great joy and pride in life is her cooking and she is very fussy about the foods she buys and what she cooks. She refuses to shop in supermarkets; she has known the vendors where she markets for years and can depend upon them for fresh, quality produce, cheeses, and meats. On Sundays the highlight of the week occurs—her daughter and son come for dinner with their families.
(Counselor's comments: Ms. S. is neat, nicely groomed, and pleasant to talk with. She does not express much animation and she talks very slowly and carefully. It took about an hour to get the above data.)

Session II: Ms. S. continued to talk about her family and cooking. She described in great detail the past Sunday—the foods and the sayings of her grandchildren, who are quite young. **(Clarification of Problem)** Toward the middle of this session we began to talk about her fear of leaving the house. She cannot remember the onset of this fear and she cannot clarify what she is afraid of. She seems to think it happened gradually and that it was nothing to get upset about. However, when I reminded her that her husband was starting a new route in a few days, she became agitated (her fingers started to play with each other and she licked her lips a lot). She then explained that she lives about eight blocks, less than a mile, from the markets and that, if her husband comes straight home from work and there is no traffic, maybe they can still make it. I asked her if she thought she would be physically able to walk that distance and she replied that sometimes on spring and fall weekends she takes walks longer than that with her husband and their son.

Session III: **(Structure/Contract)** After a few minutes of being caught up on Ms. S.'s household chores, I asked her if she would be interested in learning to be able to walk to the markets alone, to get her food. **(Exploration of Problem)** She said she didn't think she would be able to do that and we spent the entire session talking about the pros and cons. **(Possible Goals)** I suggested that we take no more than ten sessions to try it out and see if we could together enable her to overcome her fear. We went over and over the consequences of her not being able to market where she wanted to, of her husband's new routes, of maintaining the status quo. Toward the end of the session we returned to less anxiety-provoking events and she proceeded to tell me about some outfits she is making for her granddaughter.

Session IV: This session began with some more relationship discussion about my perceptions and feelings toward her and resulted in her expressing pleasure at our meetings. **(Mutual Acceptance of Goals)** We then talked about her agreeing to focus on the behaviors of being able to go out of the house alone and walk to the market, shop, and return home. **(Planning of Strategies)** She agreed to give "my way" a chance and I described a step-by-step behavioral procedure to her whereby I would come to her house each day for the next twelve days and if she was able to meet the directives for the day, I would take her marketing and/or take her to her daughter's house for a visit. When she agreed, we asked Mr. S. to come into the office, explained the procedure to him, and asked him not, under any circumstances, to market for Ms. S. or take her marketing. He agreed and Ms. S. agreed (but with reservations).

Intervention Period: The following ten-day-period consisted of graduated steps. A summary of these steps follows:

Day 1: **(Use of Strategies)** Ms. S. put on hat and coat and came to front door and walked downstairs. I said that she did not have to go any farther than that and I asked her if she wanted to go marketing with me. She said "no," she was "too nervous"; but she was pleased when I offered to go to the bakery for her and get her some of her favorite pastries (which Mr. S. had told me about).

Day 2: Ms. S. was able to walk to curb with me. During this walk, I talked calmly to her, urged her to take long, deep breaths. When we got to curb, we returned to house and I went to the butcher for her and picked up her order.

Day 3: The goal was to walk down the block to where my car was parked. When we got to the next house, Ms. S. said she was dizzy and wanted to return home. We did so. No reinforcement. I left immediately, not wanting to reinforce her with my company.

Day 4: Ms. S. expressed concern about "letting me down yesterday." As I reassured her, we left the house and we were half-way down the block before she realized where we were. She was pleased and surprised and, as we were by my car, she agreed to be driven to market. She said she was out of produce and she had been "worried sick" about how she would manage.

Days 5-8: Each day, Ms. S. was waiting for my arrival with her hat and coat on and each day we furthered our walk until Day 8, when, together, we reached the market, filled the cart with groceries, and walked home together. This called for a celebration; and we called Ms. S.'s daughter, who came over for a visit bringing the favorite grandchild. Ms. S. reported that she was so busy talking that she had not been nervous or afraid, even when crossing the 'streets.

Day 9: **(Evaluation of Strategies)** I waited for Ms. S. half-way to the markets. She arrived at the appointed time and we proceeded to the market together. She had a longer list today, as it was her son-in-law's birthday.

Day 10: Ms. S. was able to come alone to the market, where I met her. We returned home together and her daughter joined us for lunch. We agreed to add two more days to this period.

Day 11: (following a weekend) I phoned Ms. S. and told her that I would be at her home waiting for her when she returned from the market. She was about ten minutes later than I, and she explained that the produce trucks were slow in being unloaded. She was out of breath, but in good spirits and very busy bustling about the kitchen.

Day 12: Repeat of Day 11.

Sessions V & VI: **(Evaluation)** These were short sessions held in Ms. S.'s home (her husband was no longer able to drive her to my office). We discussed what had happened and her feelings. It was very hard for her to talk about her feelings, but she appeared to be O.K. and had much to report about her family and cooking.

Session VII and Session VIII: **(Evaluation/Termination)** These sessions occurred at two-week intervals and consisted of checking things out and discussing forthcoming termination. Ms. S. was continuing to do her own marketing, although she did not leave the house for any other reason, except with her husband.

Session IX: **(Termination)** This session occurred three weeks after session VIII. We talked about what we had accomplished and I asked her whether she thought she might want to go out alone for purposes other than marketing. She wasn't sure about that and seemed reluctant to discuss it. As we had fulfilled our contract with each other, I did not pursue the matter.

Session X: **(Follow-up)** This session occurred six weeks after session IX. Ms. S. was still totally involved in her family, household, and culinary efforts. She accepts her husband's changed route now that she can market herself, but she has not made any attempts or expressed any interest in expanding her independence out of doors.

Discussion: The objective of being able to leave the house to market was accomplished. At the time of follow-up, there was no generalization of this to other situations, but it could be that there was no reason or motivation for Ms. S. to go other places alone, since her family readily came to visit her, as did neighbors and friends. No attempt was made to resolve depression or underlying causes of phobic behavior.

Case of Martha

General Description and Presenting Information: Martha, age thirty, entered counseling to find out whether or not she wanted to have a baby. She's been married for eight years and reports a relatively happy marriage. She's an elementary school teacher with many activities and interests and Bill, her husband, is a middle-level research scientist in an industrial laboratory. They have never tried to have a baby, but what precipitated this entrance into counseling was a chance remark by Martha's physician during her annual check-up to the effect that if Martha and Bill were going to have children, they ought to think about getting started.

Session I: Martha arrived early for her appointment and was eager to talk about herself. **(Initiation/Entry)** She told me that she is the second of four daughters from a traditional Jewish middle-class background. She recalls a relatively placid, happy childhood, although she remembers a lot of squabbling between the sisters. Her lingering impression is of an all-female, matriarchal home. Her father seemed almost nonexistent and Martha was vague in her references to him. Martha was an above average student, although not as academically gifted as her older sister. She was easygoing, anxious to please, and easily led by others.

   Her older sister went to a prestige college, but Martha attended the state university, where she maintained a B– average and where she dated a moderate amount. She met Bill during her senior year and they were married right after graduation. She has been teaching ever since (fourth grade) and she says she likes teaching and maintains a well-organized, well-run classroom. She does express disdain at parents and teachers who don't know how to "control and discipline" children. Martha supported Bill while he studied for his master's degree. They live in a two-bedroom apartment in a suburb now. When they got married, they did not discuss having children, as they decided that was a long way off.

Martha described Bill as "quiet," "introverted," "a loner." They don't see too much of each other as she has her women's group, her art class, and her cards group during the week. However, on Saturday nights they either have company or go out. Sundays are for visiting families, who live nearby.

Martha was "shocked" at her doctor's comment. She had no idea she'd have to start thinking about children. A friend suggested she come for counseling and she eagerly accepted that suggestion. (Counselor's comments: Martha is attractive, bright, and very outspoken. She was eager to talk and speaks rapidly and egocentrically [practically every statement begins with "I"]. Near the end of the session, I asked her about Bill and she seemed genuinely startled. She does not know how Bill feels about having children, but she has decided that she needs to figure out how she feels first before she discusses it with him. She definitely does not want him to come to counseling with her.)

Session II: Martha arrived early again, but she seemed a little subdued, her rate of speech was slower and she was more reflective. **(Clarification of Problem)** She described her eight years of marriage as if she were relating an article from a women's magazine, with little affect. She talked about their different interests—she likes to keep busy, always doing things and doing them as perfectly as possible, to be with people, go to cultural events; Bill's idea of fun is reading a mystery novel or watching TV. While he's watching TV the evenings she's at home, she is usually reading and correcting papers. She has pretty high expectations of her students and writes long comments on their papers.

We discussed her feelings about children: no one she knows is happy with their children; too much work; being trapped and tied down; she'd hate to give up teaching, yet she wouldn't dream of working with young children; it seems like such a burden. The only positive reason she could think of was that "it's the thing to do" and that "it would please our parents." She said that Bill doesn't really care—"he wants what will make me happy."

The session concluded with Martha agreeing to keep a diary containing all the thoughts, feelings, and observations she has or makes about children during the week.

(Counselor's comments: The fact that she's come for counseling is the only behavioral evidence that there is a positive side to her feelings about having children. There seems to be some anger and fear underneath the bright exterior.)

Session III: Martha produced her diary for the week, which elaborated her ambivalences. **(Clarification)** On the one hand she's afraid that if she decides not to have children, she'll regret it when it's too late and on the other hand she has many "shoulds" in her head that she's afraid of, such as "I should have children because it is expected of me.", "If I have children, they should be perfect.", "If I have children, I should stop teaching and stay home and be the perfect mother." We spent much time talking about these beliefs and what they mean to Martha and the feelings behind them. She has great difficulty experiencing her own feelings. She can talk about, but not experience them.

(Structure/Contract) We decided to set up seven more sessions, one per week, to see where we can go. Martha agreed to continue her diary and to read some books that I've selected for her.
(Counselor's comments: Slowly but surely, she's becoming a little less guarded and more relaxed. She's not trying to impress me so much. Less talk about all her activities and achievements and today she expressed some genuine feeling [compassion] for one of her students.)

Session IV: (Exploration) We talked about where Martha got some of her beliefs and what kinds of things occurred in her childhood to reinforce these beliefs. As she talked about her mother expecting her to live up to her older sister and to keep on trying harder, she began to get in touch with some anger. (Use of Strategies) I explained the TA ego states to her and she decided she had definitely been an "adapted child." Using some Gestalt strategies, I encouraged her to experience the anger and she did remarkably well for the first attempt.

Sessions V & VI: (Exploration and Possible Goals) We decided to focus on Martha's feelings about herself and her self-understanding, rather than the decision making about children. (Mutual Acceptance of Goals) It became apparent that there is much material to work through before a decision can be made. Martha decided that she really doesn't like herself very much and that she hides behind lots of activities and fast talk. (Counselor's comments: She seems somewhat relieved, although anxious, that she doesn't have to play "perfect games" anymore and that she can say and do what she feels like here.)

Sessions VII - X: (Planning of Strategies) In these sessions, I explained how we could use some Rational-Emotive, Gestalt, and Transactional Analysis techniques to help her get in touch with and understand her feelings and beliefs. She agreed and easily got into dialoguing, developing fantasies, and so forth.

Martha came into the ninth session disturbed by the anger she's feeling toward her family. She finds now she's feeling angry every time she speaks to or thinks of them. (Use of Strategies) We emphasized that it is O.K. to be angry and that she will be able to work it through once she allows herself to feel it. During a dialogue session with her imagined mother, some anger spilled over to her father and Bill, both of whom she sees as "passive," "almost not there." We spent the rest of the ninth and all of the tenth sessions dealing with the anger toward men. (Recontracting) At the end of the tenth session, we agreed to meet for five more sessions.

Sessions XI-XIV: We continued intense exploration and working through of anger and early script decision vowed always to try harder.

(**Use of Strategies**) Each session ends with a behavioral contract for the interval between sessions, such as talking to Bill about a particular feeling or doing something that is fun and enjoyable. The contract after session XIII was to tell both families that they would not visit that Sunday because they were going to spend the day together alone. Session XIV, Martha came in glowing: she had had a wonderful day with Bill and they had really talked for the first time in years. (**Evaluation**) She says she is seeing and hearing things she never saw or heard before, one such thing being Bill's caring for her and wanting her to stop running around so much and to pay more attention to him.

Session XV: This is the final session contracted for. (**Termination**) Martha says that she wants to feel her own way from here on and that she believes over the next few months she and Bill will be able to decide about having children. She feels good knowing that whatever they do decide will be fine for them and she agreed that she is now able to balance the scales a bit by seeing and looking for people who enjoy having children.

Three month follow-up: Martha reports over the telephone that although they still have not made a final decision with regard to children, they are getting there. She reports that she is able to continue to refute her "crazy" beliefs and that she is able to relax and to enjoy Bill's company more. She thinks that one day they will both want to come in for some counseling together, as she knows there are marital issues they can be helped with.

Discussion: You will note that I use bibliotherapy (the assigning of pertinent reading material) and weekly homework assignments regularly. I find that these behavioral strategies go hand-in-hand with more experiential strategies used in sessions. In this case, it was important not to rush into decision making but to take the time to explore underlying dynamics of the presenting concerns.

Overall Discussion

The steps of the human relations counseling model are almost cyclical, in that they flow freely and often you go back one or two steps and then return. This is not a systems model, but one could diagram it systematically using feedback loops. In any case, the purpose of presenting these two case studies was to illustrate the steps involved in the counseling process, not to discuss different strategies or diagnostic procedures.

SUMMARY

In this chapter we have discussed the six steps of the strategies stage (acceptance of defined goals and objectives, planning strategies, using strategies, evaluating strategies, termination, and follow-up).

Then we dealt with crisis intervention techniques. Although crisis intervention usually involves a helping approach different from the model developed in this book, communications skills are still paramount. Two types of crisis intervention prevail: one is where helpees go to the helpers (telephone hot lines, drop-in centers, crisis clinics) and the other is where helpers go to the helpees (outreach counseling).

We've presented two case studies to illustrate the steps of the human relations counseling model. Remember that these steps are not necessarily clear and discrete. Each case is different and flexibility and modification are encouraged.

It is essential to emphasize that the effectiveness of the strategies stage depends upon the quality of the relationship stage, as demonstrated in the case studies. Thus, the strategies stage steps can only be viewed within the context of the empathic helping relationship.

EXERCISE ANSWERS

Exercise 7-4. (1) c and d
(2) a, c, and also d
(3) c, d
(4) b, d
(5) a, b

Exercise 7-7. (1) Follow-up
(2) Mutual Acceptance of Objectives
(3) Evaluation
(4) Use of Strategies
(5) Termination
(6) Planning of Strategies

REFERENCES AND FURTHER READINGS

Ausubel, D. *Drug Addiction: Physiological, Psychological and Sociological Aspects.* New York: Random House, 1958.

Farber, M. *A Theory of Suicide.* New York: Funk and Wagnalls, 1968.

Feifel, H. *The Meaning of Death.* New York: McGraw-Hill, 1959.

Laurie, P. *Drugs.* Baltimore, Md.: Penguin, 1967.

Lester, G., and Lester, D. *Suicide.* Englewood Cliffs, N.J.: Prentice-Hall, 1971.

Lieb, J.; Lipsitch, I.; and Slaby, A. *The Crisis Team: A Handbook for the Mental Health Professional.* New York: Harper and Row, 1973.

Krantzler, M. *Creative Divorce.* New York: Evans, 1973.

Kubler-Ross, E. *On Death and Dying.* New York: Crowell Collier and Macmillan, 1969.

Parad, H. *Crisis Intervention: Selected Readings.* New York: Family Service Association of America, 1965.

CHAPTER 8

ISSUES
AFFECTING
HELPING

Understanding the two dimensions of the helping relationship model, the *skills* utilized and the *stages* followed, is not sufficient by itself to understand the entire helping process. Underlying these skills and stages in helping people are our own individual values and points of view, represented by the third dimension, issues. Unless recognized, these issues can seriously hamper our usefulness as helpers.

There are several issues that are critical in any human relationship. Consider that most of us choose our friends, those with whom we can relate easily and feel free to share our true feelings and beliefs. We enjoy being around people with similar value systems. Fortunately, we have the freedom to choose who will be our friends and we can choose not to associate with others. Helping relationships are different in that we are not always able to choose who will come to us for help, to choose with whom we will work. If we can work only with those people who share our values, it is fair that we acknowledge this to prospective employers and employees, as we will be unable to develop effective helping relationships with those who do not share our values. Values, beliefs, and ideology can have positive or negative effects on helping relationships. It is necessary to explore this to raise our own self-awareness and become more aware of our impact on those with whom we work.

There are many societal, professional, and personal issues that affect helping relationships. It is not the scope of this book to explore these issues in depth, but it is important to make future helpers aware of some of them. Some consciousness-raising exercises for you to do in groups are also presented in this chapter. There is a reading list at the end of the chapter that will allow you to study these issues further.

VALUES

What are those values that impact a helping relationship? Our attitudes and feelings about kinds of people, what is "good" or "bad," what is acceptable or unacceptable, what is important for choices, and all those questions we considered in chapter 5 lay the foundation for our value system. Our beliefs underlie our values; examining and reconsidering our beliefs can help us clarify our values.

The "traditional" models of helping maintained that if helping relationships were objective, distant, and neutral, the helper's values and beliefs would not contaminate the relationship. However, in recent years we have recognized that in any interpersonal relationship, whether or not it is a helping relationship, values are transmitted either covertly or overtly between the participants.

Thus, it is necessary for helpers to become aware of their own value systems in order to aid helpees in clarifying their value systems. The important point is that if you are aware of your own values, you are less likely to impose them covertly on others. By being aware of your own value system, you can "lay it out" on the table and declare your values as *your* values. You also will become more aware of other people's value systems, and this helps you understand and accept differences between your value system and others' value systems. Discussion of your values and the helpee's values can enhance the helping relationship if genuineness and empathy are operating. Trying to change another person's value system is fraught with dangers, but helpers can make clients aware of their own values in order to increase their self-understanding and ability to make effective choices.

"Values clarification" is a systematic, seven-step approach developed by Simon, Howe, and Kirschenbaum (1972, p. 19) that helps people process their values through structured exercises. They define a value as involving seven steps:

1. prizing and cherishing one's beliefs and behaviors
2. publicly affirming, when appropriate, one's beliefs and behaviors
3. choosing one's beliefs and behaviors from alternatives
4. choosing one's beliefs and behaviors from alternatives after consideration of consequences

5. choosing one's beliefs and behaviors freely

6. acting on one's beliefs

7. acting on one's beliefs with a pattern, consistency, and repetition

The strategies developed by Simon, et al. are designed for use in groups and classrooms, but they can be modified and used in one-to-one situations. Helpers have found their principles and concepts important for their own self-awareness and for helping others develop awareness of their value systems. Discussion of values is a form of teaching and provides information and alternative viewpoints. This differs from the imposition of values, which indicates that there is a "right" view to adopt.

Values are often confused or hidden in areas such as family, money, politics, religion, work, race, authority, culture, personal tastes, and time structure. Confusion of these values usually results in interpersonal difficulties, the major reason that many people seek help from agencies and institutions. Moreover, if helpers are uneasy about their values in any one of these areas, they may deliberately and subtly avoid these areas in helping relationships. For example, if you find that you never seem to get around to talking about sexuality with helpees who are involved in sexual relationships, you might ask yourself what's going on and whose problem it is. You may find that you, not the helpee, are uneasy about discussing sexuality.

In order for helpers to create the necessary empathic conditions for an effective helping relationship, they must be able to accept people with different value systems. This can create quite a dilemma for you as a helper. How can you be genuine and nonjudgmental at the same time with someone whose values you really dislike? How can you acknowledge the dignity and worth of an individual with whose actions, values, and ideology you disagree?

Accepting people means that you respect them as dignified, worthy individuals. It means that they have as much integrity and right to be alive as any other human being. This does not mean that you have to accept their behavior or concur with their values. This also does not mean that you cannot feel and express anger and disagreement when it is appropriate. It does mean that you can tolerate differences, ambiguity, and uncertainty, that you can accept that what is right or good for one person may not be right or good for another.

Responsive listening and sending "I messages" can help you communicate respect for the person as a worthwhile human being, your own personal values and views without imposing them, and your genuine feelings and reactions. In this way, the helper aids helpees in learning to acknowledge and evaluate their own values. By sharing values with helpees, we may be adding options and alternative values for them to consider. By the same token, we may gain insight into our own value systems. An example of this occurred recently in my office when a couple came in for marriage counseling.

Counselor:	Can you try and tell me what you see as the worst problems in this marriage?
Husband:	Yes, that's easy. She's out fooling around with her art groups all the time and the house is a mess. I don't have clean socks and underwear in the morning and dinner is never ready on time.
Wife:	You never say anything nice to me, you never talk to me, and now that I finally, after twenty years, found interests and friends of my own, you resent it and you're continually carping at me.
Counselor:	(to husband) It's important to you that your laundry be done, the house cleaned, and dinner prepared when you come home.
Husband:	Damn right it is! That's what wives are supposed to do.
Counselor:	(to husband) You feel that your wife is *not* meeting her obligations to you.
Husband:	There's no question.
Counselor:	I have a hard time with this because I do not agree with your definition of a wife's obligations. However, I do see that in your view, she is not meeting the terms of the marriage contract under which you are operating.

In the above excerpt, I expressed my views without deriding or punishing the husband. This seemed to help both husband and wife to begin to acknowledge and evaluate some of their own values and beliefs about sex roles and marriage.

Another example occurred when a nineteen-year-old college student was talking about flunking out.

Client:	My dad's going to be very angry about losing all this money. I'm going to see if I can get my tuition back.
Counselor:	You're really afraid of your dad's reaction to your flunking out again.

Client:	I'm going to tell them I was sick. I think I'll tell them I had an operation and that's why I couldn't attend classes. Don't you think they'll give me my money back? They did it for my girlfriend. She had her appendix out.
Counselor:	It seems to you that you can ease your dad's reaction and anger at you if you can at least get some money back for him . . . the money will make it all right.
Client:	Yes . . . that's what I'll do. Do you think they'll give me my money back? It's so much money . . . over a thousand dollars.
Counselor:	I'm uncomfortable with claiming illness as the reason for not going to classes.
Client:	Really? Why?
Counselor:	To me, that would be lying. You must think I'm pretty square but I want you to know how I feel.
Client:	Um-m. It's always worked before.
Counselor:	Sometimes the ends seems to justify the means for you, huh?
Client:	M-mmm. I never thought of it like that.

The session then focused on the client's need to defend herself against her father's reactions. She became more aware of the manipulative devices that have worked for her in the past. The counselor's statement of values did not inhibit the relationship. Two weeks later, the client reported that she had received a 75 percent rebate and that it had not been necessary for her to lie to get it.

Helpers who have strong ideologies are often dismayed by the philosophy that they should not impose their values on helpees. But imposition of values and beliefs rarely results in growth and independence. Rather, it results in submission to or withdrawal from the counselor. Helpers can share their ideologies and offer them as options for consideration, but it is important for all choices and decisions to be the helpee's, not the helper's.

An example of withdrawal occurred in a counseling session where the counselor was working with a couple. The wife was concerned about having children because she did not want to give up her career and her husband felt that it was important for children to be with their mothers full time for the first five years and that his job was more important than his wife's, so she would have to be the full-time parent. This couple was in their thirties and most physicians believe that it becomes more dangerous to have children as you approach middle age, so it was important that they resolve this issue before too many years passed. In order to resolve this problem, they went to a community agency for counseling. They were assigned to a female counselor who identified strongly with the wife and who immediately proceeded to berate the husband for being a selfish male chauvinist. By so strongly interjecting *her* value system, this counselor ended up completely alienating both the husband and the wife by the end of the first session and the couple chose not to return to this agency. The wife commented afterward that, despite her anger at her husband, she so resented seeing him attacked, even though she agreed with the counselor's values, that she became protective of him. If the counselor had utilized responsive listening and had spent time developing a relationship with the couple and drawing them out rather than reacting to their struggle, she would have been able to suggest some alternatives reflecting her values for their consideration. Thus, she would have had a better opportunity to expose them to different values and, perhaps, to help them.

Rogers (1967) suggests that if you continue to have negative feelings about a client, you first do some "homework" about your feelings, seeing if you can determine where these feelings are coming from and whether or not they relate to some of your own concerns. You then check them out with the client by focusing on the areas that are causing these feelings to again check out what they are all about and then, if they continue to persist, you finally confront the client, using "I statements." Examples of this might be "I find myself feeling angry whenever I hear you talk about your husband in such a deprecating way, like when you said that 'all men are really babies and Joe is no exception.' I'd like to talk about this with you because my angry feelings are getting in the way here." or "I'm having a hard time listening to you talk about spending money on fixing your TV when you know that Jamie needs to see a dentist. I know that for me a kid's health care is more important than TV. I don't want my values to get in the way and I want to try and understand. Can we talk about this some more?"

There *are* going to be situations where you find it difficult to be genuine and nonjudgmental at the same time. It would be irrational to believe you can like and work well with *all* people. If after you have tried talking it out with the helpee you are still unable to feel genuine positive regard for him or her as a person, you have certain options to consider: (1) locating another helper; (2) seeking consultation (from a supervisor or colleague) for help in working this through with the client; or (3) limiting your relationship to the accomplishment of specific, immediate, concrete goals, such as obtaining food stamps, processing papers, or providing factual information.

The following exercises will help you become more aware of how you react in uncomfortable situations.

Exercise 8-1.   In small groups, role play the roles of helper and helpee in the following situations and then discuss your feelings and reactions and see if different people role play in similar or different manners. The purpose of this is to help you become more aware of the impact of your values on your helping. Some controversial topics that will get you in touch with yours and others' values are (1) a twelve-year-old comes to see you because she is pregnant and she wants to keep her baby; (2) a nurse's aide comes to see you because she is in conflict about the issue of euthanasia with regard to a terminally ill thirty-seven-year-old woman in great pain who keeps pleading for an overdose of drugs; (3) a sixteen-year-old boy tells you that he is having a homosexual affair with his seventeen-year-old cousin; (4) a couple is considering an interracial marriage.

Exercise 8-2.   This exercise is anxiety provoking and should be used at the discretion of the trainer, who knows how cohesive and trusting the group has become. In every group there are some people to whom we are immediately attracted and others we instinctively avoid. We do not usually check out these initial reactions. Look around the room and pick out the person with whom you would least want to be. Go over in your mind all your reasons and feelings as you continue to look at this person. Then, go over and talk to this person and see if you can genuinely, empathically relate to him or her and share your feelings. See if you can get in touch with your avoidance reactions and with your own anxieties. How did you feel if you were someone picked? Process this in small groups.

Sexism

Most of us have been raised to believe in traditional sex roles, that girls are born to become wives and mothers, perhaps to work sometimes as teachers, secretaries, sales clerks, librarians, social workers, etc., and that boys are born to be doctors, lawyers, policemen, firemen, machinists, carpenters, etc., and husbands and fathers. Recent studies indicate a widespread occurrence of sexist counseling resulting from belief in traditional sex roles and have shown how much sex role values impact the entire helping process. One notable study by Broverman, et al. (1970), clinical psychologists known as researchers in sex roles, indicated that mental health workers hold differential standards of mental health for men and women. They found that many mental health workers perceived males as "healthier" than females and "healthy" women as more submissive, less independent, less adventurous, less competitive, more easily influenced, less aggressive, more excitable in minor crises, and more emotional than "healthy" men.

Other studies have found that the variables of the sex of the helper and the sex of the helpee are significant in the helping process. One investigator, Parker (1967), found that male therapists tended to be more nondirective with females than with males, and another investigator, Heilbrun (1970) found that dependent females tending to leave counseling prematurely showed a preference for more directive therapist responses. In areas of vocational counseling, two leading counselor educators, Pietrofesa and Schlossberg (1970) found that both men and women helpers showed negative bias toward female clients who were considering entering non-traditional occupational fields.

Sexist counseling or helping may occur when the helper, either overtly or covertly, uses his or her own sex role ideology as a basis for helping. For example, if a high school guidance counselor discourages a young lady from taking an electronics course or considering a career in carpentry because these are "male occupations," this is sexist counseling. This discouragement may be subtle, in the form of questions such as "have you really thought about how difficult it will be working with all these men?" or less subtle, in the form of questions such as "Do you really want to risk your feminity this way?" The helpers are often not even aware that they are discouraging helpees.

Another example of sexist counseling is when a helper suggests to a woman that she shouldn't think about working while her children are young because "mothers of young children should really be home full time." Sexist counseling also occurs when boys are discouraged from becoming teachers or nurses because that is "women's work," from taking home economics or child care courses, from expressing emotions and feelings, or are chastised for not being "athletic."

Still another form of sexist counseling occurs when a helper suggests to a woman that she is not being a "true feminist" if she enjoys staying home with her family and engaging in homemaking and if the helper urges her to seek a career to "fulfill" herself. The point is that any kind of counseling that imposes the helper's sex role ideology on the helpee is sexist. As discussed in the previous section, the helper's ideology may (if the opportunity presents itself within the context of the situation) be presented as one of many alternatives, but choices and decisions are left to the helpee.

Sexism exists in most organizations and is often subtle and difficult to identify. Aside from obvious sexist practices such as salary differentials for the same job functions, discriminatory promotion practices, and so forth, women are assigned to leadership tasks involving "human relations" because "women are better at that kind of stuff" in many so-called progressive organizations. Women are subtly discouraged from applying for supervisory positions over men and from assertive behaviors in staff meetings and conferences.

Although it is possible that sex role stereotyping may be changing in our society due to the effects of affirmative action programs, the women's movement, and the economic necessity for more and more women to enter the labor market, it is important for helpers to deal with their own biases, the biases of others in their work settings, and the biases that are present in testing and informational materials in order to expand, rather than restrict, options for *both* males and females.

If you want to combat sexism actively in organizations and in human relations, you can become involved in promoting day care facilities for women in your setting; helping to expand flexible hours and jobs for women with families; actively agitating for the opening of jobs, courses, programs, and activities for both males and females in your work setting and community; and helping to reduce sex discrimination in recruitment and hiring as well as in training and placement. In other words, you can put into practice what you preach with substantive action. Also, whenever possible, you can initiate group discussion among males and females within your organization and community about current sex role ideologies and possibilities for expansion into personal, family, and work lifestyles. These activities will have a ripple effect in terms of actual helping relationships in that awareness results in more open, fairer helping relationships.

The following exercises will help you begin these discussions within your training group.

Exercise 8-3.   Divide into a group of females and a group of males. Each group is first to individually rank males and females (in general) from a 1 (low) to a 5 (high) on the following dimensions: serious intellectual pursuit; aggressiveness; emotionality; physical strength; nurturance; humor. After individuals have completed their ratings, the male group and the female group each come up with a group rating, which they then post on the board or on a large piece of paper like this:

	Male Group			*Female Group*	
Males	Females		Males	Females	

1. serious intellectual pursuit
2. aggressiveness
3. emotionality
4. physical strength
5. nurturance
6. humor

Compare results and discuss as a large group. Are there greater differences between male and female groups than between male and female ratings within each group? How do you explain these differences? What helped or hindered the group consensus in each group? You might want to see how far off your group consensus is from your individual scores.

Exercise 8-4. First decide how you feel about and whether you agree with each of the following statements. Then, in small mixed groups, discuss them as freely as possible, remembering to practice responsive listening, to listen closely to the views of others, and to express your own without imposing them on others.

(1) Most women are capable of performing well as both worker and homemaker.

(2) Women are not capable of becoming policemen or firemen.

(3) Women should learn typing and shorthand regardless of their career interests in order to get their first job.

(4) Women with children under five years of age should not work.

(5) There is something wrong with people who are not married by the age of thirty-five.

(6) No man wants to work for a female boss.

(7) Women are better suited for parenting than men.

(8) Men have more leadership capabilities than women.

(9) Men and women cannot have close relationships outside of a sexual relationship.

(10) Women who are assertive and successful in their careers lose their femininity and their attractiveness to men.

Racism

Like sexism, racism exists in our society and racist counseling exists when helpers allow their biases about different ethnic groups to contaminate helping relationships. Obvious examples of racist counseling in schools are when minority children are discouraged from enrolling in college preparatory programs, are discouraged from white collar career exploration and post-secondary school education, and are discouraged from joining school clubs and seeking offices. The same discrimination and racist counseling occurs in work settings of all varieties, where minority groups are denied access to certain jobs or where tokenism is practiced. Racist counseling also occurs in family service agencies where white middle-class helpers act on false assumptions about minority groups' family roles.

Racism can only be combated with continuous consciousness raising, study, exposure to different cultural value systems, and the training of more minority helpers. It is important that helpers support equality for people of all races and that concerted effort be made to train more minority people for the helping professions so that we can all learn together to deal with our racist biases and to reduce racist helping.

The issue of how effective white helpers can be with minority helpees or how effective minority helpers can be with white helpees has been raised over and over again during the past years. I personally have seen many excellent examples of minority counselors helping white clients and vice versa. It is my belief that a skilled competent helper who is conscious of his or her biases and values can work effectively with a wide variety of clients, regardless of sex or race. However, conclusive research findings do not exist. I base my view on the belief that all people have the same kinds of psychological needs and problems, despite the obvious differences in circumstances, situations, and societal opportunities. Helpers' skills and specialized knowledge are more important than helpers' color, race, religion, or sex.

It is important for helpers to seek out nonracist information and tests, to provide for group interaction between people of different races, and to attempt to expand horizons for all people. Likewise, it is useful for helpers at all levels to keep up with current literature and research regarding sexism and racism and to continue to expand their knowledge and consciousness about different sexes and races.

Horror stories illustrating racist counseling abound. One Chinese-American student recently reported her dismay when her high school counselor told her she should not attempt to go to college because her father disapproved and because it was "important for her to stick to her heritage." A very talented black graduate student was told "kindly" by his college counselor that he was not "appreciative enough of how far 'your people' have come and you want too much too soon . . . it takes lots of time and patience."

Many white helpers report that they feel uneasy when working with minority clients. They feel they will be considered "racist" if they confront or direct in any way. Black and white helpers who work with minority clients recommend that the helpers themselves bring up the issue of race during the initiation/entry stage of helping. An example of this might be "You're probably wondering how I, a white person, can possibly understand you and your experience as a black person." If the helpee is concerned about the race of the helper, then it can be discussed and explored at the outset. If, on the other hand, the client is surprised at the introduction of the racial issue and states that this is not an issue for him or her, then the helper can proceed to identify whatever issues are presented by the helpee.

A more subtle form of racism exists when white helpers apply different strategies with black clients than with white clients or modify the helping process in any way based on race rather than on the nature of the problem. Some helpers have been heard to say that "responsive listening" is not effective with black helpees, that directive, behavioral techniques are more effective. Quite the contrary, responsive listening has been found to be effective in developing helping relationships with white and minority helpees who possess normal verbal skills.

Exercise 8-5. This is a much used exercise with many variations that helps you to get in touch with discrimination. Divide into two groups—they may or may not be even. The leader arbitrarily assigns one group to be the "haves" and the other group to be the "have-nots." The have-nots use armbands or some other means to distinguish them from the haves. For the next thirty minutes, the haves are to practice every form of discrimination they can conceive of, such as to place all the have-nots together in a corner of the room, eat and have fun in front of them without letting them participate, taunting them, whispering about them, and so forth. At the end of the thirty minutes, without any processing, switch the groups for the next thirty minutes. After this, process: How did you feel as a have and as a have-not? What was easy and difficult for you? What kinds of leadership emerged in each of the groups? Who did you find yourself allying with and staying away from? What did you actually do or not do?

Ageism

The issue of the elderly presents a less obvious "ism," that of "ageism." Ageism is defined as imposing our own beliefs and values about what a person can or should do at different ages on helpees. We know that age discrimination does exist in the labor market; some people are considered "too old" for a job and some "too young." Age discrimination also exists in human services when some helpers believe that older people cannot really be helped and therefore avoid them.

Helpers can try to understand that there are wide varieties and differences in individual development and that restricting opportunities by age may not be valid. Likewise, each developmental stage or age has something unique to contribute to our society and we can begin to think more about the positive aspects of old age than about the problematic aspects. Ageism usually refers to the problems of being elderly rather than to the problems of being too young.

As the older portion of our population rapidly increases in our country, helpers are becoming more and more concerned about providing adequate human services. A recent report (Offir, 1974) predicts that if the current population trends continue, one-half of the total population will be over the age of fifty and one-third over sixty-five by the year 2000. Currently, almost 10 percent of our population is over sixty-five. A recent report (Eisderfer and Lawton,

1974) from the American Psychological Association points out that almost one-fourth of the citizens over sixty-five are poor and many of them are faced with increased problems in health, housing, employment, and finances. The report also indicates that only about one-fifth of those sixty-five and older who require mental health services receive them. Older Americans, then, tend to have symptoms of mental and emotional problems for a long time before they receive help.

Helpers need to study the age changes that occur in sensory, cognitive, motor, and affective areas and the effects of environmental, social, and health factors on older people. For example, older people often feel inadequate because they no longer can financially support themselves. We can let them know that their poverty is not of their making, that we understand that their concerns often result from inappropriate societal opportunities.

Time, patience, and empathic communications skills are essential to provide effective helping relationships with the elderly. In addition, reminiscing is an important strategy for helpers to use with the elderly. The older person's strength is in his or her past. In contrast to younger people, the elderly are really quite secure in their pasts. Having already lived, they needn't worry about ruining their lives or dying while young. However, with reduced coping, the elderly may regress and become upset about some difficulties that occurred many years before. Reviewing with the elderly all they have done with their lives and focusing on the positive (this is similar to crisis intervention strategies) can be helpful.

Advocacy seems to be one of the best strategies in working with the elderly. Helpers need to learn about the services and resources for the elderly within their communities, need to identify key people within helping organizations, and need to familiarize themselves with bureaucratic procedures and barriers (e.g., Medicaid and Social Security).

Again, we need to become conscious of our own attitudes and beliefs about the elderly. We need to examine our stereotypic assumptions of different ages. An example of ageist helping occurred when an eighty-six-year-old man informed the social worker in the home for the aged that he wished to marry his eighty-three-year-old lady friend down the hall and they were wondering if they could obtain a double room. The social worker reacted with horror and told him that he was behaving immorally, like a "foolish child," that "everyone knows people your age don't sleep together!" Another example of ageism is something that happened to this author. When I applied for admission to a doctoral program, I was told that I would have to complete my studies before the age of thirty-five in order to have enough time to make a worthwhile contribution and justify my education. It is important for the helper to remember that although age factors may be important for a particular decision, there are many other factors that are also important.

Helpers can educate families and members of the community about facts of old age and options for dealing with aged relatives. It is hoped this education will lead to the reduction of discrimination and segregation in schools and work settings because of age and in more facilities for the aged and more involvement of the aged in the mainstream of our society. A group of volunteer workers in a neighborhood day care center recently arranged for senior citizens to participate in activities with the children. This has proven to be so successful for the children and the senior citizens that plans are underway for expanding this involvement of the elderly in the care of the young.

Other Values Issues

Other values issues may include economic and social biases, dress and appearance, language differences, and religious differences. The principles of dealing with these issues are the same as just discussed: clarifying and expressing your own values in a nonjudgmental manner.

ETHICAL CONSIDERATIONS

Professional organizations such as the American Personnel and Guidance Association (for counselors and personnel workers), the American Rehabilitation Counseling Association (for counselors who work in rehabilitation settings), the American Psychological Association (for graduate psychologists), and the National Association of Social Workers (for graduate social workers) have developed codes of ethics that may be applicable for human services workers. These codes of ethics protect the helpers from the public at the same time as they protect the public from unethical helpers. Helpers who develop a consistency between themselves and their definition of helping will find that their helper definition decides how they will answer ethical questions.

It is possible that ethics differ among settings, although the principles can remain the same. The issues of ethics that particularly affect human relations workers are (1) privileged communications and sharing of confidential information, (2) conflicts of interests, (3) record keeping, and (4) testing.

Most helpers do not have *privileged communication*, which means that they could be called upon to testify in a court of law as to the nature of their discussions with helpees and that their records can be subpoenaed. In some states certified counselors and certified psychologists do have this privileged communications, but such laws are not uniformly applied.

There are two kinds of *confidentiality*: legal and personal. The former depends upon the laws of your state. The latter is of your own making, regardless of the policies of your work setting. In other words, if, because of your setting (such as in a school or correctional institution), you are unable to treat information obtained in a helping session confidentially, you *must* make this clear to the helpee in advance of his or her sharing of concerns with you. Then the helpee can choose whether or not to tell you whatever may be controversial. If, on the other hand, you are able to promise personal confidentiality, you must maintain this confidentiality and under no circumstances reveal to anyone what has been told to you in confidence.

There are times when you may experience a *conflict of interests* between your obligations to your organization and your obligations to your helpee. There are no definite solutions in such cases. Each person must find an answer that can be lived with. For example, a school counselor recently related hearing from one of his clients the names of the students who had participated in a serious act of vandalism the previous week at school. The counselor was torn between his desire to protect his client and his desire to deal with the offenders in a helpful manner. After several difficult sessions with his client, he was able to persuade the boy to tell his friends that he had told the counselor about the vandalism and to bring his friends with him to the counselor's office.

In another case, a street worker was told by a youth that the gang was going to break into a jewelry store that night. This street worker, after much soul searching, called the youth back and told him that he was going to have to warn the owner of the jewelry store that a gang was planning a burglary. The counselor explained to the youth that he was worried about the physical safety of the owner of the jewelry store. He warned the store owner and, to his surprise, the youth kept returning and sharing confidences with him, thus indicating to the helper that perhaps the boy had hoped for this outcome.

It is important for helpers to remember that their primary responsibility during the helping process is to the helpee, not to any other individual or group. Thus, if a conflict of interests arises, helpers must assure themselves that they do not breach a helpee's confidentiality because of helper ignorance, insecurity, or ineptness or because of the good of some organization or group. The only justification for a breach of confidentiality is that the welfare of the helpee or some other human being is at stake.

In regard to *records*, you may find it a good idea to write down only objective, behavioral information and to be sure and exclude your own values, attitudes, and, above all, interpretations. Some helpers keep rudimentary information and their own coded personal notes in their office files. If tape recordings are used, it should be with the full knowledge of the helpee and with a full explanation of the intentions and purposes of the recordings and the helper's guarantee that the tape(s) will be destroyed after they fulfill their purposes.

Some human services workers may become involved in *testing* helpees. They may employ interest, aptitude, or achievement tests or some paper and pencil personality inventory that could be used for screening, placement, or some other kind of classification. It is ethical for helpers to administer tests only if they have had sufficient training and supervision in the administration of the particular test to be used. In addition, helpers are ethically bound to determine and explain clearly to helpees the rationale for and purposes of the testing process.

A related issue concerns the use of test data—who receives it and what kind of use will be made of this data. Does the helpee receive feedback in order to increase self-understanding? Is the helper able to interpret test data accurately to helpees and explain what the test means and how valid it is? The helper must determine how best to act on his or her ethical responsibility with these issues.

Remember not to discuss helpees with anyone in their family, another staff member of your organizations, teachers, supervisors, or employers without the helpee's expressed permission. This is necessary to insure trust and to communicate the helper's interest in the helpee's welfare.

No code of ethics can cover all situations and all circumstances. There may be times when you need to violate confidentiality (e.g., in the case of future crime or fraud or to protect the helpee). You will have to decide for yourself what course of action is right for you.

RELATED ISSUES

We will just touch on some of the other issues that frequently occur in helping relationships. The readings at the end of the chapter will provide more in-depth coverage of these areas.

A frequent concern of helpers in certain institutions centers around the *reluctant client*, the individual who is told he or she must seek help. This may cause an ethical dilemma for helpers who believe in the self-determination of helpees. After all, if people have the right to determine for themselves whether or not they want to be helped or "get better," how can we force our services on them? If you feel this way, you can say just this to the helpee and communicate empathy and concern for his or her position, while at the same time explaining your position.

Allowing sufficient time and exhibiting a great deal of patience and empathy can help to diminish the resistance and defensiveness of reluctant clients. Genuineness, which includes discussing alternatives and their consequences, enables the reluctant client to decide whether or not it will be in his or her best interests to cooperate with you. The client will not be able to make this decision, however, unless you can spell out just who you are, what you are doing there, and what you see as the nature and objectives of your prospective helping relationship.

Helpers often become enmeshed in a "game" with reluctant clients that does little more than pass the time away. It is the "I'm only here to help you" kind of game that is perceived as threatening by the client due to its implication of helper omniscience. One way of combating this game is to encourage the reluctant client to take the initiative for structuring the relationship. An example of this occurred in a halfway house where the youth worker just stayed in close physical proximity to the reluctant client, shrugged off the verbal abuse, and communicated caring and genuineness more by nonverbal presence than by any words. After four days of testing out the youth worker in every conceivable fashion, the fourteen-year-old boy began to shed his bravado and share some of his real feelings and thoughts. It was almost a test of endurance—who could outlast whom.

Try not to feel guilty or hurt by rejection from a reluctant client. Instead, you can try to become aware of possible aspects of your approach to this helpee, as well as aspects of your setting and situation, that may be contributing to this rejection. You may find that your style of helping is not working for this particular client in this particular setting. In that case, you can either modify your style or arrange for a referral. Modifying your style could include judicious use of humor or self-disclosure or use of more open support and acceptance or some temporary diversion, such as changing the subject. Other techniques include reflection of the resistance and clarification of the consequences of not working together.

Self-disclosure, the technique whereby helpers talk about themselves with helpees, is another controversial issue. At one time this was considered "disastrous" and "unethical," but now many helpers believe that judicious self-disclosure can enhance the helping relationship and can provide inputs into problem solving. The guiding principle is that the helper's self-disclosure is for the helpee's benefit. This means that the helper does not burden the client with his or her problems but regulates the quality and timing of self-disclosure to help the client focus more on his or her concerns and to encourage exploration and understanding.

If self-disclosure is used to further the helpee's exploration and self-understanding, it will allow the helper to be a positive role model, both in terms of revealing the helper's "humanness" in sharing a similar problem or experience and in providing a look at the possibility of coping effectively with whatever the issue is. It will not distract the helpee from the pressing concerns nor will it adversely affect the relationship by showing up the helper's "flaws." Rather, it will help focus on the central issues of the moment and teach the helpee that all human beings have problems and can make mistakes but that there is the possibility of learning from our mistakes and working through our problems.

An example of self-disclosure occurred recently in a pregnancy advisory service, where the volunteer helper was discussing the possibility of abortion with a single nineteen-year-old woman. The helpee was hesitant about considering abortion, but she felt trapped and unsure. When she began to contemplate what guilt feelings might result from an abortion, the helper shared her own painful, guilty feelings after a similar experience and explained that there would most likely be guilt and discomfort resulting from any of the options being considered. The helpee seemed relieved to be talking to someone who had experienced these feelings and lived through them.

It is important that helpers have the capacity to share themselves intimately with some others, although they certainly must choose carefully with whom and when to do so. We expect helpees to share themselves, and we need to experience and understand this very same process of sharing and relating. The underlying principle here is that we do not ask others to do what we cannot and would not do.

Change-agentry or *advocacy* occurs when helpers take active roles in bringing about political and institutional changes to combat discrimination and inequality. (Examples of change-agentry were mentioned in the sections on sexism and racism.) This issue is currently permeating the role of helpers. More people in the helping fields are taking active stands against racism, sexism, and ageism; against poverty and other forms of inequity; and against discrimination against those politically and organizationally involved and active. The rationale for this increased activity is that consistency between what one practices and what one preaches is necessary in order for changes in systems to occur and in order for effective helping relationships to occur, given that we are becoming more cognizant of social influences on psychological discomfort.

We are becoming more and more aware of the problems that systems and institutions impose on helpees. These problems subsequently become labeled as the helpee's problem. As helpers become frustrated struggling against the limitations institutions impose on them and on helpees, they become more politicized and radicalized.

This does not mean that they revolutionize or seek the destruction of the institution, but that they try to foster systemic, innovative change within the institution.

Issues that might necessitate change-agentry strategies involve program control, budgets, the political process involved in staffings, organizational decisions, and public policies. Techniques of change-agentry include generating public support by disseminating written materials; organizing support groups; training the staff; providing public education; mobilizing local, state, and national election task forces; pressuring elected officials; writing legislators; and participating in confrontations such as boycotts, demonstrations, and strikes when they are part of a total strategy campaign.

Change-agentry involves the planning of strategies; the determination of goals; and the design of a structure to reflect these goals, of a tentative implementation plan, and of an evaluation plan. Although the change agents or innovators may assume initial leadership, one of the frequent priorities in institutional change is a more broadly based power sharing among all members of the institution. If staff recruitment and training in human services institutions can result in the availability of facilitative helpers rather than "authoritarian experts," then the needs of the helpees will assume a higher priority than the needs of the helpers and the needs of the organization to maintain itself.

As an example, let's consider a federally funded mental health agency that experienced a great deal of chaos a few years ago. This chaos was reflected in high staff turnover, a large number of written and verbal client complaints and no-shows for appointments, and resistance to the agency by other community groups. The feelings of the staff were that the agency was being run to meet the needs of the director and senior staff more than to meet the needs of the community it was supposed to serve. Two of the staff helpers became very frustrated with the bureaucratic red tape they encountered every time they brought up the idea of any change. They finally recruited some active support from members of the clerical and volunteer staff as well as from members of the community. As a task force, they prepared a written report of what they perceived to be the problems of the community and of the agency and the conflicting directives and policies and they presented this to their director and the senior staff. The report included a written proposal for a pilot project that would change the staff loads and include members of the community and some representative helpees at regular agency meetings.

Because their proposal was fully documented and specific, the director agreed to a two-month trial. At the end of the trial period, modifications were suggested and some changes in leadership occurred when some senior staff members realized that they would be unable to muster up the support necessary to revert to the previous way of operating. The new leaders involved members of the community in agency policy and decision making and were successful in effecting many of the changes recommended in the original proposal.

Dedicated helpers are becoming more aware that communities must have a hand in the development of their own institutions and that these institutions must become more responsive to the needs of their client population. This means that services must be adequately provided to meet the unique needs of a particular community, not to provide research data for an erudite report or to provide training for paraprofessional and professional helpers from other communities. You must decide for yourself, as you consider your helping role and your own personal and professional ethics, just how involved you will become in systemwide changes.

The following exercises are to help you to become more familiar with the issues just discussed.

Exercise 8-6.   The purpose of this exercise is to become familiar with the feelings of a reluctant client and with the helper of a reluctant client. In pairs, assign the roles of helper and helpee. It might be helpful if the helpee keeps in mind something that he or she would not want to share under any circumstances. Engage in a role play where the helpee knows that he or she does not want help and the helper is trying to effect a helping relationship. Switch roles and then process your experiences, feelings, and reactions. In this exercise, most helpees learn that there is no way someone can make them reveal what they do not choose to reveal.

Exercise 8-7.   What are the issues in the following cases? What would you do as the helper in each case? Role play and discuss in small groups.

(1)   You are a youth street worker and you overhear a gang of boys talk about a store burglary they committed yesterday. Later, one of the boys tells you that this gang is having trouble fencing some of the loot and asks you to help. He offers you a free color TV. It's taken you a long time to gain the trust of this boy.

(2)   You are working as a volunteer in a crafts program for the aged. An eighty-five-year-old man with whom you've established a helping relationship tells you that he wants to marry a seventy-eight-year-old woman in the program. His children are raising strenuous objections and want to pull him out of this program to keep him away from "foolish temptation." He wants your help.

(3)   You are a white paraprofessional working in a community school as a vocational counseling aide. A black couple comes in with their eleventh-grade son. They had just received notice from the guidance department that their son, on the basis of an I.Q. test, was being sent to trade school for the rest of the year. The parents are very upset. They want him in a college-bound track.

(4) You are a personnel worker and Ms. White, a very competent administrative assistant in the advertising department, comes in to complain that a male administrative assistant with less background and experience has been promoted over her.

(5) You are a helper in a drop-in center for teens. A fourteen-year-old girl tells you she thinks she is pregnant and that she was seduced by her employer. She says that her parents "will kill" her if they ever find out.

(6) You are a male supervisor in a factory, supervising fourteen male fork lifters. A woman is hired because of your factory's affirmative action plan. Your men are angry and upset and come to see you to plan what to do to stop this invasion of their territory.

(7) You are a black helper in a youth activities program. A fifteen-year-old black youth who is bussed to a suburban school tells you he wants to ask a white girl to the school dance, but he is somewhat nervous about it.

(8) You are a school counselor in an upper-middle-class community. The parents of one of the students has come to see you and is very angry with you for encouraging their son with his interest in shop. They had always planned for him to go to medical school. The boy is a C student and is very talented in shop work.

(9) You are a helper in a community center. Drugs are not allowed on the premises and you find a youngster with whom you have been working smoking a joint.

(10) You are a black counselor in a prison. You notice that only black prisoners are placed in behavior modification programs and that selection is arbitrarily determined by the prison administration. Subjects have no choice and are penalized if they do not cooperate.

SUMMARY

In this chapter we have discussed some of the major values and professional issues that impact helping relationships. As helpers we must be aware of our values and be careful not to impose them on clients. We can use responsive listening and send "I messages" to communicate respect for helpees and their values. Three values we discussed at some length are sexism, racism, and ageism. There are rarely absolute answers to these issues, but we can keep informed and maintain heightened sensitivity by continuing to discuss and consider them. This process is as important as the learning of communications skills and understanding the stages of the helping relationship.

Ethical considerations in counseling were also discussed. How we resolve the problems of priviliged communications and confidentiality, conflicts of interests, record keeping, and testing will help determine our effectiveness as helpers.

REFERENCES AND FURTHER READINGS

Alinsky, S. *Rules for Radicals.* New York: Vintage Books, 1972.

Broverman, I.; Broverman, D.; Clarkson, F.; Rosenkrantz, P.; and Vogel, S. "Sex-role Stereotypes and Clinical Judgments of Mental Health." *Journal of Consulting and Clinical Psychology* 34, (1970): 1 - 7.

Codes of Ethics, APGA, APA, ARCA, NASW.

Cook, D. *Guidance for Education in Revolution.* Boston: Allyn and Bacon, 1971.

Dustin, D., and Dustin, G. *Action Counseling for Behavior Changes.* New York: Intext, 1973.

Eisdorfer, C., and Lawton, P., eds. *The Psychology of Adult Development and Ageing.* Washington, D.C.: American Psychological Association, 1974.

Halleck, S. *The Politics of Therapy.* New York: Science House, 1971.

Heilbrun, A. "Toward Resolution of the Dependency-Premature Termination Paradox for Females in Psychotherapy." *Journal of Consulting and Clinical Psychology* 34 (1970): 382 - 386.

Lawton, M., and Gottesman, L. "Psychological Services for the Elderly." *American Psychologist* 29 (1974): 689 - 694.

Offir, C. "At 65 Work Becomes A Four Letter Word." *Psychology Today* 7 (1974): 40 - 42.

Parker, G. "Some Concomitants of Therapist Dominance in the Psychotherapy Interview." *Journal of Consulting Psychology* 31 (1967): 313 - 318.

Pietrofesa, J., and Schlossberg, N. *Counselor Bias and the Female Occupational Role.* Detroit: Wayne State University Press, 1970.

Rogers, C. "The Necessary and Sufficient Conditions of Therapeutic Personality Change." *Journal of Consulting Psychology* 21 (1967): 95 - 103.

Simon, S.; Howe, L.; and Kirschenbaum, H. *Values Clarification.* New York: Hart, 1972.

POSTSCRIPT

We have now come full circle in our introductory overview of helping relationships. We have achieved three major objectives: (1) we have explored the human relations counseling model, which is designed to explain how effective human relations skills can develop helping relationships; (2) we have reviewed the major theoretical approaches to helping; and (3) we have applied this model to actual cases and practice via the exercises and case studies.

HUMAN RELATIONS COUNSELING MODEL

The human relations counseling model postulates three major dimensions of a helping relationship: stages, skills, and issues. These three dimensions interrelate and impact upon each other.

The stages dimension represents the step-by-step development of a helping relationship from initiation/entry of the relationship stage through the follow-up of the strategies stage. The relationship stage precedes the strategies stage and consists of establishing rapport, trust, empathy, and genuineness, as well as identification, clarification, and exploration of the helpee's concerns. In order for strategies and approaches to work, it is necessary to allow for the development of these relationship qualities.

The strategies stage involves clarification of the objectives of the helping relationship and action-oriented approaches to problem solving and working through helpee concerns. The strategies used are drawn from established, formal theory (i.e., psychoanalytical, phenomenological, behavioral, cognitive, transactional-communicative) and deal with feeling, thinking, and acting. They are client-centered in that they deal with the concerns that the client chooses to work with, not those that the helper thinks should be worked on.

The communications skills focus on responsive listening. They involve teaching helpers to perceive nonverbal messages, to hear both apparent and underlying messages, and to respond to both. Such responsive listening leads as reflection, clarification, and interpretation focus on surfacing underlying affective content of the verbal message. With training and practice, we can learn to heighten these communications skills so we can move through the development steps of the stages. These communications skills are essential for developing an empathic helping relationship as well as for effective human relations in any type of relationship.

However, the communications skills and the stages can be hindered inadvertently if we do not consider the issues dimension, which includes clarification of the helper's and the helpee's values, ethical considerations, and specialized helping issues. Because helpers cannot separate their persons from their effectiveness as helpers, their helping effectiveness is dependent upon their self-awareness; acknowledgement of their own values, attitudes, and beliefs; and their ability to accept others with different value systems as well as on their communications skills and conceptual understanding of human behavior and the helping process.

THEORY

We have examined the theory underlying helping relationships by turning to research for data on those qualities, behaviors, and knowledge necessary for effective helping. This, in turn, has helped us to define and explore the nature of helping relationships as well as desirable helper characteristics.

In studying the major theoretical views about helping we have focused on their philosophical assumptions about human behavior and development and their concepts of change as well as their views of the helping relationship. When we compared these theories we found that they all, to varying degrees, consider the helping relationship a crucial variable in the helping process. This review of major theories served as a foundation for our introduction to strategies and approaches of helping. We were then able to classify theories and strategies according to the domain (affective, cognitive, behavioral) they affect.

If we believe that our thoughts, feelings, and behaviors are interrelated, we can see that our thoughts about helpees and our helping relationships stem from both personal and formal theories and cannot be separated from our feelings and our techniques (behaviors). Thus, we take a multimodality view in selection and use of strategies and in the way we interact with others in that we are interested in all three aspects of the total person, in all three domains.

APPLICATIONS

Throughout this book, we have had the opportunity to apply the communications skills and our understanding of the steps in the stages and the strategies through written and group experiential exercises. The purpose of these exercises is to provide some opportunity to experience personally and to react to the material in the text. These exercises are designed to heighten your awareness of your own behaviors, thoughts, and feelings as well as to give you a taste of translating conceptual material into experience.

Whether or not the case material is appropriate to your setting and level of helping, it illustrates the stages of helping and many of the issues discussed. Most of the examples and case studies are from my own, my trainees', and my colleagues' practices; so our own biases, competences, and skills prevail. However, this model is an open one in that it does not, as a model, favor any approaches over others.

WHERE DO YOU GO FROM HERE?

Now that you have a foundation, you can choose whether or not you want to further your skills development and your understanding of the helping process and the use of strategies. If you wish to become a more effective helper, it is important for you to receive some supervised field experience as well as pursue academic courses in helping and the social sciences. Only by continuous practice and application, however, can we improve our communications skills. Reading about and studying them can only serve as a foundation; laboratory and field work application are essential.

The applications of strategies can be learned in course work, field work, and specialized training institutes and workshops. In the past years, a growing number of these institutes and workshops have been offered throughout the country. Although their quality and legitimacy vary, there are some excellent training opportunities available for discerning helpers. These workshops are often sponsored by professional associations at local, regional, and national conferences. Some are sponsored by local human relations groups or by professional institutes such as the Rational-Emotive Institute, the International Association of Transactional Analysis, the Gestalt Institute, Essalen, and the Psychodrama Institute. Keeping an eye on local announcements and human services bulletins will alert you to available opportunities.

Certain approaches require more advanced training and experience than others. However, this does not preclude you from having a basic understanding of the major approaches. Having this basic understanding can serve as a stimulus for pursuing further training in a particular area now or at any time during your helping life. As training and opportunities open up, there is more opportunity for lay helpers to become paraprofessionals and for paraprofessionals to become professionals. One need only look at the age and backgrounds of students enrolled in different levels of training programs to recognize that people are coming into human services fields at all ages, with all kinds of experiences and backgrounds.

COMMON PROBLEMS YOU MAY ENCOUNTER

Regardless of the amount of your training and experience, you will often feel insecure and question your own adequacy as a helper. Perhaps this type of self-doubt is one of the necessary qualities for an effective helper; it keeps us on our toes, prevents us from becoming cocky and overconfident, and constantly reminds us of our own frailty as a human being. Working with people in a helping relationship is awesome and often frightening in that we become aware of the importance and vulnerability of human life. On the other hand, this kind of self-doubt can protect us from getting in over our heads, from attempting to work with people and problems beyond the scope of our training and capabilities.

Another problem that beginning helpers often experience is that of becoming too emotionally involved with helpees, of wanting to take responsibility for them and do for them, rather than teaching them to do for themselves. It is because of this problem that we spend time developing our own self-awareness and examining our apparent and underlying motivations for becoming helpers as we study the helping process. As we learn about ourselves and about the helping process, we can learn to take care of ourselves and allow others to take care of themselves.

A common problem you may encounter is that of total frustration with the limitations your organization or some of your community institutions impose upon you and others. Learning what your options are and then deciding what you want to do about these options, what risks you can incur, and what resources you can muster up can be painful and difficult and cause you to feel lonely and isolated from others. Along the same line, you will often feel anger and frustration with other members of human services professions. You will question the quality and methodology of some of the services provided. This can happen in any area of endeavor associated with human beings and their welfare and it requires using your communications skills and knowledge to consult effectively with other human services workers to see if you can bring about change. The problem-solving model is especially applicable here in that we can team up with others to identify problems and brainstorm for alternative solutions.

A final problem I want to mention is that of your own resistance to changes and new ways of delivering services. We sometimes get so used to doing things in a certain way that, without realizing it, we become very set in our ways. Keeping open channels of communications with peers in your setting and others, attending meetings and conferences, reading new materials, and taking advantage of inservice training whenever possible all help us to keep abreast of new developments and opportunities in our fields.

RECENT TRENDS

Over the years we have seen increasing evidence of the helping effectiveness of beginning professional, paraprofessional, and lay helpers. There is evidence that the helping skills and strategies we have discussed are applicable, to varying degrees, to all three groups of helpers.

For example, telephone crisis intervention services report that short telephone calls utilizing these same communications skills can provide sufficient help to callers to avert a pending crisis, such as a suicide or crime. Just the trusting, understanding human contact is very often sufficient to begin the helping process. Also, a recently developed telephone career education counseling project demonstrates that vocational counseling can be effectively delivered by trained lay helpers via telephone.

Likewise, in many school and mental health settings a team approach involving professional, paraprofessional, and lay helpers has proven to be an effective way to provide human services. Professional helpers have reported that lay and paraprofessional helpers are invaluable in developing helping relationships and effecting behavior and attitude changes among the client population.

There is a need to demystify the helping process and allow for sufficient inservice and community-based training so that increasing numbers of human services and community workers can deliver services on their own turf. Only by so doing do we have the slightest chance of being able to expand vital human services to all who are in need. There are many natural helping resources available within any community; we need to identify them and train them to assume these needed helping roles. At the same time, it would behoove us to offer supervisory and consulting training to professional helpers so that they can provide supervisory services as well as more intensive care when necessary.

Recent trends indicate that we will be attempting to integrate larger numbers of populations traditionally housed in residential institutions back into our communities—the elderly, the mentally ill, prisoners, retardates, physically handicapped, etc. Halfway houses will be needed, but we will also need to consider and develop alternative programs and settings for this integration. This trend highlights the need for recruiting helpers from within the community and for using community-based helpers to assist other members of their neighborhoods in accepting people who have been traditionally kept out.

GLOSSARY

Affective: *pertaining to feelings and emotions. The affective domain consists of the feeling and emotional aspect of experience, of willing. These feelings may be conscious or unconscious.*

Anal stage: *the psychoanalytic stage occurring between two and three years of age where the child focuses on pleasure from the anal-erogeneous zone. This is a pregenital phase of sexual development during which bowel training becomes important.*

Approach reaction: *when a person's behavior is directed toward a situation or stimulus, regardless of positive or negative emotions. This tendency to deal with whatever issues are at hand connotes a positive ability to work through difficulties.*

Assertiveness training: *a behavioral technique whereby the client gradually learns progressively more assertive behaviors (standing up for own rights without impinging on the rights of others) through such means as modeling, role playing, instruction. Assertive behaviors include saying "no" without feeling guilty and learning to ask directly for what you want.*

Avoidance reaction: *when a person tends to withdraw from or avoid a situation or stimulus that might have threatening or adverse emotional aspects. This indicates a refusal to work through or check out problems and issues.*

Behavior: *some observable physical action or performance; a concrete response one makes to a stimulus situation. Behaviors may be motor, perceptual, or glandular.*

Brainstorming: *when a group of people propose possible alternative ideas for a particular purpose. Every one of these proposed ideas is considered before evaluative screening occurs. This is an important step in problem solving, allowing for all possible inputs before a decision is reached.*

210

Castration complex: *fear of losing penis that psychoanalysts believe boys experience during the phallic stage after they discover that girls do not have penises. The idea of this deprivation causes fear and anxiety and may be partly or wholly repressed.*

Clarification: *a verbal response that helps the client to better understand issues and needs, what has been said or felt.*

Client-centered: *Rogerian term meaning the direction of the counseling (the goals, course, and process) is wholly determined by the client, not the counselor.*

Cognitive: *pertaining to thinking and knowing. Covers all modes of knowing—perceiving, remembering, imagining, conceiving, judging, reasoning. Cognition is a conscious process.*

Cognitive restructuring: *Rational-Emotive-Therapy technique where irrational thinking is identified and replaced by rational thinking through didactic teaching. One is taught how to correct faulty belief systems through unlearning of irrational beliefs and learning of rational beliefs.*

Compensation: *psychoanalytic defense mechanism whereby one substitutes a satisfying activity for a frustrated one to reduce tension. One covers up a weakness or defect by exaggerating the showing of a less defective or more desirable characteristic.*

Conditioned: *something that is learned as opposed to instinctive. Conditioning is a process by which a response is elicited by a stimulus, object, or situation other than that to which it is the normal or natural response.*

Confrontation: *a verbal technique whereby helpers present helpees with discrepancies between their verbal and nonverbal behaviors or between the helpee and helper's perceptions. Confrontation is often used to facilitate approach, rather than avoidance, reactions.*

Congruence: *a client-centered concept meaning what one experiences correlates with what one is aware of within oneself. In other words, one's behavior is in tune with one's values and beliefs. One is said to "practice what one preaches."*

Contamination: *a Transactional Analysis concept meaning one of the ego states (parent, adult, or child) overlaps another ego state and interferes with the effective functioning of that other ego state. Racial prejudice is an example of contamination, whereby the parent ego state is saying that "all blacks are bad" and the adult ego state does not check that out with the real world, but merely accepts what was taught or thought during childhood.*

Content: *the material or constituents of an experience, as different from the form or process of an experience. The "what" as opposed to the "how."*

Contingency contracting: *a positive behavioral contract between the helper and the helpee specifically stating the desired behavioral outcomes and the consequential reinforcements to follow performance of each stated behavior. An elaboration of the "If you do X, you will get (to do) Y" formula that is clearly stated, agreed to by all parties, and systematically applied.*

Defense mechanism: *psychoanalytic construct of unconscious or involuntary strategies that one uses to protect oneself against painful negative feelings associated with a situation that is extremely disagreeable. The situation may be physical or mental and occur frequently or infrequently.*

Denial: *psychoanalytic defense mechanism whereby one's mind refuses to acknowledge and experience something that would cause anxiety and distress if acknowledged. A firm belief that what happened did not happen or is not so.*

Directive therapy: *a form of therapy where the therapist guides the course, objectives, and process of therapy. The therapist is a director, a teacher, a guide and has full control of the therapeutic relationship.*

Discrimination: *learning theory term involving the ability to differentiate among slightly different stimuli. Reinforcement has been present or stronger for some stimuli than for others.*

Displacement: *psychoanalytic defense mechanism whereby the psychic energy, often anger or some other emotion, directed toward a particular person or object is transferred to another similar person or object. Frequently occurs in dreams, where feelings are shifted from one item or person to another item or person to which it does not really belong.*

Dissonance: *occurs when two parts or aspects of experience do not blend or fuse, resulting in discrepancies and discomfort. The dissonance may occur between two behaviors, between behavior and feeling, or between inner and outer experiences.*

Ego: *psychoanalytic concept of the partly preconscious, partly conscious part of the personality in contact with the external world, the reality of the world. That part of the person in direct touch with external reality that includes the representation of reality as given by the senses in consciousness and exists in the preconscious as memories, together with those selected impulses and influences from within that have been accepted and are under control.*

Ego states: *Transactional Analysis concepts of the personality. There are three ego states: the parent (providing criticism and nurturing), the adult (providing thinking and reasoning), and the child (providing feelings, intuition, creativity). These ego states are conscious and observable and one can learn to identify and choose the one appropriate for a particular situation.*

Electra complex: *psychoanalytic concept occurring during the phallic stage, where a girl is jealous of her mother's sex role and directs her erotic feelings toward her father. This is acted out with the girl expressing attachment to her father and antagonism to her mother.*

Empathy: *the ability to see the world the way the helpee sees it, from the helpee's "frame of reference." Empathic communication is when one can communicate levels of feeling and experience deeper than those communicated by another, within a nonjudgmental and clear range of expression.*

Empty seat: *Gestalt technique whereby a client uses an empty chair as site of an imagined partner in a dialogue or role play game. The client sits in the empty seat when speaking as the person the seat represents.*

Exclusion: *Transactional Analysis concept meaning that one of the three ego states (parent, adult, child) is missing and not functioning. This results in imbalance of the personality system and ensuing faulty transactions and communications.*

Existential: *philosophical viewpoint dealing with the here and now, the presence of time, people's freedom to choose for themselves, purposes of life, potential, humanness. Existential psychology deals with those aspects of experience that can be observed introspectively (sensory and imaginal processes) together with feelings.*

Extinction: *behavorial technique whereby one discontinues any reinforcing consequences for a particular behavior resulting in that behavior being diminished and eventually discontinued. Extinction techniques are used to unlearn (erase) a specific behavior that is deemed inappropriate.*

Free association: *psychoanalytic technique where patients tell analysts everything that comes into their minds. The subject is asked to give ideas continuously as they come to mind in response to a word or concept stimulus.*

Generalization: *learning theory term meaning a learned response can be used in other situations with similar but different stimuli or a general concept is formed based on several component ideas.*

Genital stage: *adult psychosexual stage of development that occurs as a child reaches puberty and his or her interests become heterosexual rather than self-centered. At this stage, the earlier psychosexual stages are fused and genital eroticism predominates.*

Gestalt: *German word meaning "whole." The form, pattern, structure, or configuration of an integrated whole, not a mere summation of parts. Gestalt psychology contends that mental processes and behavior cannot be analyzed into elementary units because wholeness and organization are built-in features from the start. A psychology of perception.*

Id: *psychoanalytic concept of primitive, unconscious source of psychic energy, a part of the personality that demands immediate gratification in order to reduce tension and increase pleasure. The inner determinant of conscious life.*

Imagery techniques: *those techniques whereby helpees imagine people, scenes, and events, recalling or imagining sights, smells, feelings, and thoughts as vividly as possible.*

Implosive therapy: *a form of behavioral therapy involving the client's vividly imagining massive exposure to aversive stimuli in order to extinguish anxiety. After repeated imaginal exposures, the client is able to deal with the aversive stimuli in vivo with reduced anxiety.*

Incongruence: *client-centered term meaning there is a discrepancy between a person's actual experience and his or her picture of the experience. Someone's behavior is not in keeping with what he or she says.*

Intellectualization: *psychoanalytic defense mechanism whereby one emphasizes the intellectual or cognitive aspects and neglects the emotional and volitional aspects to avoid experiencing and dealing with emotional content.*

Interpretation: *a technique that adds the underlying meanings and relationships to the apparent verbal content of a helpee statement or behavior. This may involve connecting different aspects of experiencing for the helpee or explaining relationships and causal factors.*

Isolation: *a psychoanalytic defense mechanism whereby an idea becomes detached from its affective or emotional content. There may be a blank pause between a highly unpleasant or personally significant experience and the reaction.*

Latency stage: *a psychoanalytic stage of psychosexual development occurring between the age of four or five and emerging adolescence that separates infantile from genital sexuality. During this period, there are no conscious sexual interests or activities.*

Leading: *a verbal skill that elicits client responses in an open-ended yet focused manner. Leads include "door openers" such as "Tell me more . . ." and "I'm wondering about . . ." as well as questions, reflections, clarifications, and so forth.*

Libido: *psychoanalytic concept referring to psychic energy that includes the sexual and survival instincts. Libido is a dynamic force that includes both sexual and ego drives. It is the life force that serves to neutralize the destructive impulses in the system.*

Modeling: *a learning theory principle whereby new modes of behavior are learned or old ones changed by observing others' actual or simulated behavior and its consequences. Modeling is based on imitation.*

Neurosis: *in the psychoanalytic sense a functional disorder of the nervous system that is psychological rather than organic in origin. This disorder can result in somatic and behavioral symptoms. Because the adequate satisfaction of subjective needs is the function of the ego, neurosis can be understood as a disturbance of ego functions.*

Oedipus complex: *may occur during the psychoanalytic phallic stage, when a boy directs his erotic desires toward his mother. He expresses antagonism to his father and attachment to his mother.*

Operant conditioning: *a principle of behavioral learning theory whereby the actual consequences of behavior, rather than the original cause (stimulus), is of concern. These consequences of a behavior "operate" on the behavior and on the environment, causing the behavior to recur.*

Oral stage: *psychoanalytic term for the infantile stage of psychosexual development when pleasure is centered around the mouth, around sucking and eating activities.*

Organismic: *pertaining to the individual as a whole entity. Emphasis is placed upon the organized system of interrelated and interdependent parts.*

Penis envy: *psychoanalytic concept whereby a little girl envies boys and longs for a penis.*

Permission: *Transactional Analysis concept whereby the helper or a helpee's parent ego state allows a helpee to feel, be, or act as he or she is or chooses. In most cases the helper activates the helpee's nurturing parent to give permission to the helpee's child ego state to be whole, free, feel, etc.*

Phallic stage: *a psychoanalytic developmental stage where a child's interests shift from the anal to the genital area. During this stage, children believe that a phallus is a normal possession of both sexes.*

Phenomenological: *perceiving someone else's world through his or her eyes. Emphasizing conscious experience as real experience.*

Positive reinforcement: *rewards that have good significance (e.g., praise, money, or grades). Positive reinforcement may be social or concrete.*

Potency: *Gestalt and Transactional Analysis term implying that the helper or helpee has the power to do something, has the expertise and credibility to deliver.*

Principle of gradation: *learning theory principle whereby a sequence of intermediate or subgoals leads gradually to more complex behavior.*

Process: *a continuous series of successive, but interdependent, changes or events. Also refers to how something is happening and what the associated effect and form are as opposed to the actual facts and events (processing).*

Projection: *psychoanalytic defense mechanism whereby one unconsciously attributes feelings (e.g., guilt or inferiority), thoughts, or acts to other people. These projections are usually a defense against unpleasant feelings in ourselves and are means by which we can justify ourselves in our own eyes.*

Projective techniques: *tests or instruments that elicit unconscious material in forms of stories, pictures, or acting out. This type of mental testing helps to determine personality traits. The individual is left free to follow his or her inclinations and fantasies.*

Protection: *Transactional Analysis concept whereby helpers have the ability to take care of helpees and keep them safe. Helpers activate helpees' nurturing parent to protect their child ego state so that helpees will not be hurt by their actions.*

Psychosexual stages: *psychoanalytic developmental stages that are critical in the child's personality development. Because the Freudian view places sexual impulses at the root of all human personality problems, sexual development and sexually oriented experiences in childhood become critical for future adult development.*

Racket: *Transactional Analysis term for a feeling that occurs often and continually in one's life, which one is so used to that one sets up situations to experience this feeling as a payoff. Rackets are learned in childhood and persist into adulthood as a predominant feeling.*

Rationalization: *psychoanalytic defense mechanism whereby a person assigns a socially acceptable motive to his or her behavior. The process of justifying by reasoning after an act has been performed that helps one defend against self-accusation or guilt.*

Reaction-formation: *psychoanalytic defense mechanism where some character traits that are unacceptable to the ego are kept in check by the manifestation of the exact reverse of those unacceptable traits. The manifestation is sometimes excessive or violent in the opposite direction to the impulse or desire being repressed.*

Recall: *a psychoanalytic term meaning to revive or reinstate in memory, verbally, or in concrete imagery, a past experience.*

Referral: *when a helpee is aided to seek help elsewhere. This may be due to the need of the helpee or the skills or needs of the helper.*

Regression: *psychoanalytic defense mechanism whereby one reduces tension or anxiety by reverting to ways of behavior or to objects associated with earlier phases of one's development, when one felt more adequate. The individual expresses interests and behavior that are characteristic of an earlier infantile stage.*

Reinforcement: *behavioral term meaning the environmental event that, when it follows certain behavior, causes that behavior to recur. May be positive or negative. Reinforcements are the environmental consequences of behavior.*

Repression: *psychoanalytic defense mechanism whereby one forces to the unconscious perceptions, ideas, and feelings that would be painful to the conscious. Impulses and desires in conflict with enforced standards of conduct are thrust into the unconscious where they can still remain active, determining behavior and experience indirectly, perhaps through dreams and neurotic symptoms.*

Rubberband: *Transactional Analysis concept of a feeling associated with an early event in one's life that one feels strongly (overreacts with) in response to a present situation.*

Schedules of reinforcement: *behavioral schedules of when to use reinforcements in contingency contracting:*

1. continuous reinforcement - reinforcement following each time target behavior occurs

2. interval schedule - reinforcements occur after certain period of time (e.g., every hour)

3. ratio schedule - reinforcements occur after a certain number of responses have occurred (e.g., every third response)

Script: *Transactional Analysis concept of early life decisions that result in lifelong patterns and themes reflected in behaviors, feelings, and thoughts.*

Every individual has many scripts—to be a success or to be a failure, to be perfect—that predominate his or her life until brought into awareness by rescripting early childhood decisions.

Self-concept: *from client-centered theory, the perception we have of ourselves from significant others and from our experiences. Our image of who and what we are, what we are all about.*

Shaping: *learning theory term whereby gradually emitted responses are reinforced until a pattern of the total behavior is established. One can shape behavior by breaking the entire behavior into its smallest parts and reinforcing one part at a time, in sequence.*

Significant other: *a parent, relative, teacher, or any person whose relationship is considered especially meaningful and important. Significant others have influence over our feelings and actions.*

Social reinforcement: *behavioral term meaning attention from a significant other (e.g., a smile, nod, physical contact, praise).*

Stroke: *Transactional Analysis concept of reinforcement. Any unit of recognition a person receives from another person. Strokes may be positive or negative, conditional or unconditional.*

Sublimation: *psychoanalytic defense mechanism whereby sexual energy is expressed in the form of "higher social values" (i.e., instead of seeking sexual gratification, one might help people or engage in artistic endeavors).*

Successive approximations: *a learning theory concept whereby a desired behavior is broken into its smallest parts and behaviors resembling one of those parts are reinforced.*

Superego: *part of the psychoanalytic personality, it acts as a conscience and interjects parental and social values. The superego is a structure in the unconscious built up by early experiences with parents and significant others. As a conscience, the superego criticizes the thoughts of the ego, resulting in feelings of guilt and anxiety when the ego gratifies the primitive impulses of the id.*

Sweatshirt: *Transactional Analysis concept meaning the message that one broadcasts about oneself by manner and behavior, usually without awareness. Sweatshirts usually have two messages, one on the front and one on the back, such as "Come on and get me" on the front and "How dare you?" on the back.*

Systematic desensitization: *behavioral technique of counterconditioning to reduce anxiety by associating negative events with positive experiences so that negative stimuli lose their averseness. Desensitization begins when a client learns complete muscle relaxation (antithetical to anxiety) and establishes an anxiety hierarchy. An anxiety situation is then paired with the mental images and process of relaxation. The pairing continues until the entire hierarchy can be imagined without domination by anxiety.*

Token economy: *a behavioral reinforcement program whereby desired behaviors are rewarded with tokens having reinforcement value by association with a variety of backup rewards. The tokens can be awarded immediately after the behavior is emitted and the exchange can occur later.*

Transference: *psychoanalytic relationship whereby the patient unconsciously places the analyst in the place of one or more significant others in his or her life and attributes to the analyst the attitudes, behaviors, and attributes of the significant person(s). Transference refers to the patient developing a positive or negative emotional attitude toward the analyst.*

APPENDIX A

This observer's guide can be used for the exercises on communications skills in chapter 3. The helper will not use these behaviors for every role play, but over a period of time the ratings will indicate to the helper verbal and nonverbal behaviors that need further development as well as those currently operating effectively. Using this guide will help both observer and helper understand and recognize just what communications behaviors we are defining as necessary to enhance helping relationships.

OBSERVER'S GUIDE FOR COMMUNICATIONS SKILLS

Rate the following behaviors: 0 = did not occur, 1 = occurred but needs improvement, 2 = occurred adequately, 3 = helper especially strong on this point.

Nonverbal Behaviors

1. The helper maintained eye contact with the helpee.
   0   1   2   3

2. The helper varied facial expressions during the interview.
   0   1   2   3

3. The helper responded to the helpee with alertness and facial animation.
   0   1   2   3

4. The helper sometimes nodded his or her head.

    0   1   2   3

5. The helper had a relaxed body position.

    0   1   2   3

6. The helper leaned toward the helpee to encourage the helpee.

    0   1   2   3

7. The helper's voice pitch varied when talking.

    0   1   2   3

8. The helper's voice was easily heard by the helpee.

    0   1   2   3

9. Sometimes the helper used one-word comments such as "mm-mm" or "uh-huh" to encourage the helpee.

    0   1   2   3

10. The helper communicated warmth, concern, and empathy by smiling and other gestures.

    0   1   2   3

Verbal Behaviors

11. The helper responded to the most important theme of each of the helpee's statements.

    0   1   2   3

12. The helper usually identified and responded to the feelings of the helpee.

    0   1   2   3

13. The helper usually identified and responded to the behaviors of the helpee.

    0   1   2   3

14. The helper verbally responded to at least one nonverbal cue of the helpee.

    0   1   2   3

15. The helper encouraged the helpee to talk about his or her feelings.

    0   1   2   3

16. The helper asked questions that could not be answered in a yes or no fashion.

    0   1   2   3

17. The helper confronted the helpee with any discrepancies between the helpee's behavior and communications.

| 0 | 1 | 2 | 3 |

18. The helper shared his or her own feelings with the helpee.

| 0 | 1 | 2 | 3 |

19. The helper communicated understanding or lack of understanding of the helpee.

| 0 | 1 | 2 | 3 |

20. The helper responded in ways that communicated liking and appreciation of the helpee.

| 0 | 1 | 2 | 3 |

21. The helper summarized statements and themes to clarify issues for the helpee.

| 0 | 1 | 2 | 3 |

22. The helper sent "I messages" when confronting or expressing lack of understanding.

| 0 | 1 | 2 | 3 |

Your Summary of Suggestions for Helper

APPENDIX B

This is an additional exercise designed to heighten our awareness of our reactions to silence. It may be used in conjunction with the exercises in chapters 3 and 4. It is helpful to repeat this exercise periodically to demonstrate how you can learn to be more comfortable with and to utilize effectively periods of silence.

EXERCISE FOR SILENCE

Silence is a necessary technique for helpers but one we often feel uncomfortable with. Work through the following series of Gestalt-type exercises in triads, rotating roles of helper, helpee, and observer.

1.   The helpee talks about a real or imagined concern and the helper is not allowed to respond in any way, either verbally or nonverbally. After five minutes, share reactions and feelings.

2.   Maintaining the same roles, the helper is now allowed to make two nonverbal responses within a five-minute period. Again, process.

3.   Now the helper can make one verbal and two nonverbal responses within a five-minute period. Process after completion.

4.   The helper may make four responses, either verbally or nonverbally.

5.   The helper may respond in any way and as often as he or she chooses.

In processing, share your thoughts and feelings as well as your frustrations and choices.

INDEX

also Communication in counseling; Relationship in counseling; Strategies in counseling

Objectives. *See* Goals
Offir, C.: 193
"O.K. participation": 64
Operant conditioning: 102
Oral stage: 95
Organismic balance: 98
Outreach counseling: 169, 170 - 171
Overanalyzing: 20
"Overparticipation": 64

Paraphrasing: 52, 55
Paraprofessional helpers: 134, 207, 208; capabilities required, 2, 4, 7, 15, 17, 30, 35
Parent ego: 106, 107, 145, 146, 147
Parker, G.: 189
Pastimes: 106
Perceiving nonverbal messages: 48 - 50, 74
Perls, Fritz: 96, 117
Permission: 107
Personality: 92, 93
Personal theory of counselors: 91 - 94
Phallic stage: 95
Phenomenological helping theory: 29, 109, 110, 111, 114, 116, 132, 147 - 150, 205 - 206; approaches to helping, 97, 99 - 100; client-centered therapy, 5, 8, 9, 49, 60, 96 - 98; Gestalt therapy, 5, 9, 51, 66, 96, 98 - 100; implications, 97 - 98, 100; theoretical assumptions, 86 - 97, 98 - 99; view of helping relationship, 97, 100
Phobia: 140, 141, 159, 174 - 177
Pietrofesa, J.: 189
Planning strategies: 158 - 159, 168, 175, 179
Potency of counselor: 100, 104, 107
Poverty: 194, 199
Practice of counseling skills: 40, 43, 45, 206
Present time: 99, 117, 120, 130, 131
Privileged communication: 195 - 196, 201, 202
Probation officers: 3, 4, 17
Probing: 47, 52, 54, 55
Problem-oriented helping: 66
Problem ownership: 77, 122
Problems: clarification of, 74, 76 - 78, 84 - 86, 88, 90, 174 - 175, 178, 204; exploration of, 74, 81 - 82, 89, 90, 175, 179, 204; solving, 63, 113
Procedures: 106
Process: in Transactional-Communicative theory, 107, 109, 110

Processing: 40, 84
Professional helpers: 134, 207, 208, 209; capabilities required, 2, 3 - 4, 7, 15, 17, 30, 35
Projection: 30 - 31, 38, 45, 65
Projective techniques: 95
Protection: 107
Psychiatric aides: 4
Psychiatrists: 3
Psychoanalytic theory: 109, 110, 111, 114, 147 - 150, 205 - 206; approaches to helping, 95; implications for helpers, 96; neurosis, 94, 109; techniques for helping, 125 - 126; theoretical assumptions, 94 - 95; unconscious, 95, 109, 125; view of helping relationship, 95
Psychodrama Institute: 207
Psychological counseling: 78, 80, 81 - 82, 127 - 128, 129 - 130, 151, 159, 162, 163, 164, 173, 174 - 177
Psychological disequilibrium: 169
Psychologists: 3
Psychosexual stages: 94 - 95
Punishment: 133

Racism: 11; counseling and, 191 - 193, 199, 201, 202
Rackets: 107
Rape: 32 - 33, 168, 169
Rapport. *See* Trust relationship
Rational-Emotive-Therapy: 6, 103 - 104, 109, 110, 114, 126 - 130, 132, 147 - 150, 161, 179
Rationality: 96, 105, 114, 122; cognitive-behavioral theory, 103 - 104, 126, 127, 128 - 129, 132
Real: 118
Reality therapy: 6, 103, 104 - 106, 109, 114, 126, 130 - 132, 133, 147 - 150
Recall: 95
Recontracting: 179
Record keeping: 73, 90, 195, 196 - 197, 201, 202
Referral: 78 - 80, 163, 170, 171, 173, 198
Reflecting: 52, 55, 97
Reinforcements: 8, 144; behavioral helping theory, 101, 102, 109, 110, 114, 136, 141, 142
Relationship in counseling: 10 - 11, 12, 15, 18, 19 - 39, 70 - 90, 204 - 205; behavioral therapy, 102, 109; clarification of problems, 74, 76 - 78, 84 - 86, 88, 90, 174 - 175, 178; client-